The Chinese Journalist

China, the most populous country in the world, is also the country that is probably changing the fastest. From a sullen backwater, China is becoming a recognized force in world politics and the international economy, and the principal mediators, reflecting these changes to the Chinese and the rest of the world, are journalists. But who are the journalists in China, and through what kind of transition are they undergoing as the economy is freed up and the administration rethought?

The Chinese Journalist provides an intriguing introduction to Chinese journalists and their roles within society for students of media and students of Asian Studies. The book initially offers a background history of journalists and the media in Communist China before examining the origins and development of Chinese journalism in the nineteenth century. Subsequent chapters explore:

* how young people become journalists;
* the norms of the profession;
* the developing identity of the journalist;
* the gulf between beliefs and reality.

Drawing upon sinology, social psychology, history and sociology, this book will inform readers from many disciplines about the increasing power journalists have, as well as providing new perspectives on familiar debates for students of media and communications.

Hugo de Burgh is Senior Lecturer in the Department of Media and Communications at Goldsmiths College, University of London. Until 1995 he worked as a television reporter and producer in the UK.

The Chinese Journalist

Mediating information in the world's most populous country

Hugo de Burgh

RoutledgeCurzon
Taylor & Francis Group
LONDON AND NEW YORK

First published 2003
by RoutledgeCurzon
2 Park Square, Milton Park, Abingdon, Oxon, OX14 4RN

Simultaneously published in the USA and Canada
by RoutledgeCurzon
270 Madison Avenue, New York, NY 10016

Transferred to Digital Printing 2005

RoutledgeCurzon is an imprint of the Taylor & Francis Group

© 2003 Hugo de Burgh

Typeset in 10/12pt Mono Baskerville by
Graphicraft Limited, Hong Kong
Printed and bound in Great Britain by Antony Rowe Ltd., Chippenham, Wiltshire

British Library Cataloguing in Publication Data
A catalogue record for this book is available from the British Library

Library of Congress Cataloging in Publication Data

ISBN 0–415–30573–X

For C.S.

Contents

Preface

[T]o understand China's media you must comprehend China's history, since they cannot be extracted one from the other.

(Wang Qianghua, editor, *Law and Democracy*, formerly of *The People's Daily*)

I am indebted to those who agreed to be interviewed, to those at Renmin, Fudan, Zhejiang and Sichuan Universities who made the interviews possible and to the Chinese Journalism Educational Association. I regret that I have thought it best not to mention them by name. Mary Hodge and Professor Sandra Harris read the manuscript in early draft and their comments were very valuable. Assistance in garnering data was rendered to me by Patsy Widukaswara, Qiu Ling and Thomas de Burgh. Two visits to China were funded thanks to the generosity of the Universities China Committee. I thank Dr and Mrs T. Sciplino and Dr and Mrs A. Montalbano whose hospitality made it possible for me to work on holiday over three summers.

The original research which forms the kernel of this book was undertaken under the supervision of Professor John Tomlinson, NTU, and Professor Stephan Feuchtwang, LSE. Professor James Curran and Professor Lee Chin-chuan read and commented upon the book proposal; I am indebted to them.

None of the above bears any responsibility for what follows.

Some of the material presented in this book has also been used in 'What Chinese journalists believe about journalism' in Rawnsley, G. (ed.) (2002) *Political Communication in Greater China*, London: Macmillan; 'Chinese concepts of the journalist', *Communication*, March 2002; 'Great aspirations and conventional repertoires: Chinese regional television journalists and their work', *Journalism Studies*, spring 2003.

The purpose of this book is to provide students of the media with a case study to supplement their usual fare, heavily biased towards anglophone examples and instances. In an old Chinese story a prince was cross with a scholar who claimed that he knew nothing about the subject which he had been studying for years; but when the scholar made an excuse by likening himself to a thirsty man who takes a sip from the lakes, the prince understood. In seeking to write about the media I feel like that thirsty scholar. How can you say anything about that which is around you to such an extent that you can never grasp it? As for trying to get a hold on the Chinese media today, another story comes to mind, of the man who dropped his sword out of his canoe and then cut a notch on the boat, that he might record where the sword had gone down.[1] Despite these warnings, I hope that readers will find that what is provided here will supply them with the wherewithal for broader discussion and comparisons of the development of journalism. It is written in memory of Gareth Moor (10/7/50–9/6/70) who gave me my first book on China.

Chronology

1911	Xinghai Revolution. Overthrow of the Qing Dynasty and collapse of Manchu power throughout China. Republic of China established.
1912	General Yuan Shikai becomes President of the Republic of China. Nationalist Party (KMT) founded.
1913	Sun Yatsen flees to Japan following the failure of his putsch against Yuan.
1916	Death of Yuan Shikai. Although the Republic continues to exist in name, China is in fact ruled by a succession of warlords, dominating different fiefs.
1919	4 May Movement. Demonstrations against Japan and the Versailles Treaty. Language reform.
1920	Sun Yatsen establishes a new Republican government at Canton.
1921	1st congress of the Chinese Communist Party (CCP).
1923	Moscow's Comintern and Sun Yatsen's Nationalist Party (KMT) initiate collaboration.
1924	1st congress of Nationalist Party.
1925	Death of Sun Yatsen.
1926	Northern Expedition.
1927	Government launches Anti-Communist Campaign, ending the Nationalist Party–CCP alliance. The Red Army is founded.
1928	Mao Zedong and Zhu De found a guerrilla base in Jiangxi, on Jinggangshan.
1930	First government campaign of extermination against CCP.
1931	Chinese Soviet Republic proclaimed, capital at Ruijin. Japanese occupation of Manchuria.
1934	The Long March. The CCP flees westwards.
1937	CCP and KMT agree to cooperate against the Japanese invaders.
1938	The government of the Republic is transferred to Chunking, in Sichuan.
1941	War breaks out between CCP and KMT.
1942	At Yanan, Mao Zedong launches a Rectification Campaign to liquidate opposition.
1949	Government flees to Taiwan, where it re-establishes the Republic of

China. CCP proclaims People's Republic of China in Peking. Media nationalized.

1950 Invasion of Tibet and East Turkestan, existing governments overthrown.
Sino-Soviet Agreement. Land reform.

1956 Hundred Flowers. Ends 1957.

1957 Anti Rightist Movement.

1958 Great Leap Forward. Creation of Rural Communes.

1959 Mao Zedong resigns as Head of State to Liu Shaoqi, but retains position as Chairman of Chinese Communist party. Tibet uprising.

1960 Sino-Soviet split.

1962 Famine. Liu criticizes the Communes.

1966/76 The Cultural Revolution starts with an article in *Wenhuibao*.

1969 IX Party Congress, Lin Biao announced as Mao's heir.

1971/72 Attempted *coup d'état* by Lin Biao is foiled.

1972 US President Richard Nixon visits China.

1976 Death of Mao Zedong and fall of Gang of Four. Accession of Hua Guofeng.

1979 Advertising introduced to Chinese television.

1980 Zhao Ziyang replaces Hua Guofeng as PM. China admitted to IMF and World Bank.

1981 Public criticism of Mao.

1982 Population reaches 1bn.

1983 Special Economic Zones are announced for the Pearl River area.
Campaign against spiritual pollution from the West.
Regulations on Chinese–Western Joint Stock Ventures are promulgated.

1984 Zhao Ziyang to USA. President Ronald Reagan to China. Announcement of 'One country two systems' policy to reassure westerners that HK will not be communized.

1985 Zhao calls for freeing up of wages and prices as essential for the economy. Modernization of education called for. First public demonstrations against nuclear testing take place.

1986 Sino-Soviet border fighting. Shanghai Stock Market opens (closed 1949). Sino-British Declaration on Hong Kong. The media attack bourgeois liberalization.
Fang Lizhi makes a speech calling for openness and students demonstrate for democracy in many cities. Bankruptcy Law promulgated.

1987 *People's Daily* attacks bourgeois liberalization and hails the Four Cardinal Principles (CCP leadership; Marx–Lenin–Mao thought; People's Democratic Dictatorship and the socialist road). CCP admits that there is widespread corruption in the Party. Independence demonstrations in Tibet.

1988 CCP sends condolences to Taiwan on death of Chiang Chingkuo.
Li Peng encourages Taiwan businesses to invest in the mainland.

Most commodity prices will be deregulated and allowed to move according to the market.

1989   The first Soviet minister since 1959 visits China. President George Bush visits China. Anti-Chinese demonstrations in Tibet. Li Peng acknowledges dangers of inflation to the economy. 22 April a major demonstration in Peking calls for the rehabilitation of Hu Yaobang, just deceased, and for democracy.

Demonstrations increase in size and number through May; university students swear to remain in Tiananmen Square until democracy be granted. Soviet President Gorbachev visits and normalization of Sino-Soviet relations is declared. 20 May Martial law declared; students call for overthrow of Li Peng.

4 June Tiananmen Massacre in Peking. Arrests.

9 November Deng Xiaoping announces that he will resign as Chairman of Party Military Affairs Committee; Jiang Zemin to succeed him.

1990   Martial law lifted from Peking, many student demonstrators released.

1991   GDP growth is predicted to be 11 per cent, fastest of any economy. In December, Deng starts his 'Southern Progress'.

1992   Foreign investment to be permitted in major southern cities.

1993   Wei Jingshen released from prison as a goodwill gesture to the West. GDP grows by 14 per cent.

1994   An austerity plan to slow down the economy.

1995   Wei Jingshen rearrested and sentenced to a further fourteen years.

1996   Democratic elections in Taiwan.

1997   Death of Deng Xiaoping. Hong Kong returned to Chinese jurisdiction. Wei Jingshen released, arrives in USA. Jiang Zemin visits the USA.

1998   PM Zhu Rongji replaces Li Peng. President Clinton visits China.

1999   China's population approximately 1.243 billion.

2001   China member of World Trade Organization.

2002   November. XVI Congress of the CCP. Hu Jintao becomes General Secretary.

Notes on the text

Chinese names and expressions have been rendered as is conventional, even when this gives the appearance of inconsistency because of the originals being variously known by their English version or *Pinyin* or Cantonese transcription. Historic English versions, such as 'Peking' or 'Canton' are preferred to the equivalents of 'Napoli', 'Warsava' or 'al-Quds'. The glossary contains the Chinese for names, slogans and some particular expressions. PRC ideographs are used for all.

The names given as those of Chinese journalists interviewed are pseudonyms, the only exceptions being the two who are identified by their publications. I have used the expression 'Tiananmen massacre' to refer to the events leading up to, and the events of, 4 June 1989. The 'Tiananmen incident' names the events of 1976. The shorthand term 'progressives' is used to refer to those in favour of the next steps in marketization and opening to the world inaugurated by Deng Xiaoping; the term 'leftists' refers to those suspicious of, or actively opposed to, these policies.

1   Introduction

Why should we look at journalism and choose it as a way, one among many, of understanding a given society? Why is the subject of the media's influence on society and the behaviour of journalists in particular, more and more controversial in anglophone societies? For what reasons is China is a suitable object of study? Why it is worthwhile looking at Chinese journalists? These are some of the questions with which this introductory chapter deals. It also endeavours to make clear the assumptions that underlie this examination of the journalists of another culture and to explain the approach of the book.

Why China matters

In November 1992 *The Economist* declared China to be the world's third or fourth biggest economy and growing much faster than those still ahead of it. Since then, many more journalists, backed by the wise thoughts of many economists, have flagged China as the world's coming superpower and an economy due to overtake all others (Overholt 1993, Brahm 2001).[1] A focus on journalism, such as this book provides, raises a number of doubts about these predictions because it obliges us to look beyond economics, at political institutions, social habits and culture too. However, the statistics are undoubtedly impressive.

China is the seventh biggest trading country and is widely expected to overtake all but the USA in the next few years. Of its 2001 accession to the World Trade Organization (WTO), a Brookings study has declared:

> The implications of China's membership of the WTO for the world economy, the international trading system, and the United States are immense. China's economy and international trade are so large that the expansion of economy output and trade resulting from its membership is likely to perceptibly affect the growth of global trade and thus the pace of expansion of global output.
>
> (Lardy 2002: 134)

Despite the economic disasters China suffered under socialism between 1949 and 1978; the dissipation of its cultural capital; the exploitation and violation of the ideals of its reformers; the appalling and usually unproductive relations with the rest of the world; despite all these misfortunes it would seem that China is emerging as an economic power as befits its size and as a political power as befits its history.

The reader who is unfamiliar with the splendour of Chinese history, a civilization that has outlasted ancient rivals such as the Greeks, the Byzantines, the Egyptians and the Ottomans, will need to look elsewhere if he or she is to understand the pride which often seems to colour the outlook of even the least lettered Chinese. Many conversations in China will be enriched with references to history; the resentful attitudes and behaviour which can easily be inflamed into xenophobia are incomprehensible to those ignorant of Chinese sense of identity.

This sense of identity in itself is something, quite other than its potential for material power, that makes China matter. China is culturally huge, in the sense that its homogeneity relative to other large countries is remarkable; moreover there are substantial Chinese minorities in many other countries of the world and these minorities often have important positions in the economic or cultural lives of their host societies. There are different Chinese languages, but the common ideographic writing system and the efforts of the government to promote Mandarin as the first language of most, and the second language of everybody else, make it in effect unilingual. The People's Republic of China (PRC) is an empire, containing subject peoples of quite different races and cultures, but they are numerically few and their lands are fast being colonized by Chinese, so that, for all practical purposes, the PRC is ethnically homogenous.[2]

The intellectual and cultural life of the world, to say nothing of economic and political affairs, has now for well over a century been dominated by the anglophone countries, with other European powers and Japan playing supporting roles. The world language was French and is now English; every ambitious or educated Indian, Peruvian, Zulu, Arab or Turk will not merely speak English but also know how to operate in an anglophone society. Their American or English or Italian equivalents have no such facility in China, though its customs are different and are adhered to by nearly a quarter of humankind and although its language is used as a first language by more than any other. In no country's schools is Chinese the standard second language. This is likely to change and the change will be driven not merely by the sheer scale of China but by the dynamism of a society moving, in business enterprise as in intellectual endeavour, with astounding speed. China may offer an alternative to anglophone cultural pretension.

For a century or more, Chinese have struggled to find a way to modernize that is truly a Chinese way, that does not oblige them to become second-class westerners. In the 1960s some thought they had found a way of being Chinese, poor and yet the moral leaders of the world, but this was a chimera. The failure has been swallowed but the same search is still on. There is no reason to suppose, even today when China appears to be seizing every opportunity offered by free market economics, that the country will not remain distinct and prepared to challenge anglophone cultural domination.

There are least four different schools of thought as to the potential geopolitical impact of China in the years ahead. Overholt's *The Next Economic Superpower* (1993) and Brahm's *China as Number One* (2001) emphasize the economic power they expect China to wield in the world ahead. The antagonistic school, represented by Bernstein and Munro (1998) sees China as a military power, driven by violent nationalism, and a potential aggressor. Vogel (1997), by contrast, visualizes a China integrated successfully into the world political and economic systems. Chang (2001) and Studwell (2002) see China as unable to integrate, as self-destructive because of its social and institutional flaws, and perhaps, after great domestic disasters, pulling down many other countries with it.[3] Whatever your reading of the future of Chinese impact on the rest of the world, it is unlikely to be negligible.

But why, when the anglophone media are not only the most advanced organizationally, but are also claimed to be the least repressed politically, should we wish to study the Chinese media? Even more, why should we study what has been referred to as 'that oxymoron, the Chinese journalist'? Before tackling that, it is worthwhile stepping further back and asking why, in the West today, people concern themselves with studying journalism and why there is so much concern at the supposed ill effects of the media. For this look at Chinese journalists comes out of the anglophone world, by whose interests and obsessions it is naturally conditioned.

Media power

There is a general belief that the media, because they can command the attention of many people, because they cross borders and have developed sophisticated techniques of engaging interest, are supplanting traditional means of learning, role-modelling and sharing ideas. They are

> a central force in shaping everyday social and psychological life, the organization of economic and political activity, the construction of public culture, and the creation of new expressive forms.
>
> (QAA 2001)

Whereas the main external influences upon our grandparents' thoughts, their windows on worlds wider than the hamlets or suburbs in which they lived, were religion and the local employer, today the media may be taking their place. People say they get most of their facts from television; a large number watch a great deal of it;[4] radio is enjoying a boom[5] and other media of communication have been undergoing a massive expansion over the last twenty years.

It is difficult to clarify how the influence of the media is exerted; the empirical evidence is extraordinarily patchy (Gunter 2000). If you want to learn, for example, about the media representation of family life, you would probably need to go back to the 1980s and look at a series of studies in different countries co-ordinated by Halloran.[6] It is the only major project of its kind, yet does not go much beyond description. It does not ask why the media represent certain categories of people in certain ways, nor does it delve into the significance of the representations for the societies in which they take place.[7]

As to the promotion of unhealthy social habits and attitudes, violence and prejudice, there are many arguments over the media's responsibilities. Even those who have been looking at this question for years offer only guarded and minimalist conclusions (Philo 1999a: 16). There is also a school of thought which regards the media as the promoters of new and better behaviours, although such views tend to be held in 'developing' countries and less in the West.[8]

Nevertheless it is 'common sense' that the media influence us and are the channels of exciting and influential eye-openers.[9] This is presumably one of the reasons why media studies has become the fastest-growing subject of study in anglophone education, with other countries fast catching up.

The idea of the public sphere

While the accepted wisdom that the media are remaking us rests upon rather tenuous foundations, a slightly more concrete claim is made for journalism, that journalism assures the free flow of ideas essential to democracy and to social progress. Whereas in the 1930s many saw the media as acting as the soporific of the masses and the ally of ruthless power-mongers wanting to dupe them, for the last few decades it has been widely agreed in the West that the media in general and the news and current affairs media in particular perform functions essential to the efficient operation of society in the public interest:[10] at their best, they provide factual information and impartial reports; they question and analyse the claims of those in authority or with power in the community and they investigate problems and conflicts of interest.

It is said that the need for such media has never been greater as the state in many countries gives up its roles to private initiatives locally or multinationals globally and power is more and more difficult to pin down and hold responsible (Monbiot 2000, Hertz 2001, Klein 2001).

This social role allocated to journalism is underpinned by Habermas' concept of the public sphere. He sees the emergence of a public-spirited press in nineteenth-century England, independent of commercial or political corruption and relatively impartial, as an essential of economic, political and moral advance. It is a prime task of people in public life to defend this public sphere from contamination.

The concept of 'civil society' is closely connected and has been much discussed in relation to the apparent breakdown of moral consensus in anglophone countries and since the collapse of Eastern European totalitarian regimes, whose societies are perceived to have had their capacity for regeneration stunted. One of the weaknesses of the totalitarian societies was also one of the reasons why it was going to be so difficult to establish democratic, or at least consensual, modes of political behaviour: the absence of local, voluntary and small-scale institutions, institutions intermediate with the state. The decline of such institutions in anglophone societies, as the state has accrued more power, has caused anguish among observers;[11] their reappearance in Poland and other former Russian satellites, matters of pride. The unwillingness of the Chinese government to allow any but business organizations to develop is considered to be potentially destabilizing.

For this 'civil society' to operate an informative, detached and critical media are needed, not those dominated either by political parties or by narrow business interests. In order to take the right decisions about their businesses, their consumption, their votes, their careers or their education, citizens need reliable media as fish need water. The 'public sphere' is what we all have in common; the 'agora' or space in which the public sphere operates[12] is the media and, in particular, national broadcasts and print media used by the opinion forming and decision-taking classes.

The role of journalists: representation of cultures, cultures of representation

It is journalists, by and large, who supply the media with the data and with the analysis and critique we need to help us make judgements. Journalists believe that they are tellers of truth, that they are undertaking vital tasks, impartially (Randall 1996: 2). The selection and representation of information is the key role which journalists usually ascribe to themselves (Weaver 1998); they are also gatekeeping and agenda setting, analysing events and claims, evaluating policy and acting as public 'watchdog', in the American expression.

Yet journalists are unable – even if they are competent, by training or orientation – to realize professional norms of disinterested observation and analysis. Several decades of research by academics into how journalists operate have made the Habermas' ideal seem naive. In looking at news content, sociologists have established that news reports often merely reproduce what reporters are told by established authority, are ethnocentric, create norms of deviance, give unwarranted prominence to violence and criminality and stereotype people. The media have been found guilty of sanitizing content.[13]

Such biases are functions of journalists' social and economic position; their personal make-up including gender, cultural background, attitudes; the norms of the profession; corporate policies or proprietor influence; the current market situation and the regulatory environment; working practices. Working practices include the tendency to accept information from a limited range of official sources as 'reality' and to see certain limited types of people as experts or testimony. Journalists in their working practices also make assumptions about the audience and about news values and follow conventions of story construction, which can mean that they change the story to fit the narrative format. McQuail (1994) and Shoemaker (1996) are among the scholars who have made taxonomies of these aspects of the news production process.

The claims of journalists that they are tellers of truths are rather undermined by such sceptical analyses. The 'deconstructive turn' in intellectual life makes matters worse, since it would have it that all reporting is invention and that journalists are in the business of creating, not discovering or interpreting, meaning. The fashion for Foucault-like[14] dismissals of the very concept of truth, or reality, have not made journalists any more confident, particularly when such colleagues as Martin Bell and Matthew Parris weigh in with their repudiations of impartiality. Bell has done this by drawing our attention to the ways in which journalists create news even as they think they are reporting it and Parris by analysing how they reconstruct reality (Bell 1997a, Parris 1999). Tom Wolfe has published a witty fictional illustration of how 'idealistic' journalists might fit reality to their ambitions for it (Wolfe 1998).

Anglophone myths about scrutiny

Even when we accept that much journalism fails to measure up to its ideals, we often hold onto the belief that 'investigative journalism' makes up for this. It is commonly held that 'investigative journalism' is a good thing, that it is the genuine article and that it is thanks to reporters such as those who gave us the Watergate[15] case that politicians and the powerful are kept from doing worse wrongs than they do already.

It has often been described how tenacious and courageous reporting by *The Washington Post* led to the exposure of the links which proved the president's implication in the Watergate issue and other offences.[16] The two reporters became icons and have been extensively eulogized; British television has produced regular re-examinations of the case and reflections upon its influence. All journalism in the USA since then has been affected, if not dominated, by this feat which is interpreted either as the beginning of a new relationship between journalism and politics or as a demonstration, less of the corruption of US politics, than of the efficacy of the system and proof of the important role of journalists in it.

This interpretation has been interrogated on the grounds that bringing down the president was less the achievement of journalists and more that of other politicians and institutions (Schudson 1992); that the choice of target, given that there were many other potential targets of journalistic inquiry at the time, some of which were arguably of much greater significance, was partisan (Herman and Chomsky 1995). The point being made is that investigative journalism is no less subject to the influences and limitations which compromise other kinds of journalism.

In Britain investigative journalism is also limited, not only by its vision of what needs to be dealt with, but also by its budgets, its operatives' prejudices and the daunting hard work required to pin down evidence which will stand up in law (Moore 2000, de Burgh 2000b); large areas of our public life remain unscrutinized, leaving the impression that investigative journalism, when not sensational, amounts to minor flea bites on the body of the great moloch of power.[17] As to the effects of such investigation as goes on, whereas it is generally agreed that investigations into the activities of ministers and government MPs in the crumbling years of the Major government influenced the electorate against it and made its 1997 defeat sure, comparable revelations of corruption in the Blair government seem to have had little influence on its standing with the electorate. So much for watchdog journalism; but the myth still permeates the profession worldwide, in so far as information is available (Weaver 1998). In a study of 726 British journalists, over half rated the role of adversary of public officials as very or extremely important and 88 per cent thought the same of the role of investigating claims and statements made by the government (Henningham and Delano 1998). This belief sits oddly, though, with the widespread fear that serious journalism is in decline.

The trivialization debate

Today it is argued in the UK that changes in broadcasting regulations, relaxed in order to make commercial broadcasting more viable against foreign competition, have caused a sharp falling off in inquisitorial and public-spirited journalism (Barnett and Seymour 2000, Franklin 2001, Gaber and Barnett 2001) and made the news media more parochial (Tomlinson 2000: 171); that this is leading to newspapers following suit with more sensationalism and ephemera (Golding 1998). Those convinced of 'dumbing down' consider that where profit is allowed to be the main criterion of value in the provision of information and entertainment, there is danger that the media become less reliable as sources of information and opportunities for debate. ·

> Criticism of these recent trends in journalism and news media, however, has not been limited to the coverage of particular cases not confined to newspapers. Increasingly it has focused on a more general tendency in contemporary journalism, evident in both print and broadcast media, to retreat from investigative journalism and the reporting of hard news to the preferred territory of 'softer' or 'lighter' stories. Journalism's editorial stories have changed. Entertainment has superseded the provision of information; human interest has supplanted the public interest; measured judgment has succumbed to sensationalism; the trivial has triumphed over the weighty; the intimate relations of celebrities from soap operas, the world of sport or the royal family are judged more 'newsworthy' than the reporting of significant issues and events of international consequence. Traditional news values have been undermined by new values; 'infotainment' is rampant.
>
> (Franklin 1997: 4, quoted in Sparks and Tulloch 2000: 24)

There are other angles to, and explanations of, trivialization. Many commentators have noted the eruption of business into the public sphere. This has taken two main forms, first, the use by businesses and other lobbying organizations of increasingly sophisticated techniques with which to influence the media and second, the exerting of proprietorial influence (Gaber and Barnett 2001).

Proprietor pressure is only one kind of pressure: political parties, business interests, pressure groups and issue campaigners have long sought to use media power to their own ends through advertising or by manipulating editorial content. Many consider that their efforts to do so have recently reached new heights of sophistication such that some believe our media to be mere extensions of the promotional arms of commercial interests (Barnett and Seymour 2000, Franklin 2001) and that, because of this, the public sphere is under threat.

The media as the arena of politics

There is a more specific observation, of the relationship between politics and the media, which reflects wider changes in society.

> When the fortunes of political parties rest on opinion rather than membership and historical allegiances, the means for cultivating and shaping public opinion become crucial to electoral success. In modern society, these means are, of course, the mass media of communication . . . [they] have become the dominant source of information and entertainment in nearly every society and, in many countries, have assumed a new level of independence from which to interject their own voice into the political dialogue. Media logic leads to a style of political reporting that prefers personalities to ideas, simplicity to complexity, confrontation to compromise, and heavy emphasis on 'the horse race' in electoral campaigns.
>
> (Swanson and Mancini 1996: 251)

As these developments have taken place, the media have become central to the political process and, as they have done so, politicians have reacted to this by trying to control what is in the media. Battles between competing ideologies have been replaced by the battle for the media, as rival parties seek to dominate the media agenda, or, in the UK case, as the government struggles for mastery while the opposition looks helplessly on. The weaknesses of the British parliamentary and government systems,[18] failings which make them open to abuse or at least manipulation by those who do not wish to follow conventions or disagree that there might be a generally beneficial consensus, have exacerbated the situation in the UK, as has the failure of the opposition parties, or the left wing of the governing party, successfully to confront the executive. The trends are not so different in many other countries.

What are these trends? Politicians and their associates believe that public opinion can be won not so much by successful government but by dominating the headlines. From this general premise follow certain behaviours: huge efforts are made to control the news agenda; presentation and image become more important than achievement; stories are created in order to divert attention; discipline is imposed upon ministers, members of parliament and information professionals, making a mockery of the theory that policy is decided after open debate; the dirty tricks department is ready with smears, sometimes totally fabricated, with which to undermine the credibility of those who do not follow the line; non-political information professionals are purged from the administration and replaced by compliant allies; journalists are threatened, bought with privileges or frozen out; deals are done with media bosses to get them 'on side'[19] (Osborne 1999, Franklin *et al.* 2001, Franklin 2001, Gaber and Barnett 2001).

In a situation in which an unscrupulous political leadership can use these skills and techniques unchecked, in effect, by either institutions or conscience, what can journalists do? Very little, except from time to time resist pressure and reveal corruption and dishonesties that the government would rather hide, if it suit their proprietors that they do so. The proliferation of outlets for political news means that journalists no longer gatekeep a few precious slots and thus have lost their power to bargain; small audiences for critical and analytical media means they can be treated cavalierly. The demands on journalists, now that they are producing much more news and often simultaneously for several media, mean that there is much less time for fact checking or initiating angles different from those so obligingly provided by the spindoctors.

Technology and the end of journalism

Today, some doubt whether journalism has a future, as self-select information is provided on the Internet and the mediators are cut out (Bardoel 1996). Others see them as already merely functioning as processors – copywriters and dumbers down – for those with the real power to produce information and define truth.

But it is the role of selector, which may be of continuing if not increasing usefulness in the predicted multimedia world. Far from being rendered irrelevant by the explosion of information and the ease of its access, the journalist may be needed, albeit less as originator, as the expert who will help us to navigate through the mass of information now at our disposal; evaluate the data; analyse what interest groups – whether supermarkets or politicians or lobbyists – are claiming; provide us with the wherewithal to make informed decisions and interrogate the rich and powerful. Only journalists, perhaps allied with academics, can perform these functions; however flawed, journalists are often the only guarantors of truth telling and human rights.

The loss of purpose identified by researchers questioning journalists (Merritt 1995) may be a healthy response to their own failures, but it should be a temporary one. Skilled and honest journalists have never been more needed for the provision of information, the scrutiny of public affairs and the investigation of cases of dereliction of duty. Such journalists need media channels which allow them to perform these functions and there are many questions to be raised about the present anglophone media as public interest regulation is relaxed and they are incorporated into global business empires (Philo and Miller 2000), particularly if you consider how influential the anglophone media are, for many different reasons, on the media of other countries (Boyd Barrett 1997). If we contend that journalists are becoming more, not less, critical to the good ordering of our world, then the limitations placed on them matter.

The free market argument and its limitations

It was a widely held assumption of anglophone journalists and observers of journalism until recently that the existence of the socially responsible press was due to the free market which enables such commodities to be traded; impartial and good-quality information is a commodity with a high value. The buyers of newspapers are operating like an electorate; they choose newspapers because of good journalism, so good journalism is to the commercial advantage of proprietors; advertising, which supports good journalism, is thus the means by which the media are made independent of politicians. In the Cold War era, when a helpful contrast was provided by the media of the Soviet dominated countries, this seemed axiomatic.

Curran (1985) punctured the complacency of this argument by showing that advertising is itself very partial; that as advertising developed it supported newspapers selectively according to the wealth of the readership rather than according to its extent; thus mass market newspapers had to survive on their cover price whereas elite ones were subsidized by advertising. Radical newspapers, for example, could not compete with those subsidized by advertising, or those which transformed themselves into mass market entertainment rather than organs of serious political discussion. Furthermore, the commercial interests of advertisers, as of proprietors, impact upon content, privileging that which suits the paymasters.

Yet, at least in free societies you can still set up your own newspaper or TV station, can't you? Keane doubts it. He points to the difference between the world in which a free press developed and today's 'much more oligopolistic, monopolistic, big media conglomerate' world (Keane 2002). There are too many barriers to entry – initial investment needed, hugely capitalized competitors, the need to be big before you can cover your costs. So we are likely to see our media more and more dominated by a few big business conglomerates whose main interest in journalism is that it draw audiences and not upset good contracts.

According to other critics of the argument that the free market guarantees competing opinions, socially responsible journalism is not at all a function of the free market but of other factors. First and foremost is it a function of professional ethics shared among media managers/proprietors and journalists, ethics which enable them to resist commercial pressures and to stand up for what they believe to be in the best interests of society. Those, like Phillip Knightley, who have pointed to the work of *Sunday Times Insight* in the 1970s as the heyday of UK investigative journalism, emphasize these factors (Knightley 1997). Second, it is argued that it is government media regulation which makes possible socially responsible journalism; it is having an appropriate system that biases the media towards social responsibility; controlling the tendency to conglomeration of ownership; monitoring competition to curb its ill effects (Pilger 2001).

Concerns about the alleged irresponsibility of journalism have brought the question of regulation back to the forefront of debate. Regulation was seen by many journalists, until the 1990s, as a tool used by governments to stifle socially responsible (i.e., inquisitive, dissenting) journalism; now it is tending to be seen as a means by which socially responsible journalism may yet be saved.[20] Chalaby (1998) goes so far as to suggest that special regulations during the Second World War improved the quality of the British media.

There is some contrary evidence. The appearance of investigative journalism in Brazil, Venezuela and Argentina (as in Eastern Europe) has come about as a function of the depoliticization of the media, of the growing power of the conglomerates vis-à-vis the political elites and of their using revelatory and sensational journalism to pander to audiences (Waisbord 2001). Whether these unintended consequences of market freedom do amount to an enrichment of the public sphere is difficult to say. In anglophone countries, to summarize the view, deregulation is held to be causing flight from good journalism, to the detriment of the public sphere. This has happened just at the time that the party in power has attempted to sideline parliamentary institutions and use its strength to dominate the media with propaganda. Although Britain still has the BBC as a public service broadcaster in large measure detached from government, commercial interests, as expressed through the 2002 Communications Bill (draft law), are working to de-legitimize it.

Cultural imperialism and soft power

If, under current conditions, it is difficult for journalists to perform their functions responsibly then that (UK) Communications Bill may make this even more improbable by making available large segments of its culture industries to foreign predators, a possibility which, it is thought, will intensify the trends described above.[21] In China the government has so far set its face against all but the minimal involvement of outsiders in its media in the (possibly erroneous) belief that foreign ownership threatens sovereignty by giving persuasive power to outsiders and their interests, whether commercial or political (Clifford 2002). This is an idea which has been given further dimensions through the writings of Joseph Nye, an American political scientist, which have been greeted with interest in China. His thesis is that imparting culture and values is another manifestation of political power, possibly more efficacious though intangible or indirect (Nye 2003, Nye 2002).

Already, the US media have global scope. The world market in entertainment media is dominated by the USA (Tomlinson 1997); anglophone conceptions of news are paramount (Boyd Barrett 1997); anglophone countries are almost impervious to cultural imports from other countries (Tracey 1985). The US continues to push for the abolition of EU trade controls on US films and TV.

However, there is some evidence that US media are going to lose ground as indigenous producers gain professional experience, financial strength and audience approbation (Thomas 2003). Be that as it may, events of the last few years have not warned off the globalizers: the rise of nationalism from France and Holland to India and Chechnya; the anger of Muslim extremists against the West; the regular resurgence of xenophobia in China and Japan are all indications that involvement with other cultures may have costs as well as benefits.

These are the current concerns which form the background to any study of journalism that emanates from an anglophone society. They are sketched here to help expose the approach to the subject and warn the reader of its limitations: to an extent this book looks at journalism in China in order to gain insights about the world in which the author himself lives.

China's journalists

Yet it is not just for that, that China's journalists, as opposed to China's media, are worth attention. First, if the contention that journalists are becoming more, not less, critical to the good ordering of our world has merit, then it could be useful to explore whether Chinese journalists have characteristics that are likely to influence the good ordering of the world of over one-fifth of the world's population. This thought is itself predicated upon another which has been the subject of intense debate in recent years: that 'culture' is that which accounts for the differences between societies. 'Culture' is that which determines economic development or the evolution of political institutions; every issue and aspect of a society, including the media, should be examined in the light of this. Although the most disputed interventions in the debate have been made by Huntingdon (1996) who suggested our future would be one of cultural rivalry, and Fukuyama (1993) who, in what Gray calls his 'innocent parochialism', by contrast believes that anglophone liberalism will gobble up all other cultures, this study has been more influenced by John Gray. Gray has grappled with the implications of 'value pluralism' and advocated mutual respect for and comprehension of different cultures (1995: 140; 2000).

Second, can we learn anything about our own journalists from looking at those with different assumptions and traditions? Studies in Chinese social psychology (Bond 1999) suggest that comparisons in that field are fruitful and enriching for the anglophone equivalent, overturning assumptions, which have been widely held in the academy for generations, that psychology has no cultural differences (Goldberger *et al.* 1995). Indeed it is Chinese psychologists rather than, say, Mediterranean ones, who have started to question the homogenizing assumptions of the discipline.[22] If it is good for psychology, why not for media studies? Some questioning of western premises in media studies is now starting (Curran and Park 2000).

Third, does an examination of Chinese journalists tell us anything more generally about the society in which they operate? How have journalists come through the years in which China sought to take a very different route to wealth and power from that of the rest of the world, before it too embraced free market philosophies deriving from Hayek and Mises? China may now be changing more rapidly than any nation on earth, so what are the roles of the mediators in all this? How do they relate to their complicity in the failures of Maoist China and how are they adapting to the changed environment?

Journalism in China has undergone three broad phases. First, from the late nineteenth century to 1949, a modern type of journalism developed in response to the perceptions of Chinese intellectuals of their nation's plight, to the rapid economic development of the eastern littoral and Canton Province and in response to western models of media organization. From 1949 to around 1979 journalists were obliged to conform to a narrow (though not always as narrow as assumed) definition of their role, but from time to time they were able to break free from the limitations of that role. From 1979 to 1989 they sought to claim a professional status for journalism and to talk the discourse of impartiality; since then journalism has become engulfed in what seems to have become a very different kind of society, much more free, much more wealthy yet deeply divided and shot through with that political nihilism and greed which has so struck informed observers such as Gittings (1996), Barmé (1999) and Becker (2000). The purpose of this book is to explore what parts Chinese journalists may be playing in this new China, and to understand where they are coming from, in the hope that this helps us see where they are heading.

2 The inheritance

Since the early 1990s China has opened up economically to outside ideas and businesses. The media have adjusted and now contrast very markedly with the media of the first decades of Chinese Communist Party (CCP) dictatorship. This chapter explains how an event called the 'Southern Progress' has come to stand for a break with the past; describes the advent of Communist power, the media system it established, the relationship between the media and the leadership and the reforms of 1990s; finally, it returns to the Southern Progress, because the arguments over the publicizing of it are emblematic of still unresolved issues in the Chinese media.

The Vice Chairman's[1] Southern Progress

> Before the 'Progress' there was a feeling of despair. Then all the reporters, as soon as they heard about it, wanted to report it, but they could not. When it came out they considered that there could be no turning back again. After the 'Progress' everything changed.
>
> (Zhang Yinhuan)

Journalists looking back to understand what has been happening in their society refer to 'after the "Southern Progress"' or tour by China's most senior and charismatic politician, Deng Xiaoping, in late 1991, early 1992. We will see the significance of this shortly, but to understand it, it is essential to know the context within which it took place. Against what was Deng's progress a reaction?

From 1949–92

In October 1949 the Chinese Communist Party (CCP) won a Civil War against the party, the Nationalist Party (KMT), from which it had itself sprung. This victory came after the defeat of the Japanese invaders against whom the two parties, at least nominally, had been allied. When it established the People's

Republic of China in October 1949, the CCP's claim to moral authority rested upon its success at arms, its relative administrative competence, its doctrine of respect for the poor and the failure of the KMT, which had been in power since the 1920s, to retain the esteem of public opinion at home or abroad.

The party's pre-eminent leader, Mao Zedong, had attained that pre-eminence on account of his success as a war leader in the hinterland, his ability to manipulate social issues to the advantage of the CCP, the party's steadfast opposition to foreign depredations and his ruthless suppression of competitors. He, his colleagues and their party, were greeted with widespread enthusiasm from a population exhausted by war, hunger and mismanagement. They had not only all power, but the goodwill of most of the country, in their grasp.

Unfortunately, the CCP carried ideological baggage and traditions of behaviour which it had adapted from its Bolshevik instructors in the 1920s and which were to be the enemies of its promise to provide such leadership for China that the country would begin to re-establish itself after centuries of domestic decline, defeats abroad and political failure. The Party claimed that 'democracy' (which it called 'bourgeois democracy') had failed in China; that those of China's ills which could not plausibly be blamed upon foreigners could be attributed to the middle classes, and in particular to landlords; that China's future lay in emulating the USSR in overturning all existing institutions and creating a dictatorship to rule in the name of the virtually non-existent urban working class.

In retrospect it is easy to see that this was largely irrational nonsense. What China needed was peace, less corrupt government and the harnessing of the energies of people to their own advantage and the common good; the kind of programme Deng Xiaoping would get around to forty years later. Instead, although, at first, tactical compromises were made which allowed aspects of normal life to survive for a time, and although many senior CCP officials certainly hoped that class revolution would not be carried too far, since they knew that China needed the expertise of its middle classes, ideology and unreason gained the upper hand. In order to obliterate those with the knowledge or ability to criticize; to terrify potential opponents; and, to create a class of people profiting from the crimes of the regime, the Party exploited, exacerbated or created jealousies and hatreds in the countryside in particular, turning groups of people against each other and fomenting savagery at least as destructive of social and economic well-being as the Civil War which preceded its accession to power. This was called Land Reform, and took place in the early 1950s.[2]

However, although landlordism had long been claimed to be the cause of all discontents, much as it was for Ireland and with even less justification[3], in fact there were too few landlords and their holdings were too tiny to be of much social or economic significance.[4] They were murdered anyway, and then Party functionaries started on the wealthier peasants so that they would have some loot to distribute to their adherents. Very soon after consolidating its support and eliminating potential subversion in this manner, the Party introduced collectivization, by which peasants were obliged to help each other by pooling resources while remaining individual proprietors. At the next stage, claimed completed by

1957, all peasants had given their land to cooperative entities and were enjoying the status of employees of the collective.

In the same period the assets of foreigners and wealthy business people were expropriated and voluntary, welfare and educational institutions swallowed by the state or smashed. China's finest universities and colleges would thereafter suffer decades of neglect or wrecking, to say nothing of thousands of other products of enterprise and genius. Over the 1950s more and more of the economy became owned and directed by the government, without any democratic checks upon the arrogance and rapacity of its officials, any systemic accountability nor any efficacious mode of inquiring as to the effects on people.

The CCP, with a membership of approximately 4.5 million in 1949, would expand to 17 million by 1961. Its leaders were themselves mostly intellectuals from the land-owning, business or professional classes yet claimed to speak for the workers and peasants. Below the policy-making higher levels, the task of Party cells was to oversee the ideological status of the executive and administration and all important positions in government were filled by members; before long most management positions in the economy were also filled by members.

Party members did not have orthodoxy imposed upon them by execution, as in the Soviet Union, but through thought reform, or 'brainwashing (*xinao*)'. The CCP leaders professed to believe that they were creating a 'new man' which would be dedicated to the common weal rather than to his own, or his family's interests. The common weal was of course defined by the leaders, so that whoever might disagree with them could be found in need of psychological reprogramming as being 'incorrect' and sent to a camp where special techniques were used to force them into submission (Hsu 1995: 659–660). This process is reported in vivid detail in Liang and Shapiro (1984: 11–14).

Related techniques were used on the population at large, which was regimented into mass organizations of many tens of millions, such as the Women's Federation or Youth Federation, through which they might be indoctrinated through study sessions, by being denied information and through obligatory involvement in mass campaigns which often made them complicit in the persecution of minorities.

Of the obstructive and inhumane institutions created by the CCP the worst was perhaps the *Danwei*, or Work Unit, in which every individual was imprisoned forever and which decided his or her domestic, social and economic life in its entirety.

> The Danwei gathers together within the control of a single body all the threads of an individual's life, it measures according to its own standards the states, habits and behaviour of every person, it is the unit and norm of work, of life and of thought, it is the sole leadership of the Party in the context of daily life, it is the Party in flesh and blood.
>
> (Broyelle *et al.* 1980: 22)

As if this were not enough control, Kang Sheng, a vicious and sinister policeman, adopted the Soviet mode of dealing with people that he or his associates did not like, and set up a network of slave labour camps which has at various times been publicly admitted to contain at least 40 million souls (Bao and Chelminski 1973).

The transformation of economy and society

In 1955 the first 5 Year Plan for Industry was inaugurated, with huge investments in heavy industry made possible by Soviet financial aid and expertise. This led to a second ambitious plan for further industrial development and for scientific and technical education. Before the second plan could get under way it was decided to take the process of collectivization much further and to unite agriculture, local industry and administration into 'People's Communes', replacing local administrative divisions. Virtually all remaining private property, indeed all privacy, was expropriated. Each commune was divided into brigades (usually traditional villages) which allocated tasks to individuals and experimented with new ideas such as communal messing and childcare. The product of the commune, after the payment of state quotas, was shared. There was little incentive to improvement and low productivity; carelessness and cynicism soon became typical. Those without power or connections to power were, in effect, serfs.

Two monstrous experiments in further overturning China took place as Mao Zedong became frustrated with progress towards his utopia.[5] In 1958 the Great Leap Forward, discussed in Chapter 5, was announced as an attempt to industrialize China 'overnight' and from 1965, for approximately five years, most of what was left of Chinese culture was to be obliterated and the least indication of ambition or individualism among those not part of the ruling cliques was assaulted (the Cultural Revolution, Chapter 5). The civil service established by the Party upon its accession to power, which often contained honest and idealistic functionaries, virtually disintegrated in much of the country. By the early 1970s the position of all but the gangs of those who had managed to seize power in villages, towns and cities, subject to little or no systemic restraint, was pathetic. So regimented and repressive had the climate become that I remember, at the end of the Cultural Revolution, registering shock and fear at being greeted by a student wearing something as provoking as a brown corduroy jacket.[6]

There were positive aspects to the record of the CCP before 1978: a modicum of healthcare was made available; the position of women improved in theory, and probably in practice; the power of the clans of the south was much diminished and the arbitrary power of landlords or local thugs everywhere replaced by that of officials who could be competent; serious attempts were made to curtail exploitation of the poor and landless; education perhaps became more generalized; there was enormous infrastructure investment in the early years but it was not kept up; heavy industries probably developed more rapidly than they would have done under capitalism; security of employment was available to many more people than would have been provided for in a privatized economy. Yet even some of these achievements are now being dismantled.[7]

The people destroyed in CCP-induced famines (see Shapiro 2001: 197 on 'the greatest human-created famine in history' and also Becker 1996) and purges cannot be brought back to life, nor the hopes realized for those who lived but were ruined; there is a faint chance that the environment may be saved, though so extreme is the devastation of nature that journalists and their scientific informants despair (Liu and Link 1998). Reporters (see Chapter 10) are covering environment stories more and more, and there is an awareness of what constitutes degradation, but with widespread indifference to the public weal and the continuance of projects such as the Three Gorges Dam, there is little they can do. This is a description of the past, but some journalists believe that little has changed, despite the creation of a Ministry for Environmental Protection:

> Mao and the Party thought little more of wrenching millions from their homes and families in mass relocations than they did of violating the face of nature beyond its ability to adjust. They gave little more consideration to destroying the dreams and lives of millions of individuals than they did to rejecting centuries of publicly stated ideals of harmonious accommodation to nature. The natural world was used and misused in extraordinary ways that defied logic and were catastrophic for human beings . . .
>
> (Shapiro 2001: 202)

The reaction against Maoism

When Mao Zedong died, his acolytes, the 'Gang of Four' fell and when, finally, his successor, Hua Guofeng, gave way to Deng Xiaoping and his team in the early 1980s, there was a widespread understanding that China had failed. There was hunger, waste, cynicism, grief and despair. The Chinese had been cut off almost entirely from the rest of the world, but they did not need the rest of the world to tell them that their society did not work. At least senior officials knew that very well. Their secret sources of information – Restricted Circulation Publications (RCPs, see Chapter 9) – translated foreign media reports; journalists abroad, often amazed at the gap between China and the rest, selected whatever would most surprise their masters. Deng decided very rapidly that what China needed was opening to the advanced economies and decentralization and deregulation of the economy at home. From 1978, though slowly, he began to reverse the statism of his predecessors and initiated limited liberalization of the agricultural economy and employment; moves towards a system of law to protect ordinary people and regulate contracts; measures to make state enterprises more responsible and responsive; the introduction of Special Economic Zones where foreign investors could run enterprises according to western models and without reference to socialist norms; reform of the banking system. Between 1978 and 1989 there were very rapid gains in agricultural and rural industrial production. These and other improvements silenced the left, which was obliged to leave unexpressed its concern for the fate of the socialist revolution.

It was wise to do so, since the dissatisfaction which did develop was more with the slow pace of change than with any desire to halt it. Deng Xiaoping encouraged self-expression in the economic sphere but, both out of his own beliefs and in order not to provoke the left, stifled political and cultural expression and in particular the cries for democracy, of whom the most famous voice was that of the Peking electrician Wei Jingshen. The Democracy Movement was a campaign, uncoordinated but with widespread manifestations, for more open politics; Wei became its symbol and only the most famous of those who were imprisoned for decades simply for advocating change in the late 1970s.

The more tolerant 1980s, more tolerant because Deng Xiaoping appeared to have seen off the left and did not need to placate them with the carcasses of any more progressives for the present, brought the same topics to the fore once more, culminating in nation-wide demonstrations of 1989 in which students, industrial workers and journalists united to call for democracy and freedom of expression. The army suppressed them in Peking with the Tiananmen massacre of 4 June 1989. The mobilization of students and workers in favour of better government, an end to corruption and the granting of political freedoms were understood by the left, first and foremost, as a consequence of the policies of Deng and his enthusiastic partisans, then as having been exacerbated by foreign meddling. They seized the moment of the Tiananmen massacre to disgrace the progressives and, once again ascendant, the left got another chance to see what it might propose.

Media institutions

The institutional system[8] into which the media have fitted since 1949 comprises several distinct organizations, themselves appertaining either to the state or the CCP. Under the State Council are the Ministry of Culture, New China News Agency (NCNA) and the State Administration of Radio Film and TV (SARFT), the State Administration of Press and Publication, the State Information Office, among other things. The key representatives of these organizations may meet together in a Leadership Small Group. Each of the organizations will have provincial and local branches. For example, under the NCNA will come the vast network of NCNA branches; under the SARFT come the provincial equivalents which themselves have lower-level operations below them. Under the Ministry of Culture come organizations dealing with films, publishing and theatre with their provincial and local equivalents.

Parallel to this system is the Party's own organization, headed by the Propaganda Department of the Central Committee which has sections at every level of administration of which local newspapers and broadcasting channels must take account. The Propaganda Department answers for the information and cultural networks of institutions (*xitong*) to the most powerful decision-making body in China, the Standing Committee of the Politburo of the Central Committee of the CCP.

Media organizations (newspaper publishing companies, broadcasting bodies) are organized like other government bodies, according to rank. Thus they are ranked according to whether they are at central government level, provincial level, district level, county or township level. Every media channel has a rank one level below its sponsor such that *The People's Daily* holds the rank of a ministry whereas provincial papers have district rank and so on. This ranking, along with their characteristics and functions determines relationships with other institutions, privileges and pull. At the top of the hierarchy are the Party organs controlled by the Central Committee, *The People's Daily* and *Seek Facts* (until 1988 *Red Flag*). At the provincial or regional level there is at least one organ of the Provincial Party Committee, e.g. *Xinjiang Daily* (in this case with Turkic and Chinese editions). Below the Party organs are special interest publications such as the *Communist Youth Daily* of the Young Communist League and so forth. A full description of the system is given in Chen Huailin and Lee (1998). Technically all these publications are non-profit making as opposed to profit making.

Except in Hong Kong the mass media are owned by the state. However, regional and local media are not branches of the centre and neither need to consult with the centre in managerial or technical matters nor are subject to any financial or managerial control from the centre as their points of reference are according to their level in the hierarchy. They are answerable to the administrations at national, regional and local levels.

Policy control is nevertheless exercised through the CCP propaganda departments at the different administrative levels (Jiang 1995: 39, Huang *et al.* 1997) under the rule known as the *party principle*, by which the media must adhere ideologically to the party line, propagate the party message and obey its policies. These local departments are dominated by their central organ:

> it is the Central Propaganda Department of the CCP that really manages these elements of the ideology and propaganda system in China . . . [it] is the key implementer of instructions from the leading group.
>
> (Hsiao and Cheek 1995: 78–79)

Not only are the local propaganda departments under their central body, so are various other central bodies with roles important for the media. Perry summarizes the position as he sees it:

> The Central Propaganda Department guides and supervises the work of several state bodies within the central government, including the State Administration of Radio, Film and Television, the State Administration of Press and Publication, the State Council Information Office. In Chinese administrative terms, these bodies are within the network, or xitong [system], of the Propaganda Department.
>
> (Perry and Selden 2000: 27–28)

From the viewpoint of the individual journalist, activities in the field are circumscribed by those lower-level Propaganda Departments which are present in all significant administrative units at every level of administration. Every medium is obliged to have a party cell of some kind through which the local propaganda department, answerable to the central Propaganda Department in Peking, will control it. 'Work units' (*danwei*) have party cells, party branches or general party branches depending upon their size. A media 'work unit' with more than fifty party members has a party committee. The same formula applies to smaller units except that the Propaganda Department will delegate lower-level emissaries to liaise. This system does not appear to have changed from that which Porter found during his experience of New China News Agency in 1979 (Porter 1992: 6).

Thus the Editor of Shanghai's *Liberation Daily*, a medium of the stature of the *New York Times*, attends fortnightly meetings with the Shanghai City Propaganda Department, meetings which cause him intense nervousness because the newspaper's adherence to known or unknown lines will be judged.

> The Editor goes to a meeting with the Propaganda Department every two weeks. There the officials tell him what they think has gone bad in the recent coverage, but usually place more emphasis upon the kind of topics they want to see covered in the weeks ahead. They also discuss the work of particular reporters.
>
> (Gu 2000)

Until the 1980s the line imposed by the propaganda system was adhered to as much out of a sense of mission as from gullibility or fear. This is no longer the case:

> In a period when the Party has great prestige, this conformity is a form of discipline based on trust; when the Party does not have prestige, as is the case now, it is a form of intimidation that, while still working most of the time, generates a reservoir of resentment and alienation from officialdom.
>
> (Hsiao and Cheek 1995: 80)

Since the rules are no longer clear-cut, there are often muddles and clashes. Magazines have continued to be proscribed, either indefinitely or for short periods, because they have offended the government (IFEX 1999, Prisma 2001). The slightest favourable reference to Taiwan or to the liberation movements in Tibet or East Turkestan (Xinjiang) is impermissible.

The Southern Progress

The institutional system described above persists notwithstanding the gigantic changes which have been taking place since 1992. It is time to return briefly to the wider economic and political context in which the system now operates. As we saw above, after the Tiananmen massacre, those in power who had recently advocated opening up to the outside world, freeing up the centrally managed economy and reducing the role of ideology in society – let us call them progressives – had been eclipsed. Although the leftists (whom we may also call the conservatives) had not succeeded in stopping the existing initiatives towards opening to the West, the move towards a market economy in China was slowed. Why? Partly because the progressives were seen as having brought about the dissatisfaction which had turned into demonstrations, then chaos; they were also seen as having floundered when faced with opposition, and placed the Party in danger. These same people were those who had advocated closer intercourse with the West, and it had been the West that had first enthused about the Tiananmen demonstrations and then vilified China when they were put down. *Ipso facto*, the progressives were part of a western inspired plot to denigrate, or even undermine China. Leftists had anyway been suspicious of reforms which might harm their interest in control over the economy, or their very jobs; their hostility also reflected fear of China going down the same path as Russia, which was seen as having abandoned socialism and to be on the point of disintegrating. Deng Xiaoping did not see the relevance of the Russian example and was impatient with the failure of the left to come up with solutions to China's problems, her inability to compete economically or militarily in the world, or to satisfy the justifiable aspirations of the Chinese:

> Apparently Deng felt by the end of 1991 that the conservative-minded readjustment of 1989 had lasted too long. With the 14th Congress of the CCP scheduled for later in 1992 there was a need for some immediate action. Though clearly not in perfect health and variable both in his strength and clarity of speech – he was 88 at this stage – Deng took a much publicised 'Journey of Inspection' to the south of China and the areas of rapid economic development and close foreign economic relations: notably Shanghai, Wuhan, Zhuhai and Shenzhen.
>
> (Goodman 1994: 113)

In late 1991 Deng visited Shanghai and spoke to closed meeting of cadres to encourage more initiative in releasing the economy; he followed this up in January 1992 with a tour of the economically developed areas of the south in order to exhort them to great changes and to demonstrate to the country at large his support for them. He stopped his train in selected areas, summoned provincial governors and officials and harangued them to be more courageous about freeing up economic controls, taking advantage of foreign investment and setting up stock markets. By choosing the Special Economic Zones to call in on, he showed that he considered these boom towns to be models. He asserted everywhere that he considered a much faster pace of economic development to be essential if the CCP were to remain in power and if China were to survive internationally. None of these activities were reported in the media.

Publicizing the Southern Progress

Although Deng, confident that the left's inability to make any useful proposals was clear, left Peking so that he might appeal to progressive leaders in the south and east whom he knew to be chafing, he did so without the support of his senior colleagues. There was no public debate over policy differences in the media, the faction with the upper hand generally imposed its line, ensuring that its critics had no outlet for their views, even when those critics had the prestige of Deng Xiaoping. As was Mao Zedong in 1958 and 1965, so, thirty years later, Deng was obliged to circumvent the party politics of the capital and appeal directly to those in the provinces who might share his views. In particular he sought to appeal to constituencies of forward-thinking officials who considered that the conservative economic policies of the previous two and a half years had been damaging.

Although his 'Progress' was an event of great political significance, the release of information about it was not achieved without delays and difficulties and illustrates both how the media operate in China and the workings of the political process.

Although Jiang Zemin is believed to have been fully in the know (Gilley 1998: 186) he too was unable to persuade leftists in the Propaganda Department[9] to report the 'Progress' in the media such that while the Hong Kong, and later, world, media were reporting it as significant news, not for nearly two months did New China News Agency carry the story.

Journalists remember as notable moments in their lives the days that their own channels decided to run it. Zhang Yinhuan of CCTV put it this way:

> When CCTV decided to publicize the Progress, we were all very excited. We had been thinking about this for a long time. After it happened, everything began to change.

Kang Keming, then of *Liberation Daily*, said:

> The *Liberation Daily* has always been in the forefront of developments in China, from the Great Leap to the Cultural Revolution. It was we at *Liberation Daily* which recognized that what Comrade Deng Xiaoping had done had the support of the whole nation. We were the first.

Deng Xiaoping's 'Progress' gave his imprimatur to the business and industrial developments taking place in the south and to their social implications. It calmed the fears of the enterprising that the economic reforms might be set back or that the events of 1989 presaged another dark age; economic endeavour took off. According to one well-placed executive in CCTV, it was above all the television transmission – the visual proof – of the southern tour that had impact and confirmed its implications (Jiang 1995: 104).

Shortly after the Chinese audiences learned of the Southern Progress, change took place in ways that were so dramatic and so far-reaching as to suggest that the left was completely vanquished, at least in the coastal and southern provinces. The number of Special Economic Zones – areas where government regulations hardly ran – leapt from 117 to 1,951 in a year (Schell 1995: 391); the privatization of land, commercialization of housing, introduction of stock exchanges and the possibility of a 'free' labour market all presaged a return to the kind of unregulated capitalism that the CCP had come to power to abolish and surpass.

The Party and the media

What has the supposedly totalitarian Party said about these alternatives? The danger of subversive political views appearing in the media is the core interest, although ostensibly the main concern has been the moral one. As early as 1980 Party General Secretary Hu Yaobang 'expressed concern about the sexually permissive content in foreign films' and in 1982 regulations were issued banning the import of pornographic and anti-Party foreign products and seeking to ensure that foreign products did not dominate any TV stations' broadcast schedule (Gordon 1996: 21). CCTV's first US tele-drama caused concern on account of the violence in it and was axed after twelve episodes (Jiang 1995: 169). With China joining the World Trade Organization, concern about 'decadent' media content has not receded (Prisma 2001: 202). How the views of those in power are reflected in the media is dealt with in Chapter 6. However, it is necessary to make some general points here about the relationship between leadership and media.

Senior media personnel are usually Party members and membership is a commonsense career move for aspiring media managers, but journalists are not all Party members, nor is membership taken into account in daily work routines (Jiang 1995: 42). However, there has always been a close relationship between media personnel and CCP and, therefore, state leadership. Journalism is a recognized road to the higher reaches of Party and State and the editor of *The People's Daily* and the director of the New China News Agency, for example, are officials of ministerial rank rather than simply public figures as they might be in western countries. The current President of China Central Television (CCTV) was, until his age required his retirement from the government post in 1997, concurrently a government Deputy Minister. The current Deputy Mayor of Shanghai, a significant national politician, is a former journalist and Dean of Fudan University's School of Journalism. However, this kind of integration should not be assumed to result in a total identification between ministerial and media interests or opinions, or heavy-handed censorship. It is through self-censorship rather than the correcting or eliminating of texts that orthodoxy is maintained (Lent 1978: 19, Polumbaum 1990: 55, Jernow 1993: 22). Jenner, with his historical perspective, puts it this way:

> One thinks of autocratic regimes as imposing a harsh discipline that has everyone obeying orders, but life in China is not like that. The negative resistance to authority to which the unfree have to resort is just as far removed from the political culture of democracy as is the dictatorship that rules them.
>
> (Jenner 1994: 186)

In an example which has been cited elsewhere, Polumbaum (1990) tells how the editor of an evening paper 'spiked' the report of a stabbing at a railway station by two drunks of another race because he was afraid that such a report would feed prejudice. This conformed to official policy as does the omission of such sensitive issues as rebel 'terrorism'. Interviewees have several times revealed that arguments take place in newsrooms over, for example, the coverage of demonstrations. Usually caution wins, although reporters sometimes do.

From time to time, senior leaders make statements about the role of the media, designed to encourage and identify what they regard as the positive. In 1994 President Jiang required the media to perform four major tasks: arming the people with science, guiding the people with correct opinion, educating the people in high moral standards and 'inspiring the people with outstanding works' (Li 1998: 325).

In 1996, perhaps concerned at the steady reduction in political content of the media, President Jiang visited both the *Liberation Army Daily* and *The People's Daily* and emphasized the need to maintain political loyalty, a call simultaneously underscored by a Party Plenum resolution calling on journalists to maintain party discipline and political loyalty (Hazelbarth 1997: 15). CCTV had an important visitor in 1997. Not only did Li Peng,[10] usually regarded as the leading leftist, compliment the team of investigative journalists working on *Focal Point*, but he left them a motto in his own calligraphy, which read, according to an interviewee

> Praise the vanguard
> Criticize that which is backward
> Bring Justice to society
> (Deng Huo)

The interviewees who first described this took it as an endorsement of their own view of journalists as being themselves a vanguard; later interviewees were more cynical. Political leaders, they felt, only encouraged journalism of this kind because they could see that it helped give the appearance of greater freedom and openness. But then, the appearance might whet the appetite for the reality.

The limits of dissent

That the Chinese government is repressive is clear: it is difficult, though, to distinguish any consistent policy. In June 1999 journalists associated with the banned China Democracy Party were imprisoned for producing an unauthorized magazine and distributing articles on the Internet; the following month three journalists who tried to publish an independent magazine for workers were also imprisoned (CPJ 1999: 241). President Jiang Zemin complained that there were too many publications in circulation and greater vigilance and 'public scrutiny' by the Party was promised. The year 1999 was a particularly bad year for journalists, which may account for why those interviewed asked that their names be withheld that year, whereas they had not in 1998. There were at least eleven journalists arrested, bringing the total number of journalists in prison to nineteen (CPJ 1999: 240). Editions of *Time* and *Asia Week* were banned (Chang 2001: 152). To a great extent this can be explained by the Taiwan crisis, sensitivity over the 50th Anniversary Celebrations of the CCP and the nationwide demonstrations by the Falungong which rattled the authorities.[11]

Such control is overt in times of crisis when the Party will instruct the media to deploy the New China News Agency texts:

> The Party sets the overall tone and direction for the press implicitly through general policy statements, and more directly by specifying instructions and priorities for the press via documents and bulletins transmitted from propaganda authorities to new organisations and their Party administrators, editors and reporters.
>
> (Polumbaum 1990: 53)

And not only times of crisis, but times of potential stress. According to reports in the international media (BBC 2002a) reportage of the Party Congress was absolutely uniform across the press at the week ending 16–17 November 2002. The only minor exception was that *Weekend South* made so bold as to create a profile of the new General Secretary, from its own researches, something no other channel had dared to do.

The Internet

In the matter of the Internet, though, the government has been and intends to be decidedly proactive. Chinese enthusiasm for the Internet, as for mobile phones, has been sensational to the extent that some observers consider that Chinese will shortly be its most commonly used language. The Internet has provided the Chinese diaspora, or at least that significant and loquacious minority of it which wants to debate China's future, Chinese politics and Chinese culture, with a kind of virtual Chinese public sphere.[12] There are many thousands of Websites devoted to Chinese affairs, many of which connect with users in China, providing the kind of swift communication of events and ideas that the early reformers so badly lacked. The very style of discussion – open, subversive, crude – is anathema to the CCP which has attempted various kinds of controls since the 1990s. Over the year 2000, Internet regulations obliged private portals to be closed or be taken over by authorized sites; required Internet operatives to gain approval for the disclosure of undefined state information or state secrets. In 2001 there were police raids on major Internet service providers, partial shutdowns, enforcement of filters and 'stricter oversight of chat rooms and bulletin boards'. The effort of supervision may employ as many as 30,000 people (BBC 2002). A Chinese Web publisher was said to have been put on trial for allowing articles about pro-democracy activism, the Falungong (long a forbidden topic) and the liberation movement in East Turkestan (Reuters 20 August 2001). Reuters reported in June 2002 that around 3,000 Internet cafes were closed and 11,000 temporarily banned, of which, by BBC report, only 30 had reopened in late 2002 (BBC 2002).

Concerned about the seeping into China of foreign ideas and information, the government has limited to 50 per cent the percentage of an Internet company which can be owned by a foreign interests (no holding in telecommunications companies is allowed). China has blocked and then unblocked foreign Websites such as those of Reuters, CNN, *The Washington Post* and *New York Times*; and in September 2002 blocked Google and Altavista (BBC 2002) although, if past precedent is a guide, Chinese surfers will be using proxy servers.

Up-to-date and detailed information can be found from the Internet publications of the organization Human Rights in China and from the Websites of those listed in their Internet publication, *Human Rights Forum*.[13]

The government knows the value of the Internet and wants to increase access. However, it also wants to control content and to this end Jiang Mianheng, son of Jiang Zemin, has set up a company to create an exclusively Chinese Internet, The China C-Net Strategic Alliance, to be independent of the world Internet and thus safe from 'electronic heroin' (Fewsmith 2001: 75).

The inheritance is therefore that of a rigid system which functions in ways that are often more flexible than observers of the system might expect. There is repression, but there is growth and development. Deng's Southern Progress of 1991–2 stimulated change in the media as it did in many other sectors of society. The next chapter will characterize those changes.

3   Media characteristics

In what ways have the media responded to the relaxation of economic controls, the introduction of some free market disciplines and opportunities? The state continues to own broadcasters and publishers, and to dominate those production companies which are nominally independent. Yet this has not stifled the emergence of very different forms and contents. In this chapter we look at five areas of change, pointed out for us by editor Wen Weiping: 'The first great change has been one of quantity . . . second, the media are growing in self-determination. As chief editor [today] I must work out the function of my newspaper and respond to readers. Third, there is the new economic independence. Fourth the media have become powerful in their scrutiny of public affairs; they express this by revelation and by intervention in policy matters. Finally the media now serve the people as consumers, providing every kind of advice and entertainment'.[1]

The scope of the media[2]

The scale of the Chinese media is now vast and China is written of as 'the largest television market in the world' with '80 million multi-channel cable TV homes, 330 million terrestrial TV homes and 2000 or more television stations' (Gordon 2000: 14). Television is only one part of the story of a media explosion more rapid than any society has ever seen, although similar processes are taking place on a smaller scale in other countries, and often with less dramatic results. Below are the latest figures obtainable; rows three and four contain the equivalent for two decades earlier and US comparisons.

The growth has been generalized around the whole country and among all media. The most spectacular take-off has been in television, which we look at in more detail below. It is probably the case that Chinese-language TV programming is more extensively watched than even English-language programming, and it is watched mainly by people who consider Chinese to be their first language. But the sheer quantity of all types of media channel; the variety of distribution

Table 3.1 Chinese media in 2001 with equivalent figures for 1979 and US comparisons

	2001	*1979*	*US comparisons*
Newspapers	2,007[3]	185 (some cite fewer)	3,207 (2001)
Periodicals	8,725[4]	Not known	N/a
Radio stations	1,416	93	Over 10,000 (1998)
Radio sets	417 million (1997)		575 million (1997)
Terrestrial TV stations[5]	943	32	Over 1,500 (1997)
TV channels	390[6]		
Cable stations	1,270	Not known	9,000 (1997)
TV sets	400 million (1997)		219 million (1997)
Access to TV[7]	Over 1 billion (2000)	10 million (1980)	

Sources: Lin 1994, Li 1998, *CIA World Factbook* 2001, GGDZ 2001, Prisma 2001, ZSKXCY 2001.
Any differences between the data are not significant for the purposes of this chapter.

outlets and the shift towards entertainment and consumer journalism; and especially manifestations of less deferential and more inquiring media products are all particularly startling to anyone who visited China around 1990 and has again today: the mass media are unrecognizable. How did this come about?

Media reforms

Concomitant with the economic developments which took place following the Southern Progress, a process known as 'media commercialization' got underway, without any clear plan and in response to various pressures upon the media: the demand by domestic and foreign businesses for advertising opportunities; the inability of the state to continue to subsidize the media; the public demand for more media and the advent of new technology requiring extensive investment. However, it was never the intention of the government to relinquish supervisory powers and in essence the institutional system, described above, remained as it had always been since 1949.

The implications for television in particular would be great. Advertising had been introduced on Chinese TV in 1979. Initially the reason was not financial but to improve the provision of information. The State Council circular that authorized commercials listed the functions of advertising as disseminating information, improving production, expanding circulation, providing guidance to consumers, invigorating the economy, offering conveniences to people in their daily life and developing international economy and trade (Jiang 1995: 53). Revenues went to the state, which continued to allocate budgets as heretofore.

In 1983 that system of central allocation of TV funding was abandoned at the same time that other acts of decentralization of the economy were being undertaken; in the future the regions and localities would be responsible for their own media development, although central help continued to be available for poorer areas from the State Administration for Radio Film and Television. This was successful and between 1983 and 1993 the number of TV stations increased from 52 to 700 (Gordon 1996: 24). The government continued to fund China Central Television (CCTV).

However, the government was finding the costs of the burgeoning media system increasingly onerous and, from the mid-1980s, pushed the media to generate as much revenue as possible from their own business ventures and, in particular but not exclusively, from advertising. Launching state institutions into the market is known, graphically, as *jumping into the ocean*.

The government also experimented, in a 1984 contract between CCTV and the Ministry of Finance, with a new financing system. The Self-Sufficiency System, as it came to be called, provided a fixed budget for CCTV from the government while permitting CCTV to keep all its earnings. Certain requirements as to the provision of news, educational programmes, local production and quality were stipulated.

In 1991 this system would be further refined and, in the year of Deng Xiaoping's Progress, was generalized to the media as a whole; advertising boomed as the economy took off.

Economic independence

Media commercialization, or the permitting (later forcing) of the media to raise their own revenue, and the adoption of variations on the CCTV reform of personnel employment policies, had unanticipated impacts as those authorities with permission to publish realized that publications can be 'licences to print money', in Lord Thomson's famous phrase, and as media workers saw opportunities for themselves. This is still a very controlled society in which no endeavour can start without the correct procedures having been gone through, often entailing paying for the 'chop' of various different functionaries. Thus organizations which already had licences granted long before commercialization were in a much stronger position than those who just had dreams. Would-be entrepreneurs would go to them and suggest ways in which the licences might be exploited for profit by turning print or broadcast publications into advertising or sponsorship vehicles. Growing advertising revenue whetted the appetite of media organizations for making money and, finding themselves sitting on underused assets of buildings, machinery, distribution systems and people, they set about diversifying in order to provide themselves with varied income streams. The nation's number one news wholesaler, New China News Agency, and the foremost national newspaper, *The People's Daily*, both run over twenty businesses and their efforts are emulated by many if not most other newspapers. This gives a strength and confidence to these institutions that are useful in dealings with government. Many raise their own advertising and sponsorship revenue without the use of any intermediary and some TV companies do barter deals with foreign production houses for programming in exchange for advertising slots.

Media operations have thus expanded into conglomerates of businesses earning money in many different spheres, buying other media channels, hotels, car-hire companies and restaurants. Their investments are controlled; print media can usually not cross-invest in broadcasting and vice versa, nor can they invest outwith their province, or possibly outwith their own market area (Pan 2000). Conglomeration,[8] while often desired by executives of successful media companies wanting to find ways of spending their immense profits other than on their already magnificent office buildings, equipment, salaries and employee benefits, is not always voluntary. In August 1999 Shanghai's distinguished but dull and loss-making elite daily the *Wenhui Bao* was conglomerated with the popular and financially very profitable *Xinmin Wanbao*, a move making obvious sense to officials of the Shanghai Media Bureau but less so to the reporters of *Xinmin* who found their salary average reduced from 6,000 yuan to 4,000 yuan while the average on Wenhui went up from 2,000 yuan to 4,000[9] (Pan 2000). Chen Huailin explains conglomeration thus: 'the formation of press conglomeration in China is strictly engineered by the state, revolving around a group of "core" party organs, which serve as umbrella organizations to incorporate a multitude of auxiliary newspapers and magazines designed for various specialized areas of interest' (Chen Huailin and Chan 1998: 26). He goes on to cite the case of *The People's Daily* which at the time of writing published five newspapers and six magazines. He notes that there is a potential for a social cost which 'the Chinese authorities do not seem to have thought through because the policy change was declared by fiat, devoid of transparency, and probably masking a series of behind-the-scene bargaining with emergent financial forces' (Chen Huailin and Chan 1998: 28). There were reported to be fifteen major press groups based in Peking, Canton and Chengdu in 2001; 'they have what is known as a "red hat" meaning that they work under the supervision of someone connected with the government' (Prisma 2001: 201).

International, rather than domestic, pressures appear to be behind the major development of December 2001 when the state-backed China Radio, Film and Television Group was established, potentially the dominating force in the emergent Chinese production industry. It is to provide production services in radio, TV, film, online, newspaper and journal publishing as well as innumerable tangential services from advertising to technological R & D to property services. Similar, but regional, groupings have been set up in Peking, Shanghai and three provinces (though not Canton). The principal aim is presumably to provide an adequately resourced national producer able to compete with the likes of AOL Time-Warner. The group is made up of the already powerful CCTV, CCR and China Radio International CRI; has over 20,000 employees and has fixed assets of over £1.65bn UK (Jiang 2002: 13).

Self-determination

In the race to seize the markets, those bodies permitted to publish are licensing entrepreneurs to produce magazines and newspapers that they cannot produce themselves; cable is expanding rapidly to meet the need for local, entertainment-orientated programming; editorial departments are assigned revenue quotas. There is expansion in the number of titles of limited circulation or specialist publications of every conceivable type.

What Peter Berger calls 'the marketization of political management' has not yet extended to allowing private ownership of the media although the *Chengdu Business News*, a previously ailing Sichuan paper, has stretched the rules. *Chengdu Business News* is widely regarded as a forerunner of future developments as the first newspaper to be allowed to have private investors. The effect on journalists has been interesting. It is reported that while journalists are exposed to some more commercial disciplines than they would have been subject to under the old state management, their professional status is acknowledged and indeed underlined by the management's respect for their high educational standards, explicit acknowledgement of their professional integrity (there is a system in place to protect journalists from bribery propositions) and celebration of 'professional excellence' (Huang 2000: 24). In Peking the *Beijing Times*, headed since early 2002 by one of the interviewees for this book, aims to become the largest public-owned (rather than state-owned) newspaper in China. Private ownership may not yet be possible, but private involvement under state tutelage is given the euphemism 'public ownership'.

In the twelve years of the Cultural Revolution the only television entertainment permitted consisted of the eight model revolutionary operas sponsored by Jiang Qing. The production industry being virtually destroyed, it was understood that it would take time to rebuild, and that foreign programming might fill the gap, so in 1979 the government authorized screening of selected products and CCTV started by buying the US series *The Man from Atlantis* (Howkins 1982: 45). In 1980 foreign news was bought in as unedited general world news fed via satellite from Visnews even while foreign printed media were outlawed. It is assumed that the new leadership wanted the population to see the outside world that they might make comparisons which would encourage them to support reform, but that they wanted interpretation and explanation to remain in Chinese hands. Usually, the government has discriminated between journalistic programmes and other kinds of programmes; Rupert Murdoch of Star TV and other media entrepreneurs in East Asia have fitted in with China's policy by excluding 'journalistic' material from their transmissions (Chan 1994). In 2001, the world's largest media company, AOL Time-Warner Inc., contracted with the Chinese government to broadcast a Chinese-language cable channel into southern China. The deal was the first time that an American media corporation has been able to participate in China's cable television sector. In 2002, Sun TV, a private channel with investors closely connected to the leadership and China's first documentary channel, was established specifically to carry foreign factual programming. Later that year two organizations controlled by Hong Kong businessmen with excellent contacts in Peking obtained concessions which will allow them to compete with duopolists China Post Office and NCNA in the distribution of print publications. Since both Charles Ho and Li Ka-shing are newspaper publishers as well as distributors, it may be expected that they will try to get further involved in mainland media (Clifford 2002). In early 2003 News Corporation subsidiary Star TV was granted permission to expand its Xing Hong Weishi channel throughout China. It will only broadcast in hotels.

Serving the people

The traditional model of Chinese journalism was authoritarian and hierarchical with audience involvement restricted to letters to the editor, an equivalent to what was common in the early days of BBC television. Topics thought appropriate were limited and politics took precedence. Acceptable drama themes before and after the Cultural Revolution were those which glorified suitable Chinese historical events, especially recent history which taught how essential was the arrival of the CCP and how glorious its victory.

Since the Southern Progress and little by little, formal, official information has been confined to certain specific slots and publications while the media in general have sought to develop what is most attractive to the consumer: entertainment journalism, soft features, human interest, and the like. In some cases this started from the necessity of matching the more exciting foreign product. Competing with Hong Kong transmission, Pearl River Economic Radio introduced (in the early 1990s) an informal, live, talk-show-centred style in a remarkable break with the past which, according to Zhao (1998: 96) has shown how lessons could be learned from HK/western media to better promote party ideology and create social cohesion. It was copied by Shanghai's East Radio and later Central People's Radio which brought officials onto programmes not merely to propound but to discuss issues of concern to listeners.

Similarly, evening and weekend newspapers were able to develop a much more informal and responsive style which rapidly developed into sensationalism. The paradigm here is *Weekend South*, regularly cited as 'the best' by fellow journalists on account of its courage in publishing investigations and its calls for reform. In at least one case, that of *Qianjiang Wanbao* in Hangzhou, undercover reporting has been used to expose abuses (Zhao 1998: 131). So far only one mainstream newspaper has managed successfully the transition to being a popular newspaper while maintaining its reputation for being educative and (usually) politically correct, *Peking Youth News*. It rapidly reformed its organization to hire and reward the most suitable staff and uses readers as stringers, paying for news. It contains material that is both consumerist and anti-consumerist, evading neat categorization, exposes corruption yet successfully relates news to the greater purpose of national development espoused by the Party. Its success is demonstrated by the large readership, but also by the fact that it is 'still an official organ but makes its readers feel that it is not' (Zhao 1998: 150)

It is argued that Chinese journalists have taken on board the concept of 'audience' to complement, and perhaps replace, that of the 'the people' or 'the masses' and that this process of hailing or identifying people in a new way is changing politics and society (Lee 2000, Zhang 2000). Zhang makes substantial claims for this conceptual change:

> This change eroded Mao's 'Party-masses model' of propaganda and its prescribed political and ideological relationship between press and readers ... It also extends the basis of legitimacy for journalistic work, making

way for the possibility of pluralistic news reporting and diversified media management.

(Zhang 2000: 2)

He also suggests that once this conceptual change took place, it made possible the deployment of new techniques such as audience research and journalism of greater relevance to the audience. It might be added, from the evidence of the present interviews, that it also further helps detach the journalists from the Party's categories and enables them to distinguish between the interests of the state and the citizens. In interviews the older journalists spoke about the people (*renmin*) or, occasionally, the masses (*qunzhong*) but the younger ones seemed to refer more frequently to audience, receiving masses (*shouzhong*) or viewers (*guanzhong*).

Variety and innovation in the printed media

A much larger number of topics is now not controversial or at least of no interest to the Party. Even those that are sensitive can be aired, although treatment has to be carefully managed. Editors' sources are much wider, more akin to those of an anglophone editor.

Formerly the media were merely tools of class struggle. Now there are many types of newspaper, such as economic newspapers promoting economic development and others which are rather detached from politics such as those specializing in investment, or technology or environmental protection or computers. Equally serving the masses are those types concentrating on leisure, culture, entertainment and sport. Radio and television has just as great a variety.

(Wen Weiping)

In the recent past, the editor was obliged to depend upon New China News Agency (Porter 1992), the national organs or direct instructions from officials. Enterprise in news gathering is now esteemed and there is more use of stringers or barefoot correspondents or the public. *Peking Youth News*, for example, has run columns which examine the effectiveness of the NPC (Parliament) and criticized the higher education system as making it virtually impossible for poor students to compete; *China Women's Daily* dealt with the sensitive issue of mass redundancies due to the market reforms (Li 1998: 319). Many editions of *Law and Democracy Monthly* contain criticisms of official policies in the guise of exposing maladministration. This interesting magazine reveals that there are many local protests up and down the country against high-handed officials or corrupt deals which infringe ordinary people's rights, or debilitate their environment.

The enormous expansion of print publishing often extends to material which the Party would prefer banned (Pei 2000: 155) but presumably not enough for it to be heavy-handed, unless it is simply the case that monitoring would require resources that they are not prepared to spare. Great effort and administration would be needed to monitor the *ditan* publications, i.e., those which consist both of proper newspapers, often evening ones, and magazines ranging from professional journals to gossip or lifestyle magazines. Intellectuals' magazines which are often critical, such as *Reading*, an equivalent of *New York Review of Books*, appear to be tolerated, at least in politically relaxed periods, as providing outlets for the frustrations of the intelligentsia as well as opportunities to monitor them.

There is every variety of *ad hoc* production: in Shanghai, a few yards from the main gate of the Academy of Politics for Airforce Officers, there is often a hawker selling not only salacious books about Chairman Mao's private life, but also scurrilous biographies of Jiang Zemin and Deng Xiaoping. Many films that are not transmitted on TV are sold as VCDs or tapes. Faxes and the Internet are widely available in the big cities, with around 30 million Internet users reported in November 2001 (www.chinatoday.com/med/a.htm) and 40 million a year later (Pratley 2002).

> The media have come to serve the needs of the masses for pleasure, entertainment, leisure, sport and shopping. There are many non-political papers, many of which have no other purpose than to introduce people to shops, buying opportunities, price reductions, employment advice, skills exchange, etc. – the masses love that kind of stuff, there's everything for everyone, from consumers of books and followers of football to those who want to know how to breed fish or plant trees.
>
> (Wen Weiping)

Equally central to the modern Chinese media is the large number of programmes, newspapers, magazines, programme segments and news stories dealing with business in every sense, perhaps most usefully called 'enterprise media' since their aim is, in general, to encourage enterprise and advance product development. The enterprise medium first to hit the headlines for itself, and then to become a cynosure, was CCTV's *Economics Half Hour* because Deng Xiaoping allowed himself to be cited as watching it every day and recommending it to his political colleagues:

> The content of *Economics Half Hour* covers our country's incoming investment, business matters, market construction including ethical and regulatory systems; developments in law; environmental protection, privatization and rural developments. The idea is to ensure that people understand and are connected into the framework.
>
> (Wu Weishi)

Business is also heavily involved in the media in other ways: infomercials and advertorials (paid business info) are common, as is sponsorship and even the selling of editorial rights to businesses; it is claimed that this has led to widespread 'corruption' and fabrication of news. Reportedly current is an adage which appears to celebrate business in the media, 'newspaper sets the stage, businesses sing the opera' (Zhao 1998: 71). The issue of 'fake journalism' has caused concern in the profession.[10]

Investigative journalism and the documentary movement

Over the last ten years a genre of journalism has appeared that is muck-raking and revelatory. It is likened to the 'investigative journalism' of anglophone folk-lore and it deploys some of the same assumptions and techniques.

Although there is no equivalent (yet) in China of the Arms to Iraq affair,[11] by the standards of the first forty years of the rule of the Chinese Communist Party the range of subjects today aired in the Chinese media is quite startling. No negative reporting was permitted, even a traffic accident was forbidden, until the taboo was broken around 1980. Today, chat shows and current affairs reports place on stage contentious behaviour and public issues. A Shanghai talk show specializing in domestic violence is sponsored by a leading refrigerator manufac-turer; these, as with the investigative journalism described below, have become excellent marketing tools, the more hard-hitting the better as they attract many advertisers. 'Companies want their products associated with justice' (Li Zhengmao).

This phenomenon is symptomatic of journalists' willingness to take advantage of new freedoms, but equally of commercial opportunism and of popular scepti-cism about authority. Although circumscribed according to political fashions and administrators' prejudices,[12] the journalism is sufficiently challenging and in contrast with what went on before (at any time since 1949) as to reflect a funda-mental change. Many of the topics dealt with are quite new to the public arena; others would in the recent past only have been acknowledged in Restricted Circulation Publications (RCPs).[13]

At the same time there has appeared a documentary movement, according to two books.[14] The 'movement' is considered to have been born with the screening of *River Elegy* (see p. 68) or with *Wandering in Beijing*, which follows five Chinese underground artists who leave China to live abroad. Some documentary makers do not aim at local, but an international, audience; for others, TV has created such slots as *Life Space*, part of CCTV's *Oriental Horizon*, which tells the story of ordinary people in a John Grierson/Joris Ivens mode, radically different from early Chinese factual equivalents because of its concentration on 'ordinary people's stories'.

Television takes off

Television is probably the most influential medium, if influence be judged by penetration and by the ability to introduce, if only in a superficial manner, previously unthought thoughts (Lull 1991). Virtually everyone in China watches television (CSM 2002; AC Nielsen 2002). At the end of 1997, there were 400 million sets in private homes and over a billion people had acquired regular access to TV programmes. In 1998, in terms of household penetration of television and the number of TV sets counted on a per capita basis, China was already well ahead of all other developing countries and high above the average level for the world and Asia (Li 1998). Average consumption is of 184 minutes per person per day (CSM 2002) and television takes 72.4 per cent of the advertising market, worth 24 per cent more between 2000 and 2001 and likely to be worth another 10 per cent or more the year thereafter if recent trends continue (AC Nielsen 2002). No wonder advertisers are active if, as I suggested at the start of this chapter and as the figures just cited seem to imply, Chinese-language TV programming is more extensively watched than even English-language programming.

Political factors rather than technological or economic or commercial ones have decided the development of television in China. The old revolutionaries, of whom Deng Xiaoping, who returned to power in 1978, was the leading survivor, were very aware of the power of media to harness the energies of the population and had been mass media pioneers since the 1930s or earlier. In the 1980s they gave broadcasting high priority. A series of national broadcasting conferences in the early 1980s set it as an important part of the economic development to establish a TV infrastructure covering the whole nation and to enable the population throughout the country to watch quality TV programming. Following the meetings, the country saw more government investment in the field of television, with state expenditure on television quintupling between 1980 and 1989 (Lee, P.S. 1994).

Internal management reforms in CCTV

Two important reforms took place in the 1990s, referred to as Producer System Reform and Human Resources Reform. Under the Producer System Reform, non-news producers may generate their own advertising and sponsorship, although this does not hold for news producers. News producers are all now professionals rather than (as often in the past) generic state officials and they have responsibility for specific programmes and programme segments rather than being assigned to departments as if they were clerks in a ministry (Cai 1996, Zhou 1997, Jiang Hu). Human Resources Reform in theory permits managers in TV to hire and fire as they wish although it is by no means normal for them to exercise the right to fire owing to the powerful sense of obligation felt towards employees (Zhang Yinhuan). On the other hand, managers who previously received their allocation of graduates from the various education institutions – journalism, drama, engineering, and so forth – may now select whomsoever they wish, a change which is causing the education sector to rethink its curricula (He Zihua). Managers are no longer required to pay according to civil service pay scales but can provide bonuses related to achievement (Ou Lin).

Focal Point is the (often) investigative segment of the CCTV national current affairs show *Oriental Horizon* (see below). The Executive Producer (Foreign Reports) of *Focal Point* finds herself operating three types of employment contract: the iron rice bowl (permanent, secure posts) for people employed before the reforms and top-level staff; iron rice bowl plus productivity bonuses for those on a very low wage which is intentionally not raised (you can see the bonuses published on noticeboards outside the newsroom); the new system in place within the News Criticism Department (Ou Lin).

In *Focal Point* this works specifically as follows: the First Level Producer, responsible for the entire operation of *Oriental Horizon*, the various elements of which s/he farms out to teams each under a Second Level Executive Producer, receives advertisement income generated by the programme less taxes, overhead and facility fee all of which amount to about two-thirds of receipts. Li, as Second Level Producer, receives a sum for each programme out of which she pays her thirteen employees, all overhead plus herself. She is free to advertise for staff in *China TV News*.

With these reforms, CCTV has been able to become virtually independent of state financing; Peking Television became self-sufficient in 1993. Institutional reforms have therefore been substantial and have resulted in a hybrid and possibly *sui generis* system by which some features of the public service model have been fused with modes of income generation that liberate TV from the supposed weaknesses of that model.

Even when new TV stations have been founded that are totally financed from commercials, as with Oriental Television (OTV), set up over 1992 to 1993 specifically to provide market competition for the established Shanghai TV, they remain subject to public service guidelines, there is no question of them being free of general political leadership (Li Feishi).

The 'private' production industry

With nearly 2,000 TV stations, over 1,200 TV channels and a demand for 20,000 hours of entertainment programming a year (Jiang 2002: 9) unofficial arrangements with entrepreneurs (usually their own employees moonlighting) became common in the late 1990s before the major broadcasters and relevant government departments became aware of the advantages to be obtained from the kind of division of labour that was introduced into the communication industry by the UK's C4TV in 1982.[15]

At the time of writing about a third of programming is produced by one or more of the 1,000-odd production companies which have sprung up as the broadcasters have sought to disconnect transmission and programme production, although the figure may be as high as 90 per cent for the cable channels. Some of these companies co-produce with the broadcasters and are recompensed with advertising slots; some have contracts to supply an agreed number of hours of programming for money and some produce specific programmes.[16] There are some characteristics particular to the Chinese market.

One is that the entire industry is illegal; since the media are officially state owned and no legal provision has ever been made for the legitimizing of any independent initiatives, the sector exists in a limbo which makes them vulnerable to official exploitation or changes in political line. Since they are illegal, their contracts with purchasers have no validity in law, putting them in a weak position for bargaining; they cannot grow *qua* companies since they cannot attract shareholders and thus depend upon high gearing for any expansion plans. Their production activities are restricted to non-sensitive areas, with news and current affairs most definitely excluded. As if that were not enough, the management of the private production companies is subject to official approval; in the case of a major programme supplier, Enlight, the director and producer of its programmes for BTV are appointed by BTV.[17] In the same case, BTV reserves rights of censorship of content and commercial breaks and a veto over all matters of personnel.

Content changes

The development in content over every genre of television has been so vast that it is beyond the scope of this study to say more than that it is probable that – excepting the pornographic and extremely violent – every possible format and genre of television programme is available in China. The number of channels to which viewers have access depends upon the region but in large cities there is a minimum of ten channels (Ou Lin) and it is claimed that over 360 channels now cover 90 per cent of the country (Prisma 2001: 202).

Television since 1978 has increasingly shown its vast audiences how foreigners live. China now receives many foreign programmes which have opened the eyes of millions who knew next to nothing about life elsewhere (Lull 1994); advertisements are now very similar to those in the West and presumably create the same expectations as in the more established consumer societies. The shopping complexes of Shanghai are bigger, and perhaps almost as diversely stocked, as those of New York or London, and the prices show that there is at least a minority which has the wealth with which to buy the most expensive luxury goods.[18] Gallup's *1995 Lifestyle and Consumer Attitudes Survey* found that both rural and urban residents have a 'distinctly materialist outlook' (Gordon 1996) and this is unlikely to have lessened.

Consumer culture is not the only ideological development which has come about as a result of the changes. It is possible openly to be Christian, Muslim or disciple of heavy rock. One interviewee claimed to be an active Buddhist. Traditional cultural life, smothered and believed destroyed during the Cultural Revolution (de Burgh 1975), has returned. It is the new media which have, according to at least one observer, 'opened the eyes of the people to alternatives' to the CCP version of modernity (Chu, L.C. 1994: 17), an interesting contrast to the view commonly held in the West that the media destroy traditional culture.

The format of a television programme may be as significant as the content – as with the approach of a newspaper or radio show – in provoking change, or at least reaction to its newness. The launch of both *Oriental Horizon* (1993) and *Tell it like it is* (1996) stimulated thousands of letters and widespread controversy simply because such relatively uninhibited discussion had never been seen on Chinese TV. Over the following six years, 179 discussion programmes commenced transmission, with the top-rated topics including one in which a former Red Guard begs pardon for having attacked his teacher during the Cultural Revolution; one dealing with a 'doctor–patient' relationship; one on the 1999 Marriage Law; 'Should women remain at at home?' and a quarrel between noisy Mah Jong players and their neighbours. Other topics have included Aids, traffic accents, extinction of traditional music; euthanasia; Japanese amnesia over war crimes; children and drugs (Wang 2003). Although they are not yet as uninhibited as Jerry Springer (USA), Oprah Winfrey (USA) or Kilroy (UK) the intimate style, the legitimation of hitherto personal issues, the interaction and the informality are revolutionary.

In early 2002 it became clear that both News Corporation and AOL Time-Warner had obtained access to cable viewers in some areas of Canton Province, the first admission of foreign media business into any other than the restricted tourist hotel market. Whether this presages significant changes in content remains to be seen.

News and current affairs today

All factual programmes are 'news', but some are in-depth reports, sometimes confusingly translated as 'investigative journalism' but closer in conception to the UK's 'current affairs'. The same people work in news and in-depth work, often moving between programmes, and the Shanghai TV organization, itself modelled on that of CCTV, appears increasingly to be being copied everywhere. With this model the News Department of a TV station will have three sub-departments: general news, economic or business news and critique department. The latter will produce both news features with a special, in-depth or investigative aspect, or 20-minute features of the same approach.

The national Network News, from CCTV, is transmitted daily at 7 p.m. and relayed throughout the nation via satellite or microwave links and has an average audience of 400 million. It is then followed by the provincial or local news. Famously, Chinese news programmes in the past eschewed negative reports and concentrated upon the kind of stories of interest to the hierarchy or intended to inspire or awe the masses, such as reports of achievements in economic production or the doings of high leaders and their foreign counterparts. This was typical not only of Soviet bloc countries but also of Third World dictatorships (McNair 1991). The duty of the media, as we have seen above, was not to indulge people with frivolity but to exhort or at least to help them concentrate their minds on socialist construction. Journalists were aware that this policy neither reflected their best abilities nor attracted the customers.

Core political news may no longer have pride of place on every single medium, but on those media where there is such news it has remained much the same in the topics of which it consists or the fact that it reports not debates but results, not policy formulation but decision. There is no evaluation. Outside this, of course, the range of topics available for reporting has widened greatly but Zhao argues that this reflects not a competition in ideas but conformity to the 'new ideology of national and personal development' that the government is happy to see promoted by communicators more skilled than its own official propagandists (Zhao 2000).

In 1979 the Chinese Association of Journalists introduced a national award for good journalism and the first prize that year went to *Liberation Daily* for a little story about a bus accident. 'Before *Liberation Daily* published 200 to 300 ideographs about the number 26 bus in Shanghai, there had never been an accident in China. So this was a simple, dramatic moment – when the culture of journalism changed' (Li Zhengmao).

Today, although official, positive stories remain a staple of the Chinese media, already in 1979 it became possible not only to report difficulties but also to criticize aspects of official behaviour and to expose official malpractice in certain types of programmes (Yu 1990: 78). Programmes giving space for ordinary people to voice their opinions and human interest stories appeared (Chu 1983) and, with a hiatus in 1989 to 1990, there has been a continuous development along these lines. Radio has often been a trendsetter in this respect with its phone-in shows, opinionated chat hosts and airing of every kind of grouse or enquiry of the public authorities (Crook 1997). By 1990 most households had a radio (Lull 1991: 20). According to Polumbaum (1994) it was the radio that recreated journalism in China, by showing a new model which was audience led rather than elite led or, as some put it, 'from we speak you listen to you speak we listen'.

Accidents, disasters, crime, price rises, inflation and environmental problems have become routine. There are probably many reasons for this change, but one is surely the awareness by managers – journalists knew this all along – that much of their previous output was simply not credible. The audience was now to be taken into account. A principle of 'Three Proximities' has been widely adopted, meaning proximity to the public, proximity to reality and proximity to day-to-day life. The new formats, with less hierarchical presentation of subject matter and more informal styles, most obviously with talk shows and phone-ins where people participate as themselves rather as representing an institution, can be interpreted as being modernization of technique in accordance with the old rule, so well articulated by (then President of China) Liu Shaoqi in the 1950s, that to be effective propagandists the media must always be close to the people's concerns. By seemingly allowing people to articulate their problems themselves and by allowing the mediators to counsel and sympathize, it can be argued that the Party reduces pressure upon itself.

The *Oriental Horizon* TV magazine mentioned above was launched on CCTV in 1993. It is an hour-long programme started very tentatively, only mornings and with only an audience of 1 per cent to 2 per cent, in 1993. It was to contain several segments, of which the most famous segment is now the feature or documentary *Focal Point*, started in 1994. While ratings for network news are around 40 per cent of maximum audience ('over 900 millions'), for investigative and critical features on *Focal Point* they can be as high as 70 per cent. *Focal Point* receives 80 per cent of CCTV's mail, 3,000 to 4,000 letters a week, along with many thousands of calls, all dealt with by a full-time staff (Ou Lin). It is widely believed that ministers watch the programme before making policy. President Jiang Zemin has been known to call in, and former Premier Zhu Rongji is believed to have instructed ministers to watch it.

Soon regional TV stations started to copy the *Focal Point* format. Peking TV was the first, and by some accounts the best, but Shanghai TV, Zhejiang TV and Sichuan TV and many other provincial broadcasters all have current affairs reports of this type, lasting between 10 and 25 minutes after the provincial news which itself follows the national news. Principal current affairs[19] programmes available in Shanghai and Peking are listed in the appendices of this volume, along with descriptions of some of the stories, to indicate the range of subject matter. For example, Shanghai Television's *News Tale* also appears to do some challenging reporting exposing social issues and bad officials in a populist way, such as the story of a young criminal, whose life and crimes were reconstructed, as were his imprisonment, parole and rehabilitation. Peking TV is in reality national rather than local, as it is received in most provinces (Lu Weidong); in fact in many provinces it is possible to receive the channels of other provinces and localities (see also Perry and Selden 2000: 26).

Journalists of Sichuan TV interviewed by the author considered that there are wide differences in the quality of this kind of output. In Sichuan, for example, both production standards and journalistic courage were more highly developed on the Chengdu Television version and sometimes on the cable channel CDCTV. Informants Lee and Xie were very scathing of their own work on news and longed for the privileged position of working in current affairs, preferably with a more daring channel. In the same week in which they were interviewed, the week beginning 19 June 2000, Sichuan TV's current affairs stories included features on education reform, with the reporter representing the case of the students on teaching and learning methods; forestry problems and the loss of soil due to deforestation (a staple topic), and rice purchasing. In the rice story the villagers had complained about both methods and price and, thanks to the intervention of TV the problems were resolved to the satisfaction of both sides.

Reporter Fang Chih was particularly proud of a report on the pollution of the Dadu River. Fishermen were called in and took the journalist to see quantities of dead fish. The report was shot on location and featured interviews with 'peasants of the area'[20] and the local housewives. The reporter was seen going to get scientific analysis organized and thence to the Provincial Fisheries Office to lodge a complaint. Part two was to contain the resolution of the story. Fang also drew attention to the fact that he had managed to get righted an injustice involving overpayments. He had discovered the cost of installation of telephone lines in a certain area of the province was nearly double that elsewhere. In his film he is seen questioning officials and putting them on the spot. 'Who authorized the rise and why?' The officials respond that it was all a great mistake (!) and are obliged by the reporter to attend a confrontation with the consumers. At the filmed meeting the officials are contrite and a solution is found in the form of a rebate to all concerned and we see the cash payout to the happy victors. We are told that the telephone office was fined 5,000 rmb, indicating that the story was all put to bed a long time before transmission.

Chengdu TV's equivalent transmitted similar types of story, for example that of dangerous gas escapes from domestic housing, a situation to which the safety authorities had failed to respond until those affected alerted the TV station which then undertook its own investigation, confronted the authorities and had them shamefacedly putting the situation right. The programme then broadened out into a wider look at gas appliances in general and the monitoring procedures that supposedly exist.

Chengdu TV also transmitted an up-to-the-minute[21] report on the Orbis Flying Eye Surgery. This was remarkable to anyone who had been in China a few years before in its unembarrassed and frank acknowledgement of the help being given to Chinese doctors by non Chinese. The Chinese were depicted quite clearly as learning from the anglophone and German surgeons, represented as being at a much more advanced stage. It was well planned and shot and gave a rounded picture of the processes involved in eye surgery, the training techniques, the organization of the missions and the motivations of the visitors.

The cable operator CDCTV, which broadcasts four channels in Chengdu and area, is held up by the young journalists interviewed as the most 'advanced'. The most striking current affairs story seen during this visit dealt with the sale of a baby by its father. The baby was identified at the purchasers' end as having been bought and the reporter, with the help of the police, then traced it with difficulty back to a village in another province where he eventually located the child's grandparents by showing photographs to people in the village (the grandparents at first denied knowledge of the child) and through them the mother and then the culprit, the father who was seen confessing and contrite.

Some of these topics equate to what are common on anglophone consumer magazines, others have more in common with (USA) *60 Minutes* or (UK) *Dispatches* in that they deal with topics of wider implication. Reporters with whom these programmes were discussed agreed with the suggestion that, ten years ago, much of what is now being screened might well have been researched but only published in Restricted Circulation Publications (RCP). The main differences between the similar genre in anglophone countries are, first, that there is so much more of it and second, that there is a clear emphasis upon the solution of the problem rather than the joy of revelation. This is further indication of how journalists see themselves – not simply as providers of information, or investigators, but as brokers.

Helter-skelter, the Chinese media have raced to embrace the opportunities provided for them by the new directions in economic policy, whether leading or following public opinion it is difficult to say. Though the media appear more and more to share their characteristics with equivalents elsewhere, there are important differences in approach which seem likely to persist, because of the influence of history which we explore in the next chapter.

4 The burden of the past I: from Yanan to the great proletarian Cultural Revolution

In this chapter we see why, in talking about their work, Chinese journalists (especially but not exclusively the older ones) hark back to past debates and past personalities. We look at the significance, in this lore, of the Yanan experience, the Hundred Flowers and the role of journalists in the Great Leap Forward. Beliefs about journalism are coloured by memories of persecution and realization that the persecution was not aberrant but systemic.

Old ideas

Totalitarian leaders of the twentieth century were all convinced of the importance of mass communications. Totalitarian regimes in Germany, Russia, Italy and China put enormous efforts not only into controlling the media but into using them to change minds and to create 'new people'. What distinguished these totalitarian movements from traditional authoritarianism is that they desired to extend their power everywhere and to mobilize people through the use of mass communication and the manipulation of information. They may well have been deluded about the capacity of the media to have those effects; recent studies (Morley 1986, Gunter and Svennevig 1987, Kitzinger 1999, Philo 1997) suggest a much more complex situation in which the recipients and the context condition the reception. However, the myth that propaganda works as the propagandists intend was very potent in the 1930s to 1950s; it was not only politicians who believed it, writers such as Koestler and Orwell were also convinced by it.

In traditional societies 'the king's writ stopped at the village gate'. Communist and fascist governments were not content with that. They desired to bring the majority of the population into the political process.

> We can attribute to Lenin the formulation of the totalitarian approach to politics. He did not think he was the inventor of it, for in his mind he was implementing efficiently and on a national scale an approach to mass-mobilization that had been emerging throughout the 19th century.
>
> (Pool 1973: 464)

The Nationalist Party (KMT) initially modelled itself on the Bolsheviks. The CCP grew up within the Nationalist Party and learned its Bolshevism in the 1920s and 1930s when the Russian regime was committed to creating a 'new Soviet man' through mass persuasion. By the time the CCP had come to power it had adopted this vision as well as the Bolshevik approach to communications as a tool in the power struggle. CCP activists also inherited a concept of Chineseness, with racist overtones, from the dreamy intellectuals of the generation before (Dikotter 1992: 131) who had discovered western nationalism and regretted their own land's lack of national cohesion. They seized upon Bolshevik tools to integrate a country which, they considered, had no common language, communications, civil service, means of transportation or any kind of sense of common purpose. Kang is expressing this view of the role of journalists when he describes what is to him one of their important functions:

> Journalists make the people aware of what they have in common, for example when foreigners threaten or insult China as in the Belgrade bombings.
>
> (Kang Wei)

In addition to the ideas of mass mobilization and of using mass persuasion to change people's thinking, the Bolshevik approach to communications included a clear line on truth. The main consideration was not whether statements be true or false but the consequences they might have and their 'class nature', i.e., whether they could be interpreted as representing the interests of a particular social class, with both the definition of class and the interpretation being made by the leaders. No statement or fact is without its class nature and is to be judged by that rather than by any supposed 'objective criteria' which can determine its truth impartially. This is reflected in what Chinese textbooks tell their journalists about truth in reporting.[1] It accounts for the slogans, or, more accurately, acceptable formulations, which are repeated unendingly in the media to the bewilderment of those starting to learn Chinese.[2]

The CCP style

In the 1940s, disgust at the perceived incompetence of the Nationalist Party government and frustration at the failure of China to defeat the Japanese had many idealistic people, particularly intellectuals, turning to the ideal of self-sacrifice in the cause of national renewal supposedly realized by the Communists, hidden away in the Shanxi mountains at Yanan. The frugality of the CCP leaders and their rhetoric of equality were as attractive as their being untainted by defeat at the hands of the Japanese. Tens of thousands trekked up the mountains to CCP headquarters, without first having properly ascertained what they would be required to believe. In 1942 heterodox views and the exigencies of internal power struggles caused the CCP to introduce ideological rectification. Those who had doubts were criticized in mass meetings, forced to sign confessions, demoted or sent to reform through labour. By 'making an example of such people through the rectification campaign, Mao strongly affirmed the role of the CCP in defining the limits of intellectual expression and enquiry' (Spence 1982: 473). A categorical line on journalism was laid down:

> The role and power of the newspapers consists in their ability to bring the Party program, the Party line, the Party's general and specific policies, its tasks and methods of work before the masses in the quickest and most extensive way.
>
> (Mao 1961: 241)

With such expectations, communication is not about providing information as the raw material to be deployed in the making of rational judgements. Nor are media campaigns planned to appeal to reason to persuade the recipients of the desirability of a particular course of action.[3] The media become vehicles of mobilization and distributors of pre-set formulae in which people can frame their words, if not their thoughts. Jiang Weihua is a senior journalist born in 1960 who nevertheless formulates her role in words which hark back to the Yanan past: 'The most important responsibility of the journalist is to keep the masses informed of the Party's decisions so that they can carry them out' (Jiang Weihua). A younger journalist puts it thus:

> First, we are endowed with *the sacred task rapidly to disseminate and propagate the policies of the government* for we work in the service of the masses of society; we have to enable them to grasp policies such that they can know and apply them. Second, once the policies, which we have disseminated, have been implemented, it may be that there are sometimes distortions in the process, that the benefits are not apparent and that there are complaints. In these situations it is our duty to reflect and explain these. In general, the authorities take this seriously such that those implementing the policies, after watching the programmes, will try to rectify their ways.
>
> (Deng Huo)

In the propaganda campaigns typical of CCP rule

> Instructions go out to local Party authorities . . . secretly to prepare for the campaign. The local organizers in the school, office, factory, or committee decide in advance who will be the victims, who will be forced to confess sins, and whether each will be forgiven or punished and in what way. Thus the secret scenario is secretly settled before the campaign even begins. At the start of the campaign the mass media proclaim the slogans to be featured, generally by describing how some group of workers or persons somewhere 'spontaneously' began raising these slogans and acting in accordance with them. Suddenly, from all over the country, as if by magic, response and imitation begin.
>
> (Pool 1973: 495)

Few contemporary factual accounts exist, although some have been written up since (Liang and Shapiro 1984, Chang 1991); fiction, does. For mild criticisms in Ding Ling's novel *The Sun Shines over the Sangan River* (1948) she was to suffer for many years. Her contemporary Zhang Ailing fled China and so survived publication of *Bare Earth* (1954). It tells of the intelligentsia in 1950s China, opening with scenes of young enthusiasts of a propaganda work team in the countryside becoming disillusioned as they seek to apply instructions from on high, based upon the analysis of a theoretical situation, to the conditions of poverty and ignorance, corruption and violence, in which they find themselves. The novel contains scenes of suffering which are painful to read.

In brief, the nationalized and strictly regimented media of the PRC was informed by the Maoist conception of the media. This originated in, and has barely developed from, the ideas of Lenin who himself was formed intellectually in the nineteenth century; their premises are more akin to those of Matthew Arnold[4] than to those of our contemporaries, and journalism students in China learn them as truth even while they are increasingly aware of other interpretations. Today the relationship of media theory and practice has become much more complex, as Deng Huo's comment, above, makes clear.

Contradictions between theory and practice

Well before Deng Huo was born, contradictions, between the Leninist theory of media and the practicalities of journalism, became apparent as soon as the victory of the CCP was in sight.

In 1948 (future President of China) Liu Shaoqi cited Lenin to justify his view of the tasks of journalism as a bridge between Party and people:

> Lenin said that the Party should maintain its ties with the masses through a thousand channels. That's right, that's what we should do. And your task, your occupation, constitutes one of the very important channels. The newspapers appear before the masses every day and acquaint them with the Party's policies. Likewise, the army, the people's representative conferences and the co-operatives serve as bridges linking the Party with the masses. Without these bridges, the contact between the Party and the masses would be severed, leaving a wide gap. Hence, these bridges cannot be dispensed with. And among the thousands of bridges or channels, the newspaper is an essential one.
>
> (Liu 1984: 395)

On establishing the PRC in October 1949, the CCP in effect nationalized the media, thus making all journalists state employees.[5] Perhaps more significant, journalists became subject to a number of institutions which limited their ability to withstand Party pressure: the life dossier,[6] the work unit and the Party committee in particular (Ogden 1992 Chapter 4). Although the CCP had driven the Nationalists onto Taiwan, it was not clear then that the Civil War really was over, or that they might not stage a comeback with US help, so that the wartime conditions could be justified. In the series of campaigns intended to destroy class enemies, mobilize behind the Party a large enough constituency of support, terrorize the opposition and carry out reforms deemed necessary for China's economic development, the journalist was to be propagandist and motivator and not to quibble. Liu Shaoqi's bridge had become a one-way route. In simply becoming the mouthpiece of authority it also became so uninteresting, so lacking in diversity as to be unreadable. Interviewee Wen Weiping was succinct:

> In the past politics dominated the newspapers but the Party began to realize that no one was reading them.
>
> (Wen Weiping)

The 'past' to which he referred was the 1970s. What he did not say – perhaps he did not know – is that this was a problem which had first been identified as early as the 1950s and indeed had been observed in Russia, soon after the Revolution, too. By the mid-1950s, as the CCP felt more confident, leaders began to admit out loud, what had soon been evident, that the newspapers were failing to attract readers. In 1955 Liu Shaoqi asked why it should be that, while bourgeois newspapers contained interesting reports, 'our own newspapers' were so uninteresting.

Because such a senior leader had opened up the topic, it became possible for discussion to take place about the evident contradiction between producing newspapers that people might want to read, and producing the kind of journalism which provided little more than features on ideology and reports of the doings of politicians, hardly likely to thrill much of the population. For a period there was a lively debate as to how journalism might serve the cause and how the fact of journalists being state employees, and so inhibited and restricted, could be improved upon. Liu expressed a wish to see journalists develop independence and a sense of personal responsibility.

> Foreign journalists have this as their watchword: news reports are to be objective, truthful, and impartial. If we merely stress the political stand but dare not stress objectivity and truthfulness in our news reports, then our news reports would be subjective and partial indeed.
>
> (quoted in MacFarquhar 1974: 76)

Moreover, Liu specifically held up for emulation US newspapers which would, he said, report criticisms of the USA by China, whereas the reverse was not the case (Ibid: 76). What the discussants of the period appear to have hoped for was to establish the kind of consensus within which debate could take place and variety would be possible, a situation which was believed to have obtained before the Nationalist–CCP split, though this time within a new consensus.

The difficulty was that not only had the CCP concentrated ownership of the media in its own hands, but that it had imposed a much more rigid ideological control. At the same time it had introduced intervention by the state into the lives of the citizenry of a ferocity which, some argue, had not been seen in China for at least a thousand years (Jenner 1994); allowed to mushroom an enormous state bureaucracy impervious to criticism or moral suasion; and forced mass mobilization for ideological campaigns which crushed all rights and rejected all questioning.

Some contemporary fiction gives a flavour of this period. For example, in Zhang Ailing's (1956) novel *The Rice Sprout Song*, set in 1950s rural China, there is a witty description of a writer, Gu Gang, sent to the countryside to gather material for a script about rural issues. He ignores totally the dramatic and tragic events around him because they do not fit his required format and, while setting his story in the village in which he lodges, transforms it to accord with his audience's expectations. It becomes the vehicle for a stereotypical tale of revolutionary heroism in a flood, though there had never been a flood in the real village. Listening to the District Officer describe the trials and efforts of the local peasants with studied disinterest as he searches for a topic that will fit the current fashions:

> [Gu Gang] waited until Comrade Wang had stopped . . .
> 'Comrade Wang, has there been a flood in this area?'
> 'Flood?' Comrade Wang was startled. 'No. What, you want to visit a flood?'
> He suddenly became stimulated, gave a great smile and looked with a great light in his eyes. Gu Gang saw that he suspected him.
> 'Oh no I was just wondering whether in summer the stream overflowed . . .'
> There was still a hint of suspicion in Wang's face.
> 'The water increases but it's never overflowed'
> 'But for example if it were to overflow' Gu explained ' I was just thinking one could base a story on the possibility'
> 'But', Comrade Wang looked at him with surprise 'I don't understand, when we've got so many significant things going on, why'd you want to write a fake story?'
>
> (Zhang 1960: 98–99 paraphrased)

From a later period, *News from Inside the Paper* by Liu Binyan (1960), deals with a journalist who uncovers a case which appears to be just what the authorities would want, yet finds that her report is suppressed and her career blocked. Liu's reporter had a conception of what she ought to be doing – exposing malfeasance – rather different to that of Zhang's. The difference, though, can probably be explained by reference to the different outlooks of the two authors. Zhang was cynical about the attempt to build socialism, with most of the activists in her most powerful novel, *Bare Earth*, being characterized as corrupt or flawed in some other way, whereas Liu continued to believe that if only the good activists (and journalists like himself) could come to the fore, the Party would redeem itself. However, the lack of any alternative channels of opinion than Party-dominated media and the concentration of power into factions made this unlikely. Rowe suggests that the Party could not close down the public sphere and then hope to resurrect it (Rowe 1990: 326).[7]

As the memoirs of reporter Liu Binyan demonstrate, leaders might call for more interesting, even critical, journalism one day, but destroy those who dared to oblige, the next (Liu 1990a: 16). The vagaries of the relationship between journalists and the political process are burned into the consciousness of succeeding generations.

Landmarks in the story of journalism

In talking about their work, Chinese journalists use phrases and formulate their views in ways which, to the informed listener, hark back to debates which may have taken place long before their births. We all do this, although it is possible that, in China, it is more the case than in the anglophone world. Chinese is replete with stock expressions[8] and a cultural predilection has become a political obsession as the Party has sought to add to the already vast national arsenal of cliché and set expression such that it is difficult to make any kind of communication without bringing into play a multitude of allusions. This is absolutely intentional and, in politics and journalism at least, is indicative of the need to express oneself only in a manner already approved by precedent authority. Some of the modern stock expressions used in the following response are in italics:

> Our task is to identify the *latest news facts* and social phenomena and to reflect them in our recording of them. Of course, we have our own objectives, one of which is to be *close to the citizenry*. If there is a topic in which the *citizenry* have shown no interest, yet you cover it, then you will create a *social effect*. There are some matters that are *known to the audience but not thought out by them* . . . we go into depth on these topics and demonstrate our view, perhaps providing revelation.
>
> (Lu Cihui)

Aside from this orthodoxy of expression, there is a stock of references to past events which are brought up regularly in conversation. There are the names of Wang Shiwei and Hu Feng; the periods called the 'Hundred Flowers', the 'Great Leap Forward' and the 'Cultural Revolution'. These terms are used as shorthand to explain the failings of journalism or to demonstrate the problematic inheritance:

> One of my colleagues said to me I should study the life of Wang Shiwei . . . a journalist who was persecuted back in the 1940s. My teacher wanted me to understand that the Party is no good, has always been no good. But my family is fishing people and we have done rather well since 1949[9] so my thoughts are rather confused.
>
> (Cao Xin)

Cao's confusion is not surprising. His parents' economic life had improved under the CCP as had their children's prospects. Of the three children of a poor fisherman and his uneducated housewife, one was a doctor, one an academic and one, 'the stupid one', a rich entrepreneur. Yet, intellectually, Cao rejected the CCP, and this appeared to have started with his learning the story of Wang Shiwei.

Wang Shiwei

The name Wang Shiwei is surely quite forgotten by all but students of Chinese Communism – and Chinese journalists. By them, his case is still cited, sixty years after. One of the best known of today's Chinese reporters has written a monograph on Wang Shiwei, itself a telling point about the perceived relevance of history to current debates (Dai 1994). Wang was a journalist in Yanan, the fastness in which the CCP and its forces were holed up in the 1940s, who criticized the leadership for living sybaritically. He charged that, not only did they eat better and enjoy better accommodation than the *hoi polloi*, but they also obliged the young women to be available for casual sex. He was imprisoned, held up as a negative model, insulted and humiliated. Eventually he was beheaded. The preface to Dai Qing's book on him argues that not only 'the abuses of the Cultural Revolution', the 'mass criticism' the fabricated 'anti-party cliques' and 'the witchhunts' but also the ludicrous but tragic purges of writers and journalists in the 1980s are:

> not examples of the violation of the Yanan Way; they are the expression of Yanan's dark side, as authentic a part of Yanan's inner 'symbolic capital' as the outer manifestations of frugality, self sacrifice and national salvation. Thus, with the insight Dai Qing provides, the narrative of Chinese communism's decline is less a story of betrayal or lost idealism than tragedy playing out its initial flaws.
>
> (Dai 1994: xxv)

Others could have told her this long before, for example Simon Leys in his series of books from the 1970s onwards. The point is that today it is the very Chinese who were the mainstays of the regime in the past, families such as Cao Xin's, who are opening their eyes.

Hu Feng

Hu Feng was a hero for the intellectuals of the Hundred Flowers period. They identified with his sufferings at the hands of those in the Party who were determined to impose the most rigid conformity even if it meant destroying the careers and imprisoning people who were, by any yardstick, loyal to the ideals of the Communist Revolution. Hu Feng, one of the few leading Communists from a poor background, developed as a writer of distinction during the 1920s and also became a committed Marxist. However, his approach to literature was different to that expounded by Mao Zedong in his Yanan talks, aimed at achieving orthodoxy, as he believed that a consensus on general aims should not lead to forcing writers into producing only narrow, stereotypical works. To Hu, literary value was not subordinate to politics (Goldman 1981). He founded and ran a popular magazine *Hope* in the late 1940s and, despite arguments with the conformist Zhou Yang, believed that his approach would win out, or continue to be tolerated, particularly as, even after 1949 he retained or gained leading posts in the new cultural hierarchies. As always, in Chinese affairs, he was surrounded by an admiring faction which was hostile to Zhou's faction so that rivalry became as important as differences on issues. Convinced of the rightness of his case and of the evidence that the literature he advocated could be shown to serve the cause better, he presented a proposal along these lines to the Central Committee in 1954. However, he had misjudged the moment since the policy of collectivization, being deeply unpopular and fraught with dangers for the CCP, required in the minds of its defenders complete unanimity. He was unjustly accused of being anti-Marxist, pilloried as a traitor and used as a warning in a nationwide campaign against heterodoxy.

The Hundred Flowers

> Today I can talk to you, like yesterday. Tomorrow – who knows?
> You know about the Hundred Flowers? Oh well you know all about us!
> (Jiang Xiaolong)

While the cases of Wang Shiwei and Hu Feng are less well known outside the profession of journalism, the expression 'Hundred Flowers' is shorthand now even in the West among people who otherwise know little about Chinese politics. The phrase was used by Mao Zedong in a speech of 1956, when he called for freedom of expression, saying 'let a hundred flowers blossom, let a hundred schools of thought contend'. When he was taken at his word, he found the results unpalatable. Journalists revealed the failures of the new government, the muddle and waste and, though they invariably put the blame on well-meaning but incompetent lower-level cadres who prevented the carrying out of the leadership's full wishes or stood between the people and the beneficent leaders (Liu 1990a), even this proved intolerable. In speaking of their own profession, the journalists' aims were not for anything as extreme as abstract rights, but they argued for the professional autonomy that would enable them better to do their job of serving the state and acting as interface between people and that state. Nevertheless, the newspapers that had allowed such views to be voiced, initially the *Guangming Daily* and *Wenhui Bao* of Shanghai, were subject to an Anti-Rightist Campaign. As always in Chinese politics, whole groups of people fell, dragged down with their patrons (Hu Yaobang and Liu Binyan among the journalists, for example). One writer sees the Hundred Flowers as presaging the horrors that were to come:

> The 'Hundred Flowers' left permanent scars. For Mao, the experiment finally confirmed the prejudices he had built up towards the intellectuals

and led him from then on to consider the modern mind as the natural and unmanageable enemy of his power. For historians studying the rise, decay and final collapse of Maoism, the 'Hundred Flowers' campaign will remain a crucial date – the turning point in an evolution and the first seeds of disintegration. This first, apparently feeble tremor was to be followed by the violent earthquake of the 'Great Leap Forward' and finally by the fatal shock of the 'Cultural Revolution'.

(Leys 1983: 19)[10]

In 1987 journalists Liu Binyan and Xu Liangyang joined with academic Fang Lizhi to plan a scholarly conference to look back at the Anti-Rightist Campaign of thirty years earlier:

Even though the movement had brought suffering to half a million people (the number persecuted to death was far greater than the number killed in the June 4 massacre), still we looked in vain for any openly published materials on the history of the movement. The only records of the movement were inside the memories of those fortunate enough to have survived it. With the passage of time, those fortunate survivors were themselves becoming fewer and fewer, and for the younger generation, the impression of the Anti-Rightist Movement was growing fainter and fainter. We wished to create a record of the movement before those who could supply oral accounts disappeared.

(Fang 1990: 271)

When journalists employ the expression 'Hundred Flowers' they appear to be using it as a shorthand for 'the bad old days' and as a way of reminding their interlocutors and themselves of the dangers of believing leaders' assurances of freedom of speech.

The Great Leap Forward

That Anti-Rightist Campaign of 1957 was to have unfortunate consequences, for when the Great Leap Forward was implemented in 1959 there was no journalist with the courage, confidence or authority to question it, no matter that they were in the best position to know the real situation as they toured from county to county, a notable privilege in a country where movement was restricted according to official rank.[11]

The Great Leap Forward was dreamed up by Mao as the means by which the Chinese would overtake the advanced nations of the world by sheer will-power, an attitude of mind known as 'voluntarism'.[12] It was a campaign to reject the laws of measured development led by experts and to seek dramatic, unheard of, economic successes simply through immense hard work, enthusiasm and by eschewing advanced technology in favour of whatever ordinary people could themselves harness. Peasants were taken off their normal tasks to work on small-scale local steel plants or to undertake building projects; food production and distribution were communalized and people discouraged from taking responsibility for their own feeding and supply. The result was almost total chaos and, while millions starved, journalists were writing tales of massive grain harvests and other production victories achieved by sheer heroism; they were without foundation (Becker 1996).

> After the Great Leap Forward journalists of the older generation knew that journalists should have more right to scrutinize the government so that disasters like that could be reported and so that the leaders could put them right. Some of the old journalists are very sad they did not succeed in grasping this opportunity.
>
> (Cao Xin)

The revelation of this contradiction between the duties of the journalist and the intolerance of the Party was to cause journalists to reformulate their view of themselves and to claim the rights of tribunes of the people. At the Party's Lushan Conference of 1959 Mao suffered a political setback when the Party concluded that reporting on the Great Leap Forward had been falsified and that, in effect, the experiment had been a total disaster. The institutions created for it were, in reality if not in name, dismantled (Leys 1983: 31).

The debate over how to interpret the Leap became highly charged as it concerned not only matters of policy, or execution, but of ideology and personality. It took place at a time when China had broken its ties with the USSR, heretofore its only important ally, its mentor in socialism and 'elder brother', and the ideological differences between Khrushchev's USSR and Mao's China were reflected in domestic debates. Mao claimed that his call to change the world through sheer will-power was aimed at keeping the revolution pure. He said that in China, as in the USSR, a new ruling class was being created whose relationship to the majority did not really differ from that between capitalists and proletarians. That was the 'top down' approach which, though it might make China rich and strong would not revolutionize society but entrench the inequalities, the injustices and the subjection of the poor. It was to avoid this that China had to try a kind of development which involved all the people, did not allow a new ruling class to develop, and showed the world that there really was a socialist way forward.

To Mao's keenest supporters this was obvious, but many senior cadres had been more attracted to the CCP as the vehicle for national revival than for its social programme, and they were not as committed as Mao to equality or populism; some were convinced that the Stalinist model was the only one. Others simply had no time for popular participation in decision-making; indeed, in accordance with what Jenner argues are virtually ineradicable tendencies within Chinese society and polity, they probably actually considered such ideas to be morally wrong (Jenner 1994: 180). In the debates at the Lushan Conference there were undertones of a much older controversy, a controversy over two approaches which, sometimes clearly defined, sometimes overlapping, had dominated Chinese attitudes to their country's predicament since the nineteenth century. On the one hand were those who sought the evolutionary solution by which the best of things Chinese might be incorporated into a new synthesis between West and East, and this was an approach which most appealed to the cultured, educated elite. In the other corner were the millenarians who wanted dramatic and radical change which might mean destroying all vestiges of old China but might equally mean driving out all taints of the foreign; in either case the intention was to bring forward the utopia of equality and general harmony known as communism. To the utopians, the journalists were suspect as much for their relationship to the old literati as for their collusion with the technocracy:

> Journalists in China are officials so far as the people are concerned. So left wing people don't like them. Of course Yao Wenyuan and Chang Chunqiao [leading leftists of the Cultural Revolution] were journalists but really they were anti-journalists because they were against all those people who wrote erudite essays.
>
> (Cao Xin)

The passion of the leftists to transform China, ostensibly to obliterate her backwardness, was to erupt violently once more a few years later, in an event with terrible consequences. Its catalyst was the former editor, Mao Zedong; its ideologists the two journalists cited above; its Robespierre was Mao's wife, an embittered actress called Jiang Qing. Together they drove The Great Proletarian Cultural Revolution.

5 The burden of the past II: from the Cultural Revolution to the Tiananmen massacre

The Cultural Revolution brought about the destruction of journalism as we, and Chinese journalists hitherto, understand it. Afterwards, so traumatic was the experience of the Cultural Revolution seen to have been that the first instinct of almost everybody – from journalists to former leading politicians to peasants and workers – was to get back to where China had been before. Mao's heirs could not hold their fort; change was demanded. However, the two conflicting strands of thinking about modernization soon reasserted themselves and ideological differences between the new leadership and the people – or at least the many of the thinking urban citizens – were very sharp by the late 1980s. For the first time journalists declared themselves, publicly and in large numbers, for a change in their social role.

Towards the Cultural Revolution

By 1962 it was generally understood among the elite that the Great Leap Forward had been a failure in almost all aspects;[1] its sceptics were rehabilitated and the press made criticisms unprecedented since the Nationalist–CCP split.[2] Typical of journalists before the Leap had been the attitude of veteran Communist, and founder-editor of *The People's Daily*, Deng Tuo. A firm believer in the subordination of the rights of the individual to those of the group (Cheek 1986: 113), when he had doubts he expressed 'loyal criticism' in private to his comrades on the Central Committee while producing the requisite leading articles promoting the centrally dictated line regardless of his own views. However, many journalists feared that they had forfeited trust much in the way that American journalists are thought to do when they cosy up to power: 'If they fail to attend to their own integrity and their own credibility with audiences, they may in fact simply become ineffective ideological institutions' (Schudson 1992: 147).

That was not their only concern; aware that the Leap had been a debacle, they feared Mao persisting in such 'extremism'. They were reflecting views widely held in the elite, many of whose members regretted not only the Great Leap and the Communes but also the split which had taken place between the Soviet Union and the PRC, hitherto so closely allied. All these policies they began to see as evidence of Mao's lack of realism, romanticism, ignorance of economics and his failure to grasp China's need of expertise and cooperation with abroad. The Central Committee had gradually come under the control of Liu Shaoqi and Deng Xiaoping as Mao spent more and more time reflecting and writing in his study, in effect being, as Mao was later to remark, 'treated as a dead man at his own funeral'.

President Liu encouraged journalists in oblique criticism of Mao and of 'voluntarism'. When the attacks were not countered, journalists believed that Mao was on the run and pressed home in the traditional way – by historical analogy, in this case using the story of Hai Rui.

Jonathon Spence (1990: 600) tells us that Hai Rui was a Ming Dynasty (1368–1644) official who had a place in the history books for having stood up for the rights of the common people against blinkered and incompetent officials. Shortly before launching the Leap in 1956, Party Chairman Mao Zedong had invited the erudite journalist Wu Han, celebrated during the 1930s for his use of analogies to criticize Chiang Kaishek, to write about Hai Rui. Presumably what Mao had in mind was using the example of Hai Rui to berate conservative or indolent cadres. Two factors contributed to making Wu Han's endeavours into a major political issue. First, those who were later to become the principal begetters of the Cultural Revolution were at that time mobilizing against 'elitists' who, by virtue of their cultural capital, dominated cultural life to the detriment (thought Jiang Qing and her circle) of the truly revolutionary and the masses. For this group, Wu Han would be a suitable target. Second, Wu Han himself chose to write not upon Hai Rui's championing of the people against bureaucracy but upon his taking to task the emperor of the day for failure to keep in touch with the people and their plight and for his failure to control abuses. Wu Han had other axes to grind, equally unpalatable to Jiang Qing's circle. Pusey (1969: Chapter IV) emphasizes that one of Wu's principal concerns was with the dumbing down of education, which cut young people off from their culture's past.

This first article, published in 1959, was followed over the next three years by others in *The People's Daily*, just at the time that the Leap was being interpreted as a failure of Mao's. The articles were not immediately subject to criticism and Wu went on to investigate directives issued during the Leap which he and his associates, including Deng Tuo, turned into hard critiques of policy and published in *The People's Daily*, *Peking Daily* and *Frontline* under the by-line *Three Family Village*. This by-line harked back to the exile in a village of that name of a dismissed Sung Dynasty (960–1280) official. In action as in their analogies, the writers had taken upon themselves a role similar to that of a tribune, taking up the concerns of ordinary people. It may be that they were compromised in that they may have been being manipulated by Mao's rivals at court.[3]

This was a time when scientists, technologists, economists and experts in general were back in authority (Brugger 1994: 234) after their relegation to a status below the masses during the Leap; equally, journalists were regaining status. There was a small minority of 'left' journalists in Shanghai who opposed the policy of upgrading the experts and still hit out from time to time, alleging that the policy of trusting experts rather than the masses risked putting the revolution in the hands of a new bourgeoisie; they believed that, in Peking, the very notion of class struggle was being buried. The two leading ones have been mentioned above: Yao Wenyuan and Zhang Chunqiao. In summary, two utterly contradictory views of how China should modernize were competing, antagonism was mounting and the crisis would come to a head.

It is instructive to compare the kind of critical journalism that was being published now with that of the Hundred Flowers period. Then, Liu Binyan and his emulators wrote denunciations of the obstructionism of stupid, or narrow or dishonest officials hindering the masses from carrying out the line of the leadership, and preventing the leadership from being advised by the masses (Liu 1990: Chapter 5). During the 1960s the criticism, still dealing with practice rather than principle, was aimed at the top, 'beating tigers' rather than 'swatting flies'. Because of the danger they posed to some in the leadership, such writings were to be the catalyst for the Cultural Revolution, which would crush journalism for ten or more years:

> When Mao and his gang read these articles in the newspapers, they got scared. They said to themselves that very soon they'd be finished, they'd got to act fast.
>
> (Cao Xin)

The seizure of power

In September 1965 Mao got no response in the Party to his call for a campaign against 'reactionary bourgeois ideology', an attempt to rally his following against press criticism of the Leap, and left for Shanghai to plot with his supporters in the media. Two journalists epitomized the sides at that point. Deng Tuo believed there was no further call for class struggle; Zhang Chunqiao claimed that the system was making good communists into class enemies. In November 1965 Shanghai reporter and associate of Zhang's, Yao Wenyuan,[4] China's Savonarola, attacked Wu Han for advancing the idea that journalists should obey individual morality rather than the will of the masses. Led by those in the *Liberation Army Daily*, several thousand articles echoing Yao's followed in a few weeks. This widened into a general attack by the provincial press on that of the capital. However, it soon became apparent that the press was not really being used as a site for discussion but as the means by which leaders demonstrated their influence or by which the politically aware in China might see who was prevailing over whom (MacFarquhar 1997: 192–194). As it fell under the influence of the 'mass line' the press failed to reflect the arguments but copied the exhortations of *The People's Daily*; journalism disappeared (Chen 1975: 190–191).

With the media on Mao's side, Wu Han recanted in December 1965. In the first six months of 1966, *Liberation Army Daily* and *Red Flag* called for the toppling

of the 'Black Gang' of writers who had dared to undermine Mao and for absolute adherence to Mao's line; supporters seized *The People's Daily*.

In July 1966, in order to demonstrate his vigour, Mao swam in the Yangtze
River and such was the coverage in the press that it was clear that there had been
a change of power at the top, for the journalism establishment failed to block the
kind of reporting that would have been inconceivable shortly before.[5]

> Chairman Mao is the red sun in our hearts and is with us forever. Just as
> the competition started, a fast launch cut through the waves and sailed
> towards the swimmers from the east, where the sun was rising . . . Radiant
> with vigour and in buoyant spirits, Chairman Mao stood on the deck and
> reviewed the large number of swimmers battling the waves . . . Now walking
> to the starboard and now to the port side, he waved to the swimmers amid
> enthusiastic cheers and called out to them in a loud voice: 'Greetings com-
> rades! Long Life to you comrades!' . . . One swimmer got so excited that he
> forgot he was in the water. He raised up both hands and shouted, 'Long live
> Chairman Mao!' He leapt into the air but soon sank into the water again.
> He gulped several mouthfuls, but the water tasted especially sweet to him. It
> was at this moment that Chairman Mao's launch arrived near the mouth of
> the Wuchang dyke. With steady steps, Chairman Mao walked down the
> gangway and dipped himself in the water for a while before stretching out
> his arms and beginning to swim. It was exactly 11 o'clock.
>
> (quoted in Chen 1975: 220)

A teenage Maoist remembered that day because he too felt the power of the
metaphor of an old man swimming that great river to transform his own life; and
because it was the first day that the *Hunan Daily* was printed in scarlet (Liang
and Shapiro 1984: 43). Mao returned to Peking, his way made ready by his supporters in the army. He called for the formation of Red Guard detachments to
root out class enemies and opponents of Mao Thought, then old customs and
outdated thinking and he reviewed millions of young fanatics in Tiananmen
Square. These invaded ministries, assaulted officials, smashed and looted homes
and offices, burned books and cultural objects they did not understand and
humiliated anyone they deemed different from themselves in much the manner
of officially licensed hooliganism of other countries and other times.

Leading colleagues of Mao, including Liu Shaoqi and Deng Xiaoping, were
purged and their equivalents in most provinces suffered similarly. By 1969 Mao's
authority and that of his small group of friends (including his wife Jiang Qing)
was unchallenged. Yet the army had to be called in to restore order, as something like civil war was bursting out in many parts of the country.

But, scarlet ink aside, what had happened to journalism? As newspapers simply
regurgitated the panegyrics printed by those under 'mass line' control, it seems
they were paralysed. The struggles for power in the offices and the bitter quarrels
bearing little relation to any of the original ideas of the Cultural Revolution, the
violence, the expulsion to the countryside of professional journalists, the fear of

saying anything except, in effect, 'long-live Chairman Mao' lest you be subjected to persecution by one or other of the multitude of Red Guard units, all contributed to a sclerosis of the press.[6] How individual journalists were affected is vividly illustrated by the memoir of the son of an editor on the *Hunan Daily*, later to become a journalist himself (Liang 1984); what he describes was repeated up and down the country. After expelling the existing staff, the Maoists factions managed to mobilize only a few writers on whom they could rely, from among their relatives and friends, a factor which also contributed to the decadence of the press.

In so far as a line on journalism was articulated it was as is revealed in the editorial of *The People's Daily* of 19 January 1967 entitled 'Let Mao Zedong Thought dominate the newspapers' (literally 'occupy the emplacements of the newspapers'). The first section is an encomium of the two papers, *Wenhui Daily* and *Liberation Army Daily* (the army paper), which were already solidly Maoist. Some newspapers were still backward, presumably, else this editorial would have served no purpose. The section section opined:

> From the viewpoint of the proletariat, the Party's leadership (that is the leadership of the Party Central Committee with Chairman Mao at its head), is indeed the leadership of Mao Zedong Thought which means taking Chairman Mao as the representative of the proletarian revolutionary line. There is a little clique of the capitalist class which has viciously made its way into the Party, overturning the Party, contradicting Mao Thought, opposing the proletarian revolutionary line. We must rise up against these capitalist gentry! Once we have risen against them, the newspapers will get back onto the road of Mao Thought and once they are back on the revolutionary road of Chairman Mao the broad revolutionary masses will be able to hear correctly the voice of the Party, Chairman Mao's voice!
>
> (*The People's Daily* 19 January 1967)

These are only words. It was the brutality that broke people. Mao's gang encouraged the Red Guards, youngsters similar in purpose to Savonarola's *Army of Boys* in fifteenth-century Florence or the *Hitler Youth* of twentieth-century Germany, to burn books and destroy anything they thought 'decadent' from domestic cats to paintings; people whose faces did not fit were beaten, imprisoned, tortured, forced to suicide or just murdered. Others were sent to starve in the countryside where they were to 'learn from the peasantry'. Virtually all institutions shut down for long periods, or failed to function properly. This was a reign of terror carried out by young thugs commanded by old crooks, of which nothing positive can be said whatsoever.

As to the media, over the next few years, the expulsion or cowing of the establishment journalists resulted not in a throwing open of the media to the initiative and imagination of the masses, but in a sterile uniformity of Mao worship and political formulae. In 1969 the combined staffs of *The People's Daily*, *Red Flag* and *Liberation Army Daily* put out a little pamphlet, *Thoroughly Revolutionizing Journalism*, which explained the contemporary line on freedom of the press:

The press must necessarily be subject to the control, which is to say the 'restrictions' of a particular class. There can be absolutely no press free of all 'restrictions'. It is subject to the 'restrictions' of the bourgeoisie, or else to the 'restrictions' of the proletariat . . . as regards all these reactionaries, we must present a unanimity of opinion, we must not allow any expression of 'different opinions', not concede them the slightest freedom.

(Broyelle *et al.* 1980: 81)

If modern readers (only thirty-five odd years later!) are repelled by this, let them remember that German and Italian journalists were saying the same kind of sinister rubbish thirty years before that, and that Russians kept it up until the 1990s. In all these countries, moreover, there had been relatively free media before. There is no reason to suppose that humankind has been cured of the totalitarian disease.

The best depiction of how television in the Cultural Revolution was supposed to differ from the earlier, decadent period was given by a western enthusiast, Roger Howard, in 1971:

Television is a tool to help the masses of workers, peasants and soldiers maintain dictatorship over the bourgeoisie. The Liu Shao-ch'i line in television had four characteristics: it advocated programmes that had aesthetic appeal, general interest, general knowledge and entertainment value. So they had 'laughing parties' (comedy shows, pure and simple), films on archaeological relics that lauded the past, and programmes on how to grow potted plants, or girls on how to make pretty dresses. They had cartoons about monkeys that were wise and bears that were loyal. These ghosts have been laid.

(Howard 1971: 992)[7]

Howard also gives a concise description of the different news values under the mass line:

We have no interest in 'hot' news or so called actuality . . . We show a consolidated view of events when they've completed the process of their formation, not the events as they happen. The loss in so-called actuality is a gain in clarity of conclusions. We give the end result, the positive resolution of contradictions: and so we show the way forward.

(Howard 1971: 992)

The disdain for timeliness has remained a characteristic of Chinese public affairs journalism but, as the media become more competitive, may diminish.

As to content, during the Cultural Revolution, which in effect lasted from 1965 to 1975, journalism was denied any role other than as conduit for the views of those Revolutionary Committees, which claimed to be expressing the voice of the masses. The memory of this period is still strong in the minds of journalists over forty-five and lessons from it burnt into younger ones; it is surely for this reason that they so heartily advocate privatization as a safeguard – and cartoons about bears.

Journalism in the aftermath of the Cultural Revolution

> In those times China was involved in class struggle, [during the Cultural Revolution] people's relationships with each other were very confused. I was dubbed a black element and sent to do hard labour. At the smashing of the Gang of Four and after the reform period began, I was to return to my work. When that happened I recognized that to understand China's media you must comprehend China's history, since they cannot be extracted one from the other. The media is formed by the historical environment. In the past we could not imagine publishing anything of what we publish now.
>
> (Wang Qianghua)

If those interviewed are representative, Chinese journalists today fall into several categories according to how they evaluate their job and its functions. All, though, concur with the view that the Cultural Revolution was a disaster for journalism. The recent past informs both hopes for, and cynicism about, the future:

> Today it is possible to be a real journalist. This is because Deng Xiaoping came to power. The *falsehood, exaggeration and empty words* of the past went out when he came in.
>
> (Zhang Ximin)

> Oh yes, things have improved since [ironical] Comrade Xiaoping stepped up to the podium. Chinese journalists yesterday shouted *falsehood, exaggeration and empty words* for Communism. Now they do it for capitalism.
>
> (Kang Wei)[8]

The reality may be that the changes have been less dramatic than either respondent opines; there have been many twists and turns since Deng came back. Mao died in 1976. He was succeeded by Hua Guofeng, candidate of the left, rather than by Deng Xiaoping, who had reappeared discreetly as that of the modernizers. Hua soon found himself in conflict with Mao's wife and her associates, the 'Gang of Four' and, after they attempted a *coup d'état* in October 1976, had them arrested. Hua then brought Deng back into government.

By 1978 Deng Xiaoping had started to return to authority those experts, where still alive, who had been sacked during the Cultural Revolution and to attempt a decisive break. Guilt for the recent past was assigned to the Gang of Four, and Maoist fundamentalism subtly denigrated with Deng's slogans 'practice is the sole criterion of truth' and 'seek truth from facts'. Economic reforms, in effect, decollectivized; the results from the new 'responsibility system' were so much better that there was no likelihood of a return to the past.

Deng renounced class struggle, rehabilitated the persecuted and abolished class classifications.

Journalists rushed to demonize the Gang. Over the following ten years, intellectuals were increasingly consulted by government and involved in policy formulation, the media tentatively started discussing alternative policies rather than simply parroting the ruling faction, although moments of repression set clear limits as to what could be aired.[9] Although there was an 'open door policy' towards the outside world, with experts of many different kinds welcomed from abroad, people were rightly chary of being seen to be too involved with foreigners.

The journalistic style of the Cultural Revolution period, characterized as '*falsehood, exaggeration and empty words*' was condemned; in tune with Deng's most famous slogan 'It doesn't matter if it's a black cat or a white cat as long as it gets the mouse!' there was a great expansion of economic news and news about business ventures and agricultural production in place of domestic political coverage. In the internal struggles within the party, Hua Guofeng, of whom Mao had purportedly declared 'with you at the helm, I am at ease', was toppled. Editor Wang Qianghua's version of how this occurred is quoted in Chapter 10.

With the success of Deng Xiaoping, the CCP promised that, modernization not class struggle now being the state's goal, effectiveness would be the sole criterion of value and that differences in viewpoint would not result in political persecution. As Wang Meng, former 'dissident' journalist later to become Minister of Culture, put it, on the understanding that the Party's supreme position was not challenged, they would be 'criticized for their views and not for their natures' (Lin 1994: 79). There were limits to what could be said and these were made evident when, in 1979, the Democracy Wall movement was suppressed (see p. 66).

Nevertheless, during the 1980s, critical coverage and journalism of a quantity and breadth that had never before been seen in Communist China could be found in the newspapers. Articles suggested that alienation, or the feeling of being estranged from society, was a feature of Chinese society; some proposed humanism as a moral basis for life and even questioned party dictatorship. This openness was closely connected to Deng Xiaoping's attempts to reform the institutions of government, attempts which were centred on the September 1980 National People's Congress (NPC) and were known collectively as the *Gengshen* reforms. The initiatives were a response both to millions of appeals against miscarriages of justice and to a welter of complaints about the rigidities of the system in dealing with planning and development. Popular 'public scrutiny' of decision-making, a wider franchise for elections and recruitment reforms were all mooted. Democratic institutions were seen as better instruments of development; at the NPC delegates cross-examined government ministers more energetically than had been known before. The media were seen as playing an important part, according to one of Deng Xiaoping's advisers:

> In order for the media to play the role of quickly and effectively propagating the policies and decrees of the Party and the government, opportunely inform the people of all important events aside from a minority of secrets

concerning national defense and diplomacy, and opportunely reflect the people's criticisms of and suggestions to the Party and state organs, we should permit, require and encourage the media, the journalists, and commentators independently to assume responsibility of reporting and publishing news, letters from the masses, and comments. I think that such broad freedom of the press, freedom of speech, and freedom of publication carried out under the leadership of the Party's line, principles and policies, is of prime importance in democratizing the Party and the state.

(quoted in Nathan 1985: 82)

Yet there was opposition to this conception of the media, or to liberalization of any kind. It was a turbulent period as Deng consolidated his economic pragmatism, overcoming his rivals within the media as elsewhere in the establishment. As Lee writes, they were

caught up in rounds of factional warfare. The media were reviled by Party ideologues during the short-lived Anti-Spiritual Pollution Campaign (1983), the Anti-Bourgeois Liberalization Campaign (1987) and the Tiananmen Crackdown (1989). Each time some of the best journalists-writers were listed on account of their investigative exposés or theoretical arguments . . .

(Lee 2000)

Despite the rectification campaigns of 1983 and 1987 referred to by Lee, there was no return to pre-1978 days. In a famous case of journalistic scrutiny – the critique of negligence which had caused the sinking of an oil platform – the minister responsible was sacked; encouraged by this thousands of people wrote in with information to reporters who investigated stories of corruption and malfeasance. Before long, the failures of government were so freely aired as to be described in the government public relations information produced for foreign consumption.[10]

Journalism itself was widely discussed. Formerly ignored exemplars of the profession such as Shao Piaoping, a reporter and editor between 1911 and his murder in 1926, who had been famous for his revelations of bribery and corruption, were claimed, not very credibly, for the CCP (*China Daily* 13 November 1984). Editors published articles on the position of journalists in other countries, in 1984 a national forum was held on truthfulness in news reporting and *The People's Daily* called for a press law to prevent the persecution of journalists such as had occurred during the Cultural Revolution. The problem, though, as foreign observers have noted, is less the absence of laws than the failure of the courts to remember what they are. It is internalization of the concept of legality that has been needed (Ogden 1992: 173).

Those in leading positions, which by 1985 would include Hu Jiwei as first president of the *National Association of Journalists*, sought a formulation for journalism which would permit it to take on the censorial tasks and yet to maintain its role as articulator of the Party's line. They also tried to differentiate the Chinese journalist from his/her opposite number in the West. At the time, thanks to

much freer intercourse between Chinese and westerners and the recommence-
ment of journalism education in China with much western input from both
practitioners and academics, younger journalists were inclined to embrace western norms wholeheartedly in reaction to the recent past (Porter 1992 Chapter 1).
This is how Chen Lung, Director of the Department of Domestic News for
Foreign Services at New China News Agency put it in April 1983:

> The starting point for the press is different in China. The mass media have
> a grave responsibility to people and society in China. Formerly China was
> controlled by foreign countries and by feudalism. If we want to overthrow
> these two yokes, we have to rely on people. So our primary task is to awaken
> the people so that they will understand the overthrow of imperialism and
> feudalism, that it is of common interest, so that they will fight for it. The
> primary role of the news is to educate and awaken the people. And you see
> the same thing now. We want to modernize China. It is a very gigantic task.
> And you have to waken the whole people to work hard for it.
>
> (quoted in Chang 1989: 100)

Though this strict sense of mission might be binding on the professional journalist, it was not to preclude a press which would have popular appeal. By the late
1980s, newspapers had changed out of all recognition, with much less politics,
soft and entertaining features and coverage which acknowledged the existence
of widely diverse interests, hobbies, and social identities. Some saw this as the
harbinger of a very different role for journalism.

Rethinking journalism

A new line was given in a major article by Hu Yaobang, now CP Secretary
General, in *The People's Daily* in April 1985:

> In China . . . the basic requirements for journalism are truth, timeliness and
> information and interest in addition to a clear-cut class character, Party
> spirit and a scientific attitude of seeking truth from facts.
>
> (*China Daily* 16 April 1985: 1)

In making a break with previous journalistic practice, Hu was both trying not
to discourage those who wanted to get as far from the Cultural Revolution as
possible – into the western 'pluralist' camp in some cases – yet also to hold the
dyke. For the myth of the Gang of Four's seizure of the state had provided an
argument for the press to put itself forward as adjudicator of the politicians and
champion of public morality. After all, they implied, had the media not been less
hidebound, could it not have alerted the nation to the Gang of Four? Some
political leaders could not but be uneasy.

By the time of Hu's speech the atmosphere was so permissive that hundreds of
protesters, representing rusticated youths (400,000 had been sent to Shanxi alone

during the Cultural Revolution), plucked up courage to demonstrate in Peking. Freedoms, despite regular statements attempting to dampen enthusiasm for them, seemed continually expanding such that the press by 1986 was carrying articles extolling 'democratic liberties', discussing the need for a new state agency to control the press and, in the *World Economic Herald*, declaring the view that barriers to economic advance were political. The same year the National Forum of Chief News Editors made clear their desire for autonomy from Party Committees, that they might themselves alone be arbiters of news value. In October 1987 Prime Minister Zhao Ziyang pleased journalists in his report to the 13th Party Congress when he advanced three principles for journalism: journalism is the agent for the 'public scrutiny' of public officials by public opinion; for keeping the public informed of important matters; that it should enable public debate on major issues.[11] In not mentioning the traditional propaganda role, these principles broke radically with the past. Yet when another National Forum on Journalism took place in autumn 1988 there was no progress on exactly how journalism could be reformed or reform be made safe (Polumbaum 1990: 44).

Concrete changes nevertheless continued to take place. Previously taboo subjects or subjects which would only have appeared as news long after the event such as natural disasters, riots or resistance to Chinese rule by the Turks[12] or Tibetans were reported. In 1989 it was Zhao Ziyang who was, by all accounts, responsible for allowing foreign journalists into the (7th) National People's Congress for the first time and it was at this conference that, also a first, there was a choice of candidate for whom to vote (a change forced upon the congress organisers by delegates from Hong Kong) and that plans to separate the Party from the civil service were first considered. A draft press law was under discussion at the very moment of the Tiananmen Massacre, after which it was shelved.[13]

Democracy Wall

The democracy movement of 1978–1979 started when it became rumoured about in autumn 1978 that there was a struggle going on between Hua Guofeng and Deng Xiaoping. Deng Xiaoping was (rightly) said to be leader of a faction which wanted both to depoliticize much of Chinese society and to free up the economy from the paralysis imposed by state control. On a stretch of wall in Peking students began to put up posters in support of Deng Xiaoping and calling for change; to their cries were added those of frustrated workers, people with grievances against officials and parents longing for the return of their rusticated children. Thousands of people collected in the dark winter days to read the petitions, acclamations and accusations; others began to publish crudely printed broadsheets, some of which turned into veritable magazines. Among many others, a then unknown electrician called Wei Jingsheng published his own magazine, *Explorations*; similar magazines often appeared to be informed by people in the leadership compound, since they reported the debates going on 'at the top'. The situation was repeated all over China.

It was on 5 December, when Wei posted his call for 'Democracy – the Fifth Modernization', that the authorities became alarmed, especially since Wei's dismissive attitude towards the CCP and Deng, whom he regarded as just another flawed Communist functionary, was taken up by others and the tone of the criticisms became ever more hostile and, from the point of view of the CCP, menacing. The wall was torn down and its aficionados directed to an obscure park. In March, Wei was arrested and sentenced to fifteen years' imprisonment. Nine years later his cause was to be taken up again, with even more disastrous results.

The democracy movement and the Tiananmen massacre of 4 June 1989

The year preceding the Tiananmen massacre of 1989 was one of widespread discontent. Pei (2000) records over 5,000 collective protests that year, though few received media coverage. The demonstrations which led up to the massacre and in which journalists were closely involved began in April 1989 with a memorial meeting for the recently deceased Hu Yaobang, initiated by students who lived in the high leaders' compound and were therefore connected to the ruling cliques, who saw a split developing and wanted to encourage the pro-Hu faction. Although there were calls for democracy, as observers (Mark 1991: 274) perceived, there was no very clear idea of how this democracy was to be arrived at or in what exactly it was to consist. As the world's media gave more attention to the students, so the assertions that they were fighting for democracy became more fervent; they used the foreign media to bolster their importance, but they also told the Americans and British what they hoped to hear (Smith 1992).

Journalists gradually came to identify themselves with the students. On May 4 as hundreds of thousands commemorated the May 4 of seventy years before, editors and reporters held a rally outside *New China News Agency* to protest against the sacking of the editor of the *World Economic Herald* on the grounds that he was advocating bourgeois values, and called for 'press freedom'. Outside the offices of *The People's Daily* they chanted, to the tune of *Frère Jacques* (familiar as the tune of a nursery song about tigers and tails)

> People's Daily People's Daily
> Oh how odd! Oh how odd!
> Always printing lies, always printing lies
> Oh how odd! Oh how odd!

And carried on their banners the slogan 'Our pens cannot write the articles we want to write, our mouths cannot say the words we want to say' (Black and Munro 1993: 164).

In time their demonstrations merged with those of the students. In retrospect and given forty years of experience of see-sawing media policy, the journalists made a mistake in joining so wholeheartedly with what became a massive demonstration of the discontented of every type from well-connected elite students to industrial workers seeking trades union representation to many seekers of redress from injustice who hailed from all over the country. The journalists' profession had some very specific, and perhaps realizable, demands encapsulated in the phrase of Hu Jiwei that 'journalism has its own objective laws' (Lee 1990: 12) whereas that wider circle with which they allowed their profession to become identified had objectives too ambitious for those times.

Polumbaum has shown the journalists argued that trying to serve both party and people is contradictory, since party officials want self-promotion and the publication of government PR, while journalists are the best judge of what should go into a paper to please readers. Their solution was diversity of ownership. Party and state functionaries were not be allowed to meddle and to stifle initiative and autonomy and journalists should be trusted to know their jobs and protected from any adverse consequences of honest investigative work (Polumbaum 1990).

One of the many journalism polemics at the time revolved around a statement signed on 16 May 1989 by several well-known journalists including TV reporter and author of the controversial television documentary *River Elegy*,[14] Su Xiaokang:

> During the student movement, the news media, as represented by the *People's Daily* and the *Xinhua News Agency*, for a time withheld the true facts about the student movement and stripped the citizens of their right to know (of it). The Shanghai Municipal Party Committee has fired Qin Benli, editor in chief of the *World Economic Herald*. These totally illegal acts are a gross violation of the Constitution. Freedom of the press is an effective means to uproot corruption, maintain national stability, and promote social development. Absolute power unchecked and unsupervised will definitely lead to absolute corruption. Without freedom of the Press, without independent newspapers, all hopes and aspirations about reform and the open policy will remain empty talk.
>
> (Li 1991: 92)

Many of the demonstrators had a less temperate and reasoned agenda yet the reporters and editors increasingly allowed their own objectives to be confused with those of the radical students. After the massacre, the first task to be undertaken would be the rectification[15] of the journalists, some of whom died, many of whom lost their livelihoods and their future and the bulk of whom would conform.

In retrospect it would seem that, given the political system in China, the Party was left with very little choice but to end the demonstrations violently. Sympathy for the aspirations of the demonstrators was present in the hierarchy, as was clear from the behaviour of both the hierarchs themselves and their media. Indeed it was this very sympathy which had allowed to emerge a dangerously explosive situation which could not be contained by, for example, elections or some other mechanism for social compromise because none exists. A tense situation was made much worse by the offensive and immature way in which some student representatives behaved towards the prime minister, losing them support.

Echoes

What does all this mean, many years later, to journalists? Pei (2000) has pointed out that the dissidents of the 1980s were theoretical and political, whereas in the 1990s causes were more populist. At least they were down to earth, concentrating on corruption, the environment and criticism of Japan for its failure to acknowledge its crimes in the Second World War. In 1998 (Pei 2000: 309) prominent intellectuals signed a letter blaming floods in Central China on government policies. However, in that year the magazine *Human Rights Observer* was suppressed as was the China Democratic Party.

One professor of journalism was asked whether he thought that what happened in June 1989 had made life more difficult for journalists. This was his reply:

> Just now everyone is rather cagey because of the two problems of *falungong* and the Taiwan crisis. Also we are coming up to the 50th Anniversary [of the PRC] so everything is a bit tense. But things will get better if there is no war with Taiwan. Situations like this recur all the time and things were certainly like this after June 1989. Then they got better. You just have to be prepared for the difficult situations because you know they will pass.
>
> What has changed for always is that journalists are not just mouthpieces. Now they are the mediators between people and government.
>
> (Jiang Xiaolong)

Similar phrases cropped up in the conversations of others:

> Journalists are the mediators between people and government. Their tasks are the communication of news and 'public scrutiny' of the administration.
>
> (Tang Musan)

Although some journalists have the idea that journalists should be social activists in what appears to be a traditional, (i.e., pre-Cultural Revolution), manner, others are forthright that things are different now:

> Certainly not. They are very different from journalists. A reporter should try to report impartially whereas a social activist has some aims. We report opinions and facts.
>
> (Tang Musan)

It is worth reminding ourselves of the situation of the media during the Cultural Revolution since, although it is now history, many of the developments in the media that contrast with that period – the loss of share by Party papers, the depoliticization of content, the responsiveness to the audience – can be interpreted less as the result of the 'opening' than as backlash, a continuing rejection, sometimes passionate, of the days of Mao. In what is probably an eccentric view, one interviewee attributed the collapse of Communism in the West to the leadership of the Chinese people who, he believed, had shown the way in standing up to their oppressors and would do so again once 'the objective conditions are right' by which he presumably meant the CCP's power had collapsed.

As the day of the 50th anniversary of the founding of the PRC approached (1 October 1999), the Party brought together media leaders and exhorted them not to allow journalists merely to extol the greatness of Deng Xiaoping and of the achievements after 1978 but to call attention to China's progress under Mao Zedong.[16] For want of anything else, the nuclear programme and its personnel, who researched away, untroubled by the Cultural Revolution, were held up to glorification by President Jiang[17] as demonstrating that progress had indeed taken place in those times. Yet it would appear that the period between 1955 and 1978 was still largely ignored in the celebratory reports and features. Perhaps the people in the Hangzhou street market where tourists can buy Red Guard armbands from a peddler selling red books, Mao badges and the like expressed it best when they said 'that was China's worst period ... only foreigners buy those things ... we don't want to remember'.

But memory plays an important part in the discourses of journalism in China. It frames them. Some journalists appear to believe that it was only by a fluke that China, after the Tiananmen incident, did not revert to the closed society that it had been under Mao and Hua; that it was the fluke of Deng just being fit enough to revive reform that saved them. Western commentators might scoff at this, seeing it as a manifestation of the Cleopatra's nose theory of history, ignoring the powerful economic and political forces driving China towards reform. But people's beliefs about their world can be at least as influential as the realities which social scientists try to reveal.

Journalism after the Tiananmen massacre

When, on 18 August 1989, New China News Agency issued its analysis of the reasons for the closure of the *World Economic Herald*, it explained that the particular offending edition, focusing on the life and work of Hu Yaobang, had gone beyond appropriate bounds by featuring opinions which were permissible expressed in private, in communications to the Central Committee or in limited circulation publications, but which the Central Committee had expressly forbidden to be aired in public. Thus was set the tenor of the post-massacre media; notwithstanding the anger of those journalists who fled abroad (Hsiao 1990, Liu 1990), this explanation of events was by no means a return to the situation before 1978. Some observers saw it as an attempt to compromise between 'conservatives' and 'liberals' (Jernow 1993).

Even if it can be agreed that 'conservatives' are indeed those who, for a variety of different reasons, wish to limit the free expression of ideas, how far is it justifiable to refer to 'liberals'? While the *Herald* had survived as an economic policy critic for several years thanks to the support it received from Zhao Ziyang (Hsiao 1990: 118), it should not necessarily be concluded that this support was for the sake of a liberal ideal; many of the articles were doubtless useful to

Zhao in the internal Party debates and it is likely that many of the advocates of more liberal economic reforms saw, however inchoately, media debate as a necessary concomitant. However, the relative openness which developed is, according to the critics, compromised by the relationship between the media and political power. How can there be debate if the Party can, at one go, close down thirty or forty periodicals as it did after the Tiananmen massacre?

Chinese officials struggled to theorize the position of journalism at that juncture, marrying a 'class perspective' with the idea of impartiality:

> Journalism work certainly has objective laws of its own. Considering this a weird question, some hold that under the Party's leadership journalistic work is no more than the propagation of the Party's guiding principles and policies . . . It should be recognized that journalism is subordinate to politics. It is an opinion tool of a given class, always serving a given class. This is the very fundamental law of journalism. Whether or not you recognize this, journalism the world over cannot escape the dictation of this law. But there are more aspects to this. Journalism transmits the various developments of the objective world to its audience as well as publicizes [sic] the audience's feedback to the world. In this process an opinion environment is formed, creating a kind of spiritual moving force. In other words, journalism builds a bridge between the objective world and the audience, and serves an important function between the two.
>
> What ought to be noted are as follows: News reporting must be objective and true, reflecting the reality as is [sic]. News reporting must be speedy and timely. Journalism must reduce its distance from the audience, making itself easy for the audience to accept. The audience's feedback or evaluation determines the survival of journalism.
>
> (Gan 1994: 44)

Policy makers also attempted to differentiate Chinese journalism from that of the West:

> Most journalists agree that we must not one-sidedly repudiate 'objectivity' or 'fairness'. Instead, we must differentiate its substantive meaning from its use by bourgeois newspapers. Under the banner of objectivity and fairness, a few bourgeois newspapers are in reality attempting to inculcate in their readers their worldviews and biases. Their objectivity and fairness are limited, even pretentious.
>
> (Gan 1994: 46)

Such was the official view. The private opinions of journalists were perhaps better expressed in this ditty:

> I am the dog of the Party, sit in front of the Party's house;
> I bite whomsoever the Party bites, when it bites me I don't grouse.

6 The political context for journalism today

Much has changed since the Tiananmen massacre of 1989. At first there was a check in the relaxation of political controls which had been the main feature of Chinese life since 1978. China was in a kind of no man's land until Deng Xiaoping undertook his 'Southern Progress' – or at least until the media managed to publicize it. The role of journalists in this period is similar to their role in earlier crises, and perhaps in crises to come: they are seen to be sometimes subject to, and sometimes negotiating with, factions in government. Here we attempt to understand the political circumstances within which journalists now operate and how those circumstances may frame the way journalism is developing.

Economic reforms and social consequences

In 1978 the economy was stagnant, production and distribution were inefficient and corrupt; there was little or no new commercial enterprise; China had fallen behind the rest of the world and would be hard put to it to feed its population. At that date most prices were set by the central government, virtually all production was managed by government ministries and innovation in response to the market was rare. Visitors to China were amused by the quaint retail shops with their domestic goods based on designs of the 1940s and characterized by shortages such that vast crowds might collect in a particular state shop if the rumour got round that some sewing machines were available. Yet by 1995 few prices were controlled and two-thirds of the economy had been subjected to market influences.

In 1978 China had $38bn of foreign trade, monopolized by the state trading ministry, and in 1997 enjoyed $300bn of trade handled by 4,000 trading organizations. There were 300,000 joint ventures and wholly owned foreign firms operating in China, accounting for perhaps half of China's foreign trade.[1]

This economic development came about in stages. It took until 1987 and the 13th Party Congress for it to be politically feasible to announce publicly that the private sector 'be permitted to exist'. The following year there took place the revision of the state constitution which legalized private businesses.

The fact that it took so long, after the fall of the Gang of Four and the establishment of Deng Xiaoping's leadership, for initiatives which had been set in motion to be admitted publicly, indicates the degree of opposition, on grounds of ideology and of practicality, that needed to be overcome.

Opposition to the marketization of the economy gained a fillip after the Tiananmen massacre and there was criticism of privatization in the media; the number of private enterprises fell. The problems to which marketization had been intended as a solution did not, however, go away; the State-Operated Enterprises (SOEs), long recognized as failing to respond to market needs in quantity, quality or type of product, were not resuscitated and, by 1996, subsidies to them outweighed their contributions to the state budget. The economy was depressed yet the left faction, which gained the ascendancy after the massacre, produced no practicable alternative policy.

Here it is necessary to write something about the use of the terms 'left' and 'right' and it may be useful to make an analogy with a western country. In the 1970s and 1980s in the UK, the left party, Labour, increasingly appeared, or was represented as, the defender of old fashioned ways of doing things to which were attributed the failures of the UK economy, poverty and low morale. The so-called right on the other hand, the Conservative Party, championed (very radical) reform and modernization. To caricature, the left therefore became associated with all that was backward – became conservative – and the right with insensate neophilia. This is a reversal of the thinking which had been common among earlier generations which had viewed right-wing parties as wanting to conserve the established order, particularly the economic order, and the left as wanting change at all costs, in the interests of the progressive classes. With China, the 'left' is normally referred to as the 'conservatives' in the sense that they want to preserve the old order, with its rigid hierarchies and special privileges, whereas the 'right' opts for ending statism, promoting private enterprise and opening to the world. This is meant to be helpful; if it at the same time illustrates the idiocy, today, of the terms 'left' and 'right' then that is a happy by-product.

The state

In the early 1950s the CCP had established formal organs of state administration, influenced by Soviet practice. With no system of democratic accountability, these could always be circumvented, nevertheless there was some element of legality and system. During the Cultural Revolution power went into the hands of those who could grab it; the chaos that ensued convinced Deng Xiaoping and many others that China needed a new system. He wanted Party and state separated, a revised version of the 1954 constitution and political restructuring to accompany economic reform. The People's Communes were abolished and the traditional administrative pyramid re-established; political supervision was separated from economic management. The Party was to reduce its role to policy generation and oversight and a profession of state functionaries developed. The National People's Congress was supplemented by local equivalents. The changes were managed by the State Commission for the Reform of the Economic System (*Tigaiwei*) and there was much enthusiasm, at least around the senior leadership of Zhao Ziyang, in effect Deng's executive arm, to reform everything, even if reducing public ownership in the economy had to be done with discretion.

Students and officials had again begun to go abroad to study in the mid-1970s and as they returned, shocked at China's backwardness and enthused by new ideas from Europe and the USA, many were recruited into think tanks and consulting bodies. Although journalists could rarely publicize the advanced thoughts of the returnees, they mixed among them and shared the dissatisfaction with the slow pace of change and the enthusiastic hopes for the future.

Among the important changes was fiscal decentralization. This gave provincial and lower tier governments authority to raise and allocate revenues. The local governments were given property rights over state owned enterprises within their jurisdictions and these became sources of funds. Some local authorities ignored central government instructions to reduce expansion and cut credit and simultaneously erected protective trade barriers against other localities. Thus Peking has found it more difficult to collect money from the provinces – its attempts to reform the tax-raising system in one crucial respect were stymied (Cheung 1994) – yet the importance of the state in other respects, for example its ability to determine key appointments, its ability to collect information, have not atrophied. It is argued that, in provincial–central relations, command and coercion have given way to bargaining and compromise (Baum and Shevchenko 1999: 338).

Observers (Baum 1999, Wank 1999, Christiansen and Rai 1998, O'Brien 1995) have noted other unintended consequences of the reforms. As new initiatives have sprung up to advance free enterprise and liberate the market, so bureaucracy has proliferated, with vast increases in the numbers of state functionaries. These functionaries' success is judged on their ability to promote enterprise and generate money; officials who lack commercial initiative become predators on enterprise, inventing new taxes and imposts in order to increase revenues. Wank calls this 'symbiotic clientilism' (Wank 1999: 269ff.) while Baum describes it as 'reversion to primitive predatory patrimonialism' (Baum 1999: 357) although he also argues that the cooperation of entrepreneurs and officials may have ensured social stability, in other words that the situation is positive simply because they are not fighting each other for spoils but cooperating to despoil the state (and the poor).

Upright officials rapidly become demoralized in such circumstances and the party appears to be withering away in some areas, while in others it has become colonized by profiteers looking for opportunities to buy state property or exploit party connections. After rural riots in 1992 to 1993, Peking encouraged farmers to voice their grievances against despotic or corrupt functionaries (O'Brien 1995), yet this may well have further demoralized what steadfast officials still existed.

The political context as the leadership changes generations

The success of Deng's 'Progress' appeared to seal the direction China would take but skill has been needed for Jiang Zemin to steer China as far as the World Trade Organization (WTO), with all the implications that membership has for China's domestic economy and politics.

Typically the Chinese polity has been thought of by non-Chinese as a totalitarian system. However, in academic eyes, already by the Cultural Revolution, it appeared that China was less totalitarian and that its leaders 'far from radiating totally penetrating power and exerting total control, seemed to lurch from crisis to crisis trying to contain or to redirect the various forces . . . that sought to challenge and erode even the semblance of unified authority in China' (Shue 1988: 16). Not only had aspects typical of pre-Communist Chinese society survived, most obviously factionalism, regionalism and personalized politics, but China's affairs appeared dominated by the competitions of rival organizations, each with their own interests and bureaucracies.

> Our studies had taught us that the state under Mao contained numerous shifting, cross-cutting, competitive (even hostile) centres of power. We had seen that the state almost never spoke to the people with one voice. We had learned that China's gargantuan and Byzantine bureaucratic apparatus acted by no means as a mechanical transmission belt for central directives, but delayed, distorted, deflected and destroyed central intentions as often as it faithfully implemented them.
>
> (Shue 1988: 17)

If that were true then, it would certainly prove to be the case in the 1990s, although some observers have held that the 1980s offered opportunities to escape from the predicaments of the past, thanks to the consensus in repudiation of the previous decades, opportunities that were lost in the gunfire at Tiananmen in June 1989.

Jiang Zemin was elected to the politburo in 1987 and, particularly since he was not part of the group of progressives around then Premier Zhao Ziyang, would not normally have been expected to rise as rapidly as he was to do. However, he pleased the older hierarchs with his handling of the *World Economic Herald*, which he suppressed on account of its free thinking (see Chapter 8). In 1989 Zhao and his, often young, progressives took the blame both for allowing discontent to rise and then for failing to deal suitably with its malign manifestations. The *open door policy* had gone too far and over indulgence in western ideas, irrelevant to Chinese circumstances, was blamed; there were many sarcastic comments about the young advisers of Zhao along the lines of their 'having doctorates from Harvard but not knowing the geography of Hunan'. While direct criticism of Deng Xiaoping was not possible, his reformist coterie, personified by Zhao Ziyang, was toppled and although *open door* itself was not officially abandoned, the economic liberalizing policies launched by Deng Xiaoping were placed in question, and checked.

Over the next few years Jiang consolidated his position as Deng's obvious heir while avoiding antagonizing Deng's enemies. He also built up his own power base – the 'Shanghai Faction' – in such a manner that he was rarely challenged until he was strong enough to see off his enemies in government (Lam 1999: 18–31). He did all this happy in the knowledge that, unlike some of his predecessors, he would likely soon be free of the old guard and their testy interference, simply because they were dying off.

The leading leftist, Li Peng, was in charge immediately after Tiananmen but he failed to find solutions for the economic difficulties so that the progressives were emboldened. The left was concerned that the private sector was outstripping the public; that in reality privatization meant selling off public assets at favourable terms to friends and relatives of officials around the country and the writing off of public debt; that China was vulnerable to foreign capitalism and foreign markets; that gross disparities of income had emerged and would cause instability; that job insecurity was undermining social life; that development was bringing with it poisonous corruption.

In deference to these concerns Jiang forbore from threatening the biggest state enterprises with dissolution and launched a campaign against corruption which led to senior officials being executed or imprisoned for embezzlement. Such cases were probably very popular with the public, which was intended to see them as indications of Jiang's serious intent at least to try to govern fairly. The public was also intended to note that the best known defendant, Chen Xitong, was the high leader who had been the most enthusiastic proponent of the hard-line solution to the Tiananmen demonstrations. It is also true that Chen Xitong was an opponent of Jiang Zemin's, and as Fewsmith notes (2001: 166) in the past such differences would have been dealt with as differences of ideology. What Jiang did was to invoke law, rather than ideology, suggesting that he did set some store by the institutional legality which had been championed by those who gave democracy the highest priority.

In these matters he showed that he wanted to avoid being easily classified as either leftist or progressive. The same instinct was at work when, while economic change accelerated in late 1996, Jiang troubled to demonstrate his sensibility to leftist anxieties, by publishing his *Resolution on Spiritual Civilization*. This declared that China would continue its policy of modernization and opening up but not at the expense of such 'spiritual' values as family first, sexual morality, social responsibility and respect for parents and for tradition. Intellectuals and publishers were exhorted to consider the 'social effects' of their activities and it was confirmed that the media and publishing would remain under political control.

The experience of Russia since Gorbachev is held up by the left as a negative example of political chaos, justifying resistance to all but the most modest political changes. Before 1989 there had been many plans for developing the National People's Congress and the People's Consultative Congress into elected parliamentary organs which would be representative and provide scrutiny of government; under Jiang there was little or no progress in this area. Village-level elections were introduced in the 1980s but there appears little likelihood of elections to township or county levels. Jiang ruled out reforms which might make China more democratic, such as universal suffrage or allowing other parties to contest elections.

Village-level elections mattered not only as experiments in democracy but also as safety valves for the frustrations of rural people which were more and more exploding into demonstrations and riots. As with city dwellers, peasants could be hit hard by the crookedness of officials re-zoning their land, cheating them out of its worth, forcing them to grow some crops at the expense of others, charging exorbitant school fees for their children's education and other impositions. Journalists often find themselves caught between the hopes of the oppressed and the conventions of the officials.

Conscious of dissatisfactions, Jiang has tried to make the ruling elite less exclusive. Business people, formerly kept out, can now join the Party, a policy which was lauded to the skies at the 2002 Party Congress. Official posts can now be filled through public examination or recruitment which is, in appearance at least, 'western-style'. Non-Party specialists are welcomed into think tanks and as consultants and even, in a few cases, given high office and administrative responsibilities (Lam 2002a).

At about the same time as the *Resolution on Spiritual Civilization*, an apparent acknowledgement of the concerns of the left, Jiang's 'policy wonks' published *Talking Heart to Heart with the General Secretary*. This volume was a defence of modernization, presumably produced at this particular moment in order to warn off the left and slap down the xenophobia, which is one of its instincts, at a time when Jiang was discussing improving relations with the USA. In its critique of the recent experience of the USSR and its successor states it disagreed with the left, which cited the Gorbachev era as the cause of that country's woes, and instead blamed Brezhnev and his failure to reform for the later instability of Russia. The book claimed not merely – as the standard argument had it – that opening up was useful for improving home technology and management but that closing the door to globalization was just not possible and that China would have to compete on the world markets if it were to survive and prosper. The aim, common to all, of wealth and power for China, was conditional on becoming a full member of the world economic system. It was a declaration that, notwithstanding setbacks in US–China relations, Jiang would pursue WTO entry.

Finally the book, as subsequent speeches and articles were to do, undertook another courageous task: the attempt to connect with China's Confucian past.[2] Up to now the CCP had repudiated the Confucian heritage utterly, but this book attempted to show how what the Communists had done expressed continuity with tradition. Perhaps even the Marxists at the top of the Party had come to see the barrenness – and the foreignness – of their creed and were scrabbling around among the ruins of what they had left of Chinese civilization to give some sense of mission and some sense of identity to their nation.

The law – and corruption

Foreign observers have been loud in their calls for China to establish a reliable legal system if they are to be able to do business with it; human rights activists have long fulminated against the limitations of China's justice system. As much to assuage this criticism and to encourage trade as in response to moral exhortation, China has made many innovations, even extending them to the devising of civilian costumes for lawyers who used to wear military uniform. It is often observed, though, that there is very little sense of equality before the law in Chinese society and that powerful individuals or institutions are able to ignore it at whim. One corollary of a political and economic system in which there are neither commonly accepted legal standards nor democratic checks is corruption, or the avoidance of rules and formal procedures and the achievement of objectives by use of bribery, threats or through mutual support networks.

Jiang Zemin has shown himself aware of the problem of corruption and encouraged numerous campaigns (almost annual) as well as calling upon the media to help in the fight, authorizing journalists' delving. However, it is not only journalists who have become cynical as their researches have been pigeon holed or as they have realized that their investigations are used as weapons in factional fighting. When ordinary citizens see that, on the one hand, thousands of petty criminals can be summarily executed after minimal trials, while on the other hand big time *mafiosi* such as Chen Xitong, Party boss of Peking, Ouyang Da, Vice Governor of Canton, or gangster sons of revolutionary leaders are given moderate treatment and allowed to protect their gangs, it is hardly surprising if they believe that anti-graft campaigns are conveniences for the bosses. It may be that Jiang and many of his government are quite sincere in wanting to get rid of graft but it is questionable whether they have the ability to escape from the factionalism which stymies their efforts, from their own family members who wallow in it,[3] or from the blinkers which prevent them from envisioning a system which might control it.

One who did envisage such a system was Jiang's rival Qiao Shi, a far-sighted official who has consistently argued since the 1980s that China needs legally based institutionalized systems if it is to progress in providing the framework for an orderly society and economy. Among the changes he and his sympathizers would like to see (and many of which were widely aired thanks to the encouragement of Deng Xiaoping in the 1980s) are: separation of Party and executive; the possibility of other parties developing; subjection of the executive to the legislature; challenged elections; subjection of the armed forces to the civil; a legislature which functions as an appraising and accounting body; civil service reform to provide impartial and meritocratically selected functionaries. Although a number of minor changes in these areas have come about, nothing has been done which changes the absolute domination of the CCP or the rule by personal whim and factional regimentation (Christiansen and Rai 1998: 83). Qiao Shi lost much of his power at the 15th Congress (1997) although his ideas still have resonance.

Instead of prosecuting such a programme, Jiang Zemin, as we have seen, tried to widen the catchment of the elite. He also attempted to attack the problems of disintegrating authority and corruption through exhortation in the media. Since appeal to Communist values has little point, he appealed to people in general to uphold 'Chinese traditional values', a gallimaufry of Confucian and Communist precepts, and to functionaries in particular to model themselves on legendary heroes of yore. His technique in other words was Maoist, though his content is neo-Confucian. In this he was very different from Deng Xiaoping, who wanted everyone to concentrate on economics as the determining factor; Jiang emphasized politics. For Jiang, while it was necessary that China learn techniques from the West, it must resist cultural pollution. By implication, all bad things come from the West; if the Chinese but heighten their national consciousness under the wise leadership of he who defends 'the spirit of the nation', then the problems will go away.[4]

It is unclear whether these pronouncements are simply obligatory to pacify the left or whether they really represented his philosophy. At any event, institutional reform was relegated, so that the only means at the government's disposal for dealing with the growing discontent were exhortation and repression. There were campaigns to improve the quality of lower-level government by re-educating cadres and prohibiting unjust corvées and taxes; there were campaigns calling upon citizens to expose extravagance and mismanagement by officials; campaigns to emulate Zhangjiagang, a model area of honest administration and economic probity. Journalists were the main mediators of these campaigns.

Another manifestation of the Jiang approach was a paternal, rather patronizing, style of showing how problems may be solved, such as the *Helping the Poor Campaign* of 1997 or his own many flying visits to impoverished or remote communities to which he brought gifts, promises of solidarity and television crews to report his fire-fighting to a grateful nation.

The Spiritual Civilization campaigns gave opportunities to the media to emphasize patriotic topics; at the height of such campaigns journalists were nervous of being seen to be doing negative reporting, even of relatively innocuous subjects such as natural calamities. Direct action was taken by the authorities against publishers of undesirable materials from pornography to politics and newspapers; intellectuals' magazines and TV stations were closed.

The WTO and the world ahead

In 2001 China became a member of the WTO, an important event in the development of world trade because China is a country with a vast population of which an ever increasing proportion is economically dynamic. China's influence upon smaller countries and different economies may be great. There is a widespread assumption that China will soon become not merely *a* powerhouse of world manufacturing, but *the* world powerhouse (BBC 2002).

The Chinese leadership undertook this step, against left opposition led by Li Peng (the only member of the Standing Committee to vote against accession to the WTO) and widespread suspicion, because it wants WTO disciplines to be a mechanism for reforming Chinese economy; improving foreign trade; reducing military expenditure and introducing new technology, new skills and new habits of mind. The accession agreement requires China to reform its economy so that it conforms with the trading, accounting, financing and reporting practices of the advanced economies. In the preparatory period China was adapting its economy by reducing tariff and non-tariff barriers to trade, reducing grain prices to conform to international prices and exhorting changes in many different areas of economic practice. The government has committed itself to adhering to intellectual property rules and the far reaching conventions which limit entrepreneurs' freedom of action, to introducing unemployment insurance programmes, to eliminating agricultural export subsidies on entry and to solving the problem of loss-making State-Operated Enterprises (SOEs) within three years. Many suspect that China is unable to adapt in these ways both because of entrenched interests and because of lack of political agreement and will; the WTO partisans appear to be hoping that the WTO will in some manner force the economy into change.

China is already the seventh biggest trading country, world leader in labour-intensive manufacture and a full partner in the world system for the production of high technology. If the rewards of WTO membership are essential to achieving the goal of China reaching western levels, then risks are equally great. One risk is that of vast unemployment as the SOE system is further dismantled. In 1997 the government confirmed its policy of letting smaller SOEs go private while keeping hold of the bigger ones to prevent undue disruption, even though they were making colossal losses. The plan was to reorganize the largest SOEs on the Korean model and to sell off or otherwise dispose of the smaller. Many tens of millions of workers have already lost their jobs, yet there are many more to follow and the government is already finding it all but impossible to cope with the scale of unemployment, although make-work schemes (such as jobs for people to help travellers onto buses, or overstaffing in hotels) and delayed automation are commonplace.

Chang (2001) is one of many commentators who fear that Chinese institutions are not capable of the changes being demanded of them. His overall argument is that politics interferes so much in Chinese economic life that no viable systems can be developed either to create trust or to facilitate proper market operations. The CCP will not relinquish its power exercised through state-controlled industries and forces the banks to act like grant-giving government bodies; the system is doomed. The discontent is such that the CCP has but a short time to live: this being China, and compromise or gradualism impossible, the end will be violent.

> In the past, China could muddle along. Now, however, its WTO agreements have put a specific timetable on structural reform. Unfortunately, the central government is not ready to fulfil the commitments Jiang has made so easily. The consequence of failure will be the end of Chinese institutions as they now exist.
>
> (Chang 2001: xix)

That the SOEs are uneconomic and take away scarce resources from the private sector is only part of the problem. Earlier in the 1990s the grants they were awarded from central government were replaced by bank loans. In April 1999 the government set up Asset Management Companies (AMC) to buy the debts with a view to conversion into equity. The shareholders would then be the mechanism by which changes would be forced on SOEs. However, political connections have been used to protect SOEs from the authority of AMCs such that no restructuring or reorienting has taken place. Since business accounts are commonly fabrications,[5] little trust can be placed in any information provided by SOEs. For political reasons any threat of bankruptcy can be nullified and state banks are obliged to roll-over loans to SOEs which are, in reality, non performing.[6]

Pessimists argue that too many interests stand to lose from reform of the remaining, massive, SOEs, and that there is no leader with the stature and power to effect such a massive reform as to break them down, given the risks to stability.

Yet the dangers for China of the SOEs continuing in their present form are acute because of the way the banking system has been tied in to their fate. When the government ended grants and had the SOEs raise bank loans it was in effect having the debt taken over by the populace at large, a very high proportion of which are savers, with one of the highest savings rate relative to income in the world (40 per cent). Chang makes the point that the huge savings of the Chinese are at risk because the main collection vehicles, the four Chinese state banks, have been obliged to lend the bulk of their deposits to SOEs which are in effect bankrupt. In theory, having private investors should force the banks into reform, but because of political interference this does not happen.

Should the SOEs default, or if confidence is lost in the banks such that depositors run for their money (there have been some localized bank runs in recent years), then the financial system will collapse. In any event, in five years from 2001, foreign banks will be able to take local deposits, after which it is a reasonable assumption that the Chinese banks, if a solution has not been found to their problems, will cease to do so and will therefore lack the funds to further bolster the SOEs.

Aside from the risks inherent in the banks being unprepared for the implications of WTO accession, there are doubts in the minds of many commentators as to whether Chinese companies really are prepared for foreign competition. If Chinese firms suddenly find that cheap imports (for example textiles) or better quality ones (cars) are destroying their safe markets then there will be fury. If Chinese companies prove inefficient they may be bought over in large numbers by foreigners. Disasters and unemployment will be blamed on foreign influences and their power be resented; xenophobia will increase.

Studwell (2001) makes the same arguments as Chang but places them within a context of other factors which militate against China successfully adapting to the challenges it has set itself. He notes that China has a record of hampering imports and that partner countries do not take account of the inability of the WTO to police the impediments which China will put in their way; the system of licensing ensures that no enterprise can be established without authority, i.e., kickbacks, and will further obstruct the opening of the markets; there are many forms of opaque subsidy; public procurement is a weapon of favouritism in the Chinese economy; bankruptcy laws do not operate; the judiciary is corrupt; banking is politically hamstrung, and so forth. He is pessimistic as to the ability of the Chinese system to change these conditions, and as to the dynamic of WTO accession to survive them.

He may be too pessimistic. There is growing awareness of these questions in the opinion-forming community.

The emergence of public opinion

Astrophysicist Fang Lizhi came to prominence in the late 1980s. He had irritated the authorities in the past, yet been protected both by his patrons and by his own allegiance to the system. This loyalty, as with so many of his contemporaries, was evaporating as he took stock of the Cultural Revolution. In 1986 *The People's Daily* carried a series of articles about Fang's reforms at the university of which he was deputy president, the University of Science and Technology (*Keda* for short), extolling the 'air of democracy' which Fang's commitment to academic freedom had brought. Late in the year the *World Economic Herald* quoted Fang as criticizing Chinese intellectuals for being supine, and exhorted them to stand up to power.

By coincidence or not, twenty of China's largest cities erupted with student demonstrations demanding reform. Faced with what it regarded as turmoil incited by academics, the authorities sacked Fang and his patron, the president of Keda, and reassigned them to research institutes in Peking. The media attacked Fang's views as reflecting 'bourgeois liberalization'; Deng Xiaoping even lambasted Fang by name.

However, as Schell has argued (Schell 1991), the Party did not want to be seen to be returning to the bad old days in which it polarized itself against the intellectuals, so that its punishment of Fang was mainly rhetorical. After all, it had declared that what, to Mao, had been 'the stinking ninth' category of citizen, the educated people, was necessary to modernization; it did not want to go back on that. It simply wanted to do a deal by which they forbore from challenging the supremacy of the Party, in return for relative freedom. Fang continued to be insulted in the media and was not allowed to meet foreign journalists, yet by February 1987 was back in public giving scientific papers and thereafter permitted to travel abroad.

In January 1989 Fang wrote a letter to Chairman Deng Xiaoping proposing the release of those held during the 1978 Democracy Wall protests. When the leadership showed its displeasure by having him excluded from the banquet in honour of US Vice-President George Bush he held an international press conference at which he condemned human rights abuses by his country's government in a manner that no one had dared do since 1949. Although he took no part in the demonstrations which began in Peking in April 1989, the moment the massacre took place Fang fled to the US embassy for protection, where he remained until a deal was done between the Chinese and US governments by which he be allowed to leave the country on health grounds. Abroad he continued to articulate what are probably now the views of many of his contemporaries, that Marxism 'no longer has any worth' and must be discarded 'like a worn-out dress'. In retrospect, the Fang case was the start of a new era in which intellectuals came to talk openly about policy and even debate policy in the media. By what stages did this come about?

Although phrases of Marxist, or at least CCP origin, are still sprinkled throughout the conversation of journalists, this may be more by habit than by conviction. When you speak to journalists about their work, the constant reiteration of the expression 'public scrutiny' (*yulun jiandu*) and the admiration evinced for investigative journalism appear to be the symptoms of an unspoken premise. The premise is that CCP orthodoxy is rejected and that the responsibilities of journalism derive from a new relationship between the people and authority. Fang's odyssey is therefore iconic and its message is reflected in the more humdrum phrases of unknown journalists:

> You become a reporter because you have a sense of justice. The tasks of a reporter are to 1. expose evil 2. give information.
>
> (Kang Wei)

> Impartiality is very necessary but the absolute is impossible, we do our best. If something is controversial, we get it said by others, we don't say it.
>
> (Tang Musan)

Here are two revelations. One is that Kang believes that the first responsibility of the reporter is to expose evil, a view rather more 'western' than that, for example, of the editor of England's *Daily Telegraph* (Page 1998: 46) and one which would not have been expressed, if thought, in China a few years ago. It is also at variance with the views expressed in Chen's 1998 survey. Second, her colleague not only champions impartiality – this could be explained by the fact that he is talking to a foreign journalist, after all – but shows that he will try to get controversial views on screen even if he has to be manipulative in the way he does it. Again, this is a very different approach to that of more conservative reporters.

These and the earlier quotation seem to suggest that journalists can now distinguish service to the country from service to the state. The traditional Chinese view is that individual interests are inseparable from those of society and society's from those of the state, ideas which both underpinned CCP ideology and were given enriched meaning by that ideology. This can account for the – to outsiders – astonishing loyalty to the state even when it persecuted your family and friends and destroyed your own career. Officials, as in Zhang Ailing's novel *Love in a Bare Land*, or Jung Chang's *Wild Swans*, did not rail against the Party but asked themselves why they themselves had done wrong. This did not work after the Tiananmen massacre. Since then, there has emerged a sense that it is possible to be a proper Chinese without identifying with the state, an idea inconceivable before 1911.

Goldman points out that in 1989 there appeared for the first time a slogan which reflected this new idea, 'We love our country but we hate our government' (Goldman 1994). Goldman argues that the Cultural Revolution was influential in undermining the relationship, but what finally destroyed the bonds which Deng had attempted to retie in 1978 were his own anti-democracy and anti-spiritual pollution movements of the early 1980s: 'by 1989 the intelligentsia saw itself less part of the state and more as outsiders fighting it' (Goldman 1994: 153). The eminent journalist and novelist Bai Hua asked the question in his novel *Bitter Love* 'you love this nation, but does it love you?' (Bai 1986).

In such a climate it is perhaps not surprising that journalists now distinguish between the Party and the people. When we remind ourselves as to how Chinese journalists have taken on board the concept of 'audience' to complement and perhaps replace that of the 'the people' and 'the masses' we see not only that it 'extends the basis of legitimacy for journalistic work' (Zhang 2000: 2) but also that it reflects a new view of society and the polity.

Political ideas since 1989

Since 1989 there has gradually developed a new consensus on China's identity and it has emerged through public argument in which both political leaders and intellectuals have been making their cases, seemingly vying for public opinion.

Before Tiananmen it would appear that the intelligentsia, responding to the horrors of the CR, were utterly alienated from the CCP; one of the results was that fiasco in which they made demands of the Party which it was impossible for it to satisfy, at very least with the peremptoriness which was demanded. Perhaps because of the shock of the massacre and its aftermath, perhaps because the leaders of the demonstrations were in prison, in exile or in hiding, few continued for long to uphold the causes espoused in spring 1989. In fact, a revulsion against them took over.

> Whereas Western commentators continued to view the image of the lone person standing in front of a column of tanks as emblematic of the aspirations of the Chinese people, more and more Chinese saw that person as symbolizing the excessive romanticism of the 1980s reform movement.
>
> (Fewsmith 2001: 160)

More now believed in gradualism; more were willing to understand the difficulties of the government and to participate in helping work them out; more rejected the ideal of western democracy which had been espoused in Tiananmen Square. Some even went so far as to blame all China's troubles on radicals whose genealogy was taken as far back as Kang Youwei in 1898 and who included the protagonists of the May 4 movement.[7]

When marketization once again was given full reign after the Southern Progress such new ideas entered the public domain and became factors in the political processes heretofore restricted to the narrow CCP elite. That they did so can be ascribed to several catalysts: the vast increase in media channels and the relative lack of control on content; the return from abroad of ever greater numbers of western-educated graduates, lending their experience; the government's establishment of think tanks and patronage of bright intellectuals and the lack of traditional, revolutionary, authority of the new leaders, particularly Jiang Zemin, who therefore had to appeal in different ways and to different supporters than their predecessors.

The rejection of radical solutions, meaning the introduction of western political and economic institutions wholesale, was accompanied by increased nationalism. This nationalism entailed both a disposition to try to find specifically Chinese approaches to the problems of failed socialism and a scepticism about the West, and the USA in particular.

In 1989 the influential *Japan can say no*, by Ishihara Shintaro, had been published and immediately translated into Chinese. It argued, in effect, that Japan would not always play a supporting role to the USA but could and should assert itself. This came about at a time when there was increasing interest in the West, picked up on elsewhere, in the seeming appearance of new expressions of capitalism which owed their achievements more to Confucian virtues than western business schools.[8] At the time Asian societies seemed successful in achieving both economic growth and social harmony, while the USA shocked Asians by its social violence, family breakdown and racial conflict. Asian success was attributed to 'Confucian values' or 'Asian values'.

Simultaneously Francis Fukuyama's writings on *The End of History* riled nationalists by suggesting that there was no viable model for modernity but the anglophone, stimulating a conscious effort to prove him wrong. Ishihara and the Malaysian Premier Mohamed Mahathir published *The Voice of Asia*, again asserting a kind of moral superiority for their values. Those enthused by such ideas welcomed Samuel Huntingdon's 1993 *Clash of Civilizations*. His idea that the future holds a division of the world according to ancient cultural tenets was taken up with greater enthusiasm in Asia than in the West, perhaps because it expressed feelings of difference repressed for long in the face of anglophone triumphalism. Such ideas fuelled the growing belief that China was right to reject the call to adopt western notions of democracy.

In 1994 Wang Shan's *Looking at China Through a Third Eye* vilified the Tiananmen protestors as having been manipulated by the USA, echoing the line of the government but doing so with an intellectual credibility and verve lacked by CCP functionaries. Two years later came *China Can Say No*, a populist tract full of vituperation against the USA and declaring that all US claims to better human rights or to stand up for the oppressed were mere hypocrisy, masks for asserting US interests and a blind for undermining China. Journalists and intellectuals who wrote *Behind the Demonization of China* claimed that the US media calumnied and disparaged their country. It is hardly surprising that in 1995 a *China Youth*

Daily opinion poll found hostility to the USA and cynicism as to US motives in the Gulf War (Fewsmith 2001: 155).

Intellectual currents in the West fed these Chinese polemics, which were influenced by the concepts of cultural imperialism and post-colonialism as well as by fears of globalization, interpreted in China as a cultural threat rather than as a danger to ecology or to the poor. Leading postmodern writers were enthusiastically quoted and books such as John Tomlinson's *Cultural Imperialism* reached the bestseller lists.[9] However, the leftists did not have it all their own way. He Qinglian's *China's Pitfall* (He: 1998), widely available on the mainland, argues that the period of CCP rule has been, in many very important ways, a 'great leap backwards' and that the problems which beset China in 1898 are still as great today as they were then.

External events have contributed too to the intensity of debate. In 1999, the year after he took over from Li Peng, Prime Minister Zhu Rongji went to Washington to discuss future trade relations, notwithstanding the unease felt by many Chinese at what they saw as the illegal NATO bombing campaign in Serbia. Membership of the WTO was seen by the leadership as necessary to ensure China's commercial future and took precedence over other considerations. The failure of Zhu's mission provoked hostility and cynicism towards the West's declarations on human rights and the rule of law, both now seen as camouflage for American imperialism. The bombing error by which US bombers destroyed the Chinese embassy in Belgrade on 8 May 1999 would compound this.

In May and June of 1998 *The People's Daily* published angry articles against US imperialism and compared the USA to Nazi Germany; on the Internet, and in demonstrations, Premier Zhu was vilified as a traitor. Even those who did not go that far accused him of being too 'pro-US pro-West' (Fewsmith 2001: 211–212). Visitors on Chinese streets were conscious of anti foreign feeling and frequent references to China's repeated sufferings under imperialism, with the implication that today's events were a continuation of western hostility to China. Even some people in leading public positions in the West find it difficult to grasp the sensitivities of Chinese in their relations with former colonial powers. In 2002 a senior British politician addressed a large group of Chinese, mainly small business people, in London. Attempting to ingratiate himself he referred to his family's longstanding connections with China, which included several relatives in the Imperial Chinese Customs. Next to me, one Chinese member of the audience remarked to another 'his grandfather forced us to import opium and burned the Summer Palace'. The facts were confused but the feelings fierce and very typical of the kind of aggrieved nationalism typical in all classes of Chinese today.[10] Given that citizens of the PRC are exposed, from primary school books to television programmes, to a view of their country as having been uniquely exploited by the savage West, it is hardly surprising that xenophobia is easily worked up.

The 1994 publication of *Looking at China Through a Third Eye* was remarkable because it went further than any in questioning international, as opposed to merely domestic, policy in public. This now became commonplace, with such works as *China's Road under Globalization* and *China's Pitfall* making sharp criticisms of policies.[11] These have been interpreted as demonstrating the public emergence of a left-wing opposition, previously confined to the hidden places of the Central Committee, an opposition proclaiming the view that the government was conspiring with foreigners and capitalists to do down the people (Fewsmith 2001: 161). That these are not merely the views of a few disaffected scribblers, but may represent powerful interests which are being impinged upon by modernization, was evident from the more judicious debates in the media. In 1996 *Economics Daily*, an organ of the State Council headed by Li Peng, published a critique of the impact of foreign investment, expressing concern at the need to protect national industries. Soon after, *Economics Daily* started its series *The People's Daily* published its refutation of the arguments, putting the case of the progressives (Fewsmith 2001: 173). The fact that the CCP leaders felt they had to respond, to take part in the debates, suggests that the media had, more than ever before, become the forum for debating public affairs or at least winning public opinion.

Skills for democrats

In discussing the development of British identity, Linda Colley draws our attention to the fact that in the Britain of the early nineteenth century, as in revolutionary France, more and more people were being drawn into politics. She quotes Lynn Hunt as writing that in France more and more people learned the micro techniques of politics from attending meetings to joining parades to wearing a badge, taking minutes or electing an official. Colley argues that such acts of 'individual initiative, commitment and participation' were equally learned in Britain. These activities had the potential to challenge the existing order even as they upheld it (Colley 1996: 242). The point stimulates some reflections on the social roles of Chinese journalists today.

Although we habitually slip into expressions which reveal our assumption that Communist China has been a totalitarian society, with all that that implies for the subjection of popular participation, in one respect at least this is unhelpful. For although most people have been denied the opportunity to find and voice views differing from those of the power-holders, the obsession of the CCP with having the appearance of participation and with forcing people to bear witness to their support may have had the effect of raising expectations. Surely you cannot talk for fifty years about the people's rights and about it being 'right to rebel' without those receiving this advice eventually applying it to their own situation? Lessons learned about revolution and protest seem now to be being applied by consumer groups and environmental organizations, pensioners and peasants. So are the practical skills required for the organization of meetings, the running of elections, lobbying and drumming up support, campaigning, public relations and media relations.[12] For example, in April 2002 it was reported that 'angry ex-workers' were marching through Liaoyang holding a banner carrying the slogan 'The army of unemployed want food and jobs' in response to redundancies, an event unlikely to be reported in the media (Gittings 2002).

Are we seeing the emergence of a less authoritarian, perhaps more democratic, society? Authority now accepts the expression of discontent, certainly in private and often in public; there is space for it, within limits (Keane 2002: 787). At the lowest level people run for elections and elsewhere they lobby and link. People are far more adept at expressing their rights and subjecting the state to criticism.[13]

The state has responded to change and to discontent: there have been major legal reforms and codes have been introduced in many areas 'from labour relations to intellectual property rights to environment and commerce' (Perry 2000: 5). People are taking advantage of their new rights, as is evidenced by the ever increasing number of disputes and burgeoning business for lawyers. There are many reasons for unrest in Chinese society and discontent is no longer muzzled by a system of comprehensive repression. One writer on 'rights and resistance' in China today quotes de Tocqueville's dictum that as repression relaxes, so demands grow (Pei 2000). In China they have and, although persecution of dissidents takes place, it is as admissible now to protest about local issues of corruption, maladministration, poverty or environmental blight (Lee Ching Kwan 2000) as it is for journalists to make programmes about them. From the president downwards, officials have wished to be seen as sincere in their condemnation of abuses and their example is taken by lower officials who tolerate complaints which only a few years ago would have been suppressed. Institutional changes from village elections to the Administrative Litigation Law have provided a climate in which people can be more courageous in commenting upon local affairs and in identifying perceived injustices or maladministration. And people are learning to use the media, tipping off reporters on everything from plans to cheat at examinations to police brutality. This can be dangerous, as reports of the arrest of whistle-blowers tell us (*New York Times* 2002).

It might be argued, notwithstanding these innovations, that the Chinese rethinking of their relationship with the state will fall short of the demands made in anglophone countries because of the absence of a similarly developed sense of rights. Wang Gongwu has argued (1991: 172) that the Confucian catalogue of duties also implies rights which flow therefrom and Pei (2000) asks why the pervasive Chinese sense of reciprocity should not be understood as one of mutual rights. Friedman (1995: 311), following des Forges and du Bary, argues that 'premodern China in fact had as wide an array of factors favourable to democracy as any society'. Whether the traditional Chinese conception of rights is attenuated and whether this has prevented the development of democratic institutions is a discussion which needs to take into account not only philosophy but also the philosophy of history since it draws upon ideas of how polities develop, which originated in the West, and upon the enlightenment discourse of rationality. These may or may not be helpful; nor urgent, since, philosophically indigenous or not, the concept of rights appears to have been caught onto anyway. It would be useful to have attitude research in this area, at the moment supported only anecdotally (e.g., Friedman 1995: 326). One simple explanation for this may be that, thanks to television and film and generally many more contacts with the world outside, Chinese are learning from other societies, even in circumstances where culture and social psychology (or fear of chaos) impede or circumscribe the conception of, or expression of, what anglophones might consider full rights.

Civil society

Some scholars have sought to demonstrate that a civil society is developing in China and that this, to a greater or lesser extent (and they disagree here) will condition the power of the state and enable the growth of democratic institutions (Gold 1990; Nathan 1985). What they appear to mean is the kind of civil society with which anglophones are familiar, characterized by large numbers of organizations, whether commercial or existing for completely uneconomic purposes, mainly independent of the state and only lightly regulated by organizations themselves often independent of the state. In China, however, the impetus of the state and party to control is the major hindrance. As Studwell points out (2001: 248–249) in another context, 'Chinese citizens cannot start a fishing club' without a whole raft of permissions. He describes the extraordinary way in which the *Falungong* came to be constructed as a threat, simply because it struggled to be recognized as a legal association for exercises spiritual and physical and, in the process, fell foul of a thuggish and corrupt Ministry of Justice. The system by which permissions are needed for everything came about in years gone by, but it is maintained now by people who live off the graft which lubricates it. In such conditions, it is not surprising that there is really no appropriate culture. In the words of He Baogang:

> The emergence of democratic politics is hindered less by a presence in the peasant population than by an absence: the absence of something compatible to the ecological concept of bio-diversity, a kind of social trellis of autonomous, self organizing associations and networks willing and able to dissociate from the policies and values of the state. This social diversity is one of the important connotations of civil society. Without this political diversity, all opposing forces tend to be penetrated or reproduced by the state.
>
> (He 1997: 1)

As far as this touches upon journalists, He Baogang has shown that by 1989 there were many study groups and periodicals which contributed to the debate about civil society. Of practical value to those looking for ways of enlarging free speech in China, there were enough non-state employers in existence to absorb those intellectuals – including journalists – involved in the democracy movement who would have been denied state employment after the Tiananmen massacre had they had the temerity to hope for it. However their dreams seem to have given way to more realistic appreciation of the limits of development in a society with imperial/Leninist state traditions and traditions of clientilism.

Journalism after Jiang

The political context in which journalists now operate is thus full of contradictions. At the 15th Party Congress in 1997 the leading role of the state sector in the economy was effectively abandoned and the risks inherent in this, of mass unemployment and destabilization, were accepted as necessary. While palliative measures are being introduced and the country is still swept by enthusiasm for entrepreneurship, institutions which can check the powerful and the rapacious and assuage the fears of the exploited do not appear to be being built. Discontent is everywhere, as is fear of the future evidenced in the desperation with which all who can appear to be trying to leave China, with the sons and daughters of the hierarchs in the van.

To foreign observers what needs to be done is clear: depoliticization of the economy; a more representative political system; accountability of executives; a legal system more independent of politics. Chinese progressives think the same way. Distilling their expectations, Lam (2002) suggests that the new leadership will begin to permit the open competition of factions within the CCP, on the Japanese Liberal Democratic Party model, and might empower the 1930s parliamentary parties, which still exist.[14] Another possibility is that the CCP forswear class struggle and turn itself into a Socialist Party; it may also renounce its army so that the PLA become the state's forces, an essential precondition for division of powers.[15]

There are some developments that suggest that such momentous changes are in the air. Li (2001: 218) has pointed out that the leadership cohort of autumn 2002, known as the '4th generation' has much less solidarity than its predecessors, made cohesive by struggle in the civil war, or training in the USSR. What its members do have in common are diversity of life experience, the memory of persecution during the Cultural Revolution, high educational levels and (often) periods of study abroad. Some were not even members of the CCP fifteen years ago and thus are far less indoctrinated in its curious theology and Leninist practices. Unlike their predecessors, who were often arrogant and remarkably narrow, these new leaders may be more aware of their own limitations. Though nationalist, they may be more aware of the global nature of many problems.

For these reasons, and given the importance traditionally placed upon the media by the CCP, together with the position of journalists as almost the only people who have the ability and the right to explore society, it can be envisaged that the problems so evident to outsiders and the proposed solutions, which fail to emerge from within the Party and yet are evident to those with different perspectives, may be drawn to the attention of more permeable rulers. Even if this does not happen openly, in the media, then at least through the RCP system and via the new channels that have opened up between CCP decision-makers and the policy world of think tanks, journalists and academics.

Journalists can be as self-interested and short term as any. They have every reason to be as cynical as anybody, since they know most clearly how information is controlled by individuals and factions in their own interests. Yet they have practices and channels that others do not have, and they are very aware of them since, particularly in China, it is from these that their status derives. More than perhaps any of their fellow-citizens they see how society works or doesn't work, mixing with the top leaders one day and those whose lives are affected by their decisions the next. As we will discuss in Chapter 9, they are biased in favour of novelty and change and have an urge to feel themselves in the thick of affairs. They also believe that they perform functions vital to society. How they know that, and what they do about it, is the subject of the next chapter.

7 The patriot journalists

Since the mid-1990s, Chinese journalism has not only been able to represent competing opinions on some political questions, but also to investigate abuses and discuss social issues previously kept under wraps. Maoist orthodoxy – that the media are tools of class power – has been abandoned and the search is on for a more nuanced understanding of the parts played by the media in society and polity.

In the course of this search, Chinese journalists today are beginning to rediscover an indigenous tradition of critical journalism, and to describe its role as 'public scrutiny'. This chapter compares the genesis of early modern English – 1850s – and Chinese – 1920s – journalism in order to see what is different about the origins of Chinese journalism.

The early history of Chinese journalism, rather than the experience of Maoism, helps to explain the gestation of the idea of the journalist as activist, partisan and patriot rather than free commentator.

Looking back to understand the future

So different does today's China appear when compared with the China of before 1992 that the foreign observer might be forgiven for imagining that the experiences of those times are as remote from the world of today's young journalists as times medieval. Yet most[1] of the journalists with whom I have talked, regardless of generation or gender, were interested in any available local models. Knowledge of pre-Communist Chinese journalism was skimpy, but as engaged journalists are becoming more aware of the limitations of the CCP's discourse of journalism so they are taking an interest in an 'alternative history':

It is good for journalists to know about great journalists before Liberation. The models we have are all communists, or they are foreigners.

(Kang Ming)

When I was studying journalism and had a chance to look through all the pre 1949 newspapers from the areas under KMT [Nationalist Party] control, I found that China had experienced every kind of journalism: plenty of 'tabloid', doorstepping journalism as in England; crimes, celebrities and social problems on the front page . . . (when I went to work) in Shanghai at the *World Economic Herald* we were very conscious that we were reviving pre 1949 practises . . . very few had direct contact with the western media so we looked to our own past.

(Li Zhengmao)

In other words knowledge of pre-1949 journalism may offer a different per-spective on the Maoist period, even role models more appropriate to the Chinese situation than the anglophone ones. This matters because, in every area of life in China, history is important: as justification, source of pride or cautionary tale. The construction of history has for well over 2,000 years been regarded as an important function of the state. History possibly matters for another reason, too. In the words of a sinologist:

[In China] history plays a role comparable to that of religious texts in other cultures . . . the religion of the Chinese ruling classes is the Chinese state, and it is through history that the object of devotion is to be understood.

(Jenner 1994: 11)

What may be happening in China is that history is gradually being rewritten as scholars come into contact with interpretations other than those of the CCP. The *grand narratives*[2] may take a long time to change, but the history of journalism does not fall into this category and so may change more rapidly. Until recently, pre-1949 journalism has tended to be written off as a period in which, after the chaos of the early years of the century in which it was possible for some left journalists to emerge, the press were tools of the capitalist class, represented by the Nationalist Party. The truth is different and journalists are beginning to look back at it. As the patina of Maoism wears off, the Chinese journalists of today are revealed to have similarities with their pre-Communist forbears.

Early modern journalism

During the latter part of the Qing Dynasty (1644–1911) five developments affected the literati[3] and began to condition the environment in which modern communications would develop. An intellectual movement aimed at subjecting Confucian orthodoxy to rational scrutiny began to undermine complacency about the Chinese world as the epitome of civilization; large numbers of Chinese went abroad to live in countries outside that world and a trickle returned wealthy and knowledgeable about lands which it was increasingly difficult to accept were barbarian, as tradition would have it; European military strength shook Chinese confidence; the need to counter the overwhelming power of the Europeans gave rise to a reform movement of intellectuals who rapidly moved from criticizing military shortcomings to identifying political and social weaknesses; European missionaries, forcing their way into China behind the traders and soldiers, learned Chinese and began to publish.

Many missionaries were committed to helping Chinese reformers and there were close and productive relationships between them and the Chinese publishing community for nearly 100 years. The first daily, *Chong Ngoi Sam Bo*,[4] came out in 1854 and the first mass circulation daily *Wahji Yatbo*, in 1864. Many early papers, much like their equivalents in eighteenth-century Europe, were directed at merchants in the treaty ports. According to the founding issue of the *Hsin Pao* in 1861:

> In general what is valuable for the conduct of commerce and trade is the circulation of reliable information. In printing this new paper we will not fail to carry all national government or military intelligence, (news of) market place advantage or disadvantage, business prices, and the coming and going of ships and cargo . . . By glancing at this new paper, you can learn that a certain cargo is to be sold on a certain day, and on the day you can personally inspect the cargo and negotiate the price. Thus you can avoid endless delay and procrastination by agents or making a bad purchase on speculation.
>
> (Lee 1985: 362)

During the 1860s to 1880s many scholarly study and discussion ('self-strengthening') groups sprang up, often publishing collections of essays or reviews. There had always been study associations, but whereas in the past they talked of poetry, calligraphy, painting and philosophy, increasingly they addressed themselves to the fact of western encroachment and the weakness of the Qing government in the face of it. It was in this period too that scholars started to learn western languages – previously only uneducated (in a Chinese sense) servants of foreigners had done so – and to translate western books into Chinese. Such changes broadened the traditional public sphere in China into something more akin to what Habermas identified in Europe, according to Rowe (1990: 310).

As the scholar-gentry and the merchants became more politicized many felt an urgent need to save China lest it be dismembered by the imperialist powers. Most young men might continue to enter for the traditional examinations, but a growing minority took part in enterprises of one kind or another which sought to come to terms with the Europeans, whether studying engineering, medicine or military skills or working among missionaries and traders. In so doing they were learning to cope with the idea that China was not the centre of the world, the cynosure and the source of all culture. It was to be from among these that the first journalists would come.

In 1895 China was defeated in war by Japan. This was a shock as few Chinese had yet appreciated the degree to which the Meiji Restoration had modernized and strengthened their neighbours. It galvanized ever-larger numbers into getting involved in public affairs, at least by reading the newspapers and discussing issues. When the young emperor's attempts to emulate his Japanese counter-part's radical overhauling of the state was thwarted by the Empress's *coup d'état* of 1898, his advisers and supporters fled abroad. Although it did not appear so at the time, this was a further impetus to the emergence of Chinese journalism.

Before they became associated with the patriotic struggle, journalists were despised. Reporters who retailed the gossip of the capital to the treaty ports and dealt as much in salacious sensation as in business information were referred to as 'scum' (Cheng 1998: 180). When the reformer Kang Youwei (1858–1927), who could not be denied to be a traditional scholar, began to use the press as a vehicle for his ideas, the image of the journalist began to change. As the image changed, so did the reality: more and more did newspaper writers come from families which had supplied officials to the imperial service for generations. While the imperial examination system continued to exist they typically passed the early stages yet chose to deploy their literary skills in the new profession. They referred to themselves as the *middle layer in society*, i.e., between ignorant masses and conservative elites, and were both more traditionally educated than the treaty-port journalists and more exposed to western ideas than the ruling classes in general. Many had studied in Japan where they learned how newspapers could be designed to be attractive to a more diverse and less erudite readership, in layout as in content (Judge 1996: 39).

Journalism became the ideal career for the patriot (perhaps the only one available for the full-time activist) and the only political journalism was patriotic, change-orientated journalism (Britton 1933 Chapter VIII). It is instructive to compare such a development with the standard accounts of the origins of English bourgeois journalism where codes of objectivity and a professional ethic grew up as functions both of the need of the business classes for factual information and of the requirement not to antagonize sections of a diverse, numerous and politically argumentative public. In this account, the 'Fourth Estate function' developed as a means of reconciling different interests to the electoral system, being only possible thanks to a wide enough consensus on general principles which the press itself had an important hand in creating (Altschull 1998: 1).

By contrast, most Chinese journalists and publishers' products were, from the start, committed; a paradigm was the *Pure Criticism Newspaper*, named after a Han Dynasty (206 BC–AD 220) student movement and founded by exiles in Japan in 1898. This was an important moment, for the new paper and Liang Qichao's equally famous *Current Affairs* became models, in terms of content and intellectual approach, to which others would aspire. Liang was disparaging of existing ones and stated his view of the purpose of the press:

> To report in detail the new government measures in the several provinces, so that readers may know that modern innovations actually do yield bene-fits; and also to realise the difficulties of those in authority, and their aims . . . To delve into and fully expose details of important Sino-foreign problems, so that readers may understand that China is not established

internationally, that because of internal disorganization China is humiliated by other nations, and that because of our ignorance of international law we are duped by other nations; and thus to stimulate the new learning, and cause readers to give thought to purging the nation of its humiliations.

(Britton 1933: 89)

Something of the effect of the changing newspapers can be gathered from the memoir of a certain Pao, a youth at the time of the Sino-Japanese War:

> Our country and Japan were warring over Korea, and the Shanghai newspapers carried news about it every day. Previously young Chinese readers paid no attention to current events, but now we were shaken. I often went out and got Shanghai newspapers to read, and I began to understand bits and pieces about current events. I began to discuss them, and I accounted myself pro-reform . . . (after the loss of the war and the establishment of a Japanese concession in Soochow) most educated people, who had never before discussed national affairs, wanted to discuss them: why are others stronger than we are, and why are we weaker?
>
> (Pao T'ien-hsiao, in Lee 1985: 364)

The discourse of Chinese journalism already had a marked 'social responsibility' bias. *The Times*, started by Liang Qichao in 1904, declared in its prospectus that it would be impartial, would eschew trivia, be impersonal, have its own foreign correspondents and contain synopses of the views of other papers, including foreign ones (Lin 1936: 136).

By the 1911 Revolution there were over 500 newspapers and probably many thousands of magazines of various kinds, and in the chaos of the period it was sometimes possible to produce some very iconoclastic and revelatory journalism:

> The [Peking] Gazette quickly made a name for itself and was itself constantly in the news. It specialized in exposes of Peking's backstage politics. It always seemed to be on the inside track of the various deals being negotiated by corrupt officials and warlords contending for power and money, and the intrigues being plotted in the Legation Quarter. (The editor) was getting information from his friends in high places. He was a sort of Jack Anderson or I. F. Stone of his day. But Peking 1913 was not Washington 1975. To play such a role in the Chinese press in those days needed foolhardy courage.
>
> (Chen 1975: 19)

Liang Qichao

Liang Qichao (1873–1929), mentioned above as a newspaper publisher, was himself the foremost of the early journalists and because of his journalism 'regarded as one of the intellectual leaders of modern China' (Boorman 1970: 349). He made himself a disciple of Kang Youwei in the 1890s and was active in the early reform movement and as a writer on international history and politics (see Liu 1983). Between 1902 and 1904 he visited Europe where he was particularly influenced by the example of Italy's Risorgimento, to the effect that he soon after published two books, one a study of Mazzini, Cavour and Garibaldi and the other a play, *The New Rome*. From these works we can see that he was inspired by the example of an ancient civilization renewing itself and he identified with the romantics and scribbler-activists of the Risorgimento (Bertuccioli 1981). By 1904 he was publishing newspapers and had a very clear idea of what journalism was for. Newspapers were to perform nine duties: 'remonstrance, guidance, encouragement, repetition, taking the large view, concentrating on main themes, propagating knowledge and penetrating society' (Nathan 1985: 133). He was the first Chinese to express views on what roles journalism might play in society. He believed that one of China's great weaknesses was that it did not have channels for communication and for the dissemination of new ideas. Further, he saw the press as performing a supervisory or scrutinizing function in society and as mobilizing public opinion to try to influence government, an idea which has regained currency today.

The influence of Liang's *Times* was diffused in ways more active than those associated with newspapers today. As in Cobbett's England, Chinese periodicals were shipped off down the canals and read aloud in the teahouses of small towns to enthralled audiences. Some were posted on walls so that all might have the chance to see. They were used as materials by schoolteachers and as foci for discussion in the debating societies that had grown up, similar to those in eighteenth-century Europe, such as the Speculative Society of Edinburgh or the History Club of Dublin. Liang's *Times* had provincial correspondents and they, as with their colleagues at head office, usually doubled as teachers in every rank and category of institution, so that dissemination was assured as they and many other teachers used the very articles as study material. Many were novelists. Early on Liang Qichao had identified fiction as a medium of enlightenment with great potential for the vast readership of traditional Chinese novels. Many young intellectuals, of whom the nonpareil has become Lu Xun, became writers of fiction out of patriotism – and a didactic inclination – rather than artistic inspiration.[5] Here again there is a European parallel, although it is with the later nineteenth century rather than with the world of Cobbett: Dickens, Zola and Dostoevsky are only the best known of Europe's journalists who became novelists with missions to change society. And, as with Zola fifty years earlier, Liang fought newspaper campaigns. *The Times* mobilized people against the government's railways policy and published articles defending the revolutionary Qiu Jin and condemning her execution by the government (Judge 1996: 53).

Liang's passionate concern suffused all he wrote; this inspired his readers. He employed a writing style that was lucid and direct; he sought to clarify complex events and issues beyond the ken of his fellow-countrymen; he explained those western concepts, inventions and habits that were a cause of wonder and the source of power. For these reasons, his influence was great.

The press and society

The critical press, of which Liang was the principal begetter, brought about changes in attitude. According to Judge (1996: 7) it weakened the political belief that *above and below are of necessity in harmony (tienxia yiti)* and made reform conceivable. Those in power were argued to be accountable to the ideal they served, if not actually to the citizenry, and implicitly to those who interpreted that ideal. It also confirmed the position of journalists, who began to see the modern media as replacing traditional scholars and teachers in the reproduction of cultural values. Journalists saw their writings not merely as passing on information but as forming and transforming ideas and opinions. Moreover it was in this period that they recast the notion of 'the people' as something which they were in the business of mobilizing and educating. 'The people' needed to know about the need for reform if China were to survive.

Even the most casual perusal of their work shows that these journalists were gripped by a vision of a global struggle for survival informed by Darwinism. In the last years of the nineteenth century, Yen Fu (1854–1921), with his limpid classical cadence, had translated the language of scholars into the dragon's teeth of revolution.[6] Darwin, Huxley and Ellis convinced Yen's readers, none more susceptible than Liang Qichao, that they were engaged in a frantic battle, with race pitted against race and nation against nation. What China needed was a shared sense of the common danger, a sublimation of personal interests in the cause, a great unity of purpose. The objective was 'wealth and power' for China.[7] Every western idea was accepted or rejected according to whether it might serve this objective, democracy included. Thus when Liang considered the use of journalism to society it was as an instrument in the cause of creating the required unity of purpose; so was it with democracy. This system of government was not to be an end in itself but an institution for political participation which would be more conducive to consensus and more competent at controlling that corruption of individual officials which ruptures unity. Characterized in terms which are, with hindsight, redolent of the rhetoric of the 1960s, there was an intermediate class of crooks which spoilt the natural solidarity of rulers and ruled. The task of the journalists was to bring rulers and ruled back together again and squeeze out the crooks!

As Nathan has pointed out (1985: 57) Liang did not deal with the problem which has exercised anglophone political philosophers, that of conflicts of interest and how they may be reconciled, and in this he is no different from either Mao Zedong or Wei Jingshen. They followed a traditional Chinese train of thought:

> When western thinkers were trying to design political systems as vessels to contain irrepressible conflict, Chinese philosophers aimed to design systems where no such conflict would be engendered.
>
> (Nathan 1985: 58)

Anglophone journalism came about in a very different set of circumstances although the relationship newspapers had to the English state at the start of the nineteenth century would have been familiar to Chinese journalists at the start of the twentieth.

England contrasted

In the first years of the nineteenth century, newspapers in England could still be bullied by the authorities through taxation, threats of prosecution, offers of help and exclusive information and the subsidy of government advertising. But by 1860 this had changed. Newspapers became relatively independent of politicians. The radical press survived attempts to stifle it, at least for a time. It has often been remarked that *The Times* and a few other papers became the modern equivalents of the ancient Greek agora or places where opinion-formers and decision-makers met to make public opinion. How had this come about?

Different historians give differing weight to the various factors at play. Traditional English histories saw the easing of government restrictions on the press as the result of the struggles of progressives (Williams 1957); others have preferred to emphasize the burgeoning power of the new business classes who resisted attempts by the political elite to dominate information (Harris 1996: 106). To Franklin 'undoubtedly the most necessary change was the removal of what opponents dubbed "the taxes on knowledge"', by which he means advertising, newspaper stamp duty and duties on paper all repealed between 1853 and 1861 (Franklin 1997: 78). Technological change made it possible to print and distribute more and larger newspapers, and thus to satisfy the growing demand. In today's parlance, moreover, the stakeholders in newspapers were many: first, the capital required was large and distributed, such that there were many ready to defend their interest; the revenue from advertisements rendered other sources of funds such as political subvention unnecessary; the readers were influential in guiding the policy of the paper; the inland transport revolution provided a much more extensive market and wide distribution gave to the opinions of the writers an influence which politicians began to fear to contravene.

The pre-eminence of *The Times* was clear. Between 1800 and 1860, Britain's position in the world consolidated and a large class of internationally aware, information-hungry and influential bourgeois emerged. *The Times* became their debating chamber. Thomas Barnes (editor of *The Times* 1817–41) was their spokesman and informant and he earned new readers by championing causes such as parliamentary reform and the victims of the Peterloo Massacre. Rising revenue meant he could spend more on finding things out and he and his successors prided themselves on their access to information and their independence from pressure.

Whereas in the eighteenth century much of the political conflict had been about personalities, cliques and corruption, now with economic development at home and an empire to exploit abroad, and new classes depending upon both, government policies were of intense interest, both those which touched upon business affairs (foreign treaties, trade policy) or which had a wider constituency (social conditions and taxation). One 1832 paper gave as its aims:

> The abolition of tithes, the repeal of the Corn Laws; a more equitable system of taxation; the abolition of the hereditary peerage; an equitable reduction of the national debt . . . a reform in the expenditure of the crown; and the abolition of all unmerited pensions and sinecures; the doing away with an expensive state of religion, and causing society to maintain its own ministers; remodelling the laws, and making the same law for rich and poor; a still more extensive franchise, Etc.
>
> (Cranfield 1978: 134)

Editors welcomed journalists who could identify the issues of the day, analyse them and communicate their relevance to a critical public. These abilities and the new power of the media are illustrated well in the career of several war correspondents, of whom William Howard Russell is the best known. He is generally celebrated for his influence over the agenda of politics; his impartial reporting; his demotic point of view and his fearless criticism of those in authority (Knightley 1975, Wilkinson-Latham 1979).

By contrast with journalists contemporary to Barnes their Chinese equivalents had to struggle against political power which was not only hostile (so were British governments) but whose power was not tempered by any institutional controls, only by either the countervailing power of the foreigners whose extraterritorial enclaves gave sanctuary to journalists, or by the limited protection afforded by faction. According to Lau (1949: Chapter V),[8] the first Chinese graduate of journalism was Hin Wong, who graduated from Missouri[9] in 1912. He was sentenced to death in 1913 but this was commuted. He was to become a leading editor and narrowly survive before becoming a teacher of journalism at Yenching University in 1928. Of this period, James D. White, a distinguished American journalist and teacher of journalism in China wrote:

> The unsung martyrs of Chinese journalistic history are so numerous that the history of western journalism does not bear comparison, for in China the political barometer was subject to sudden and catastrophic changes.
>
> (Lau 1949: 102)

Nevertheless they did begin to create and to respond to a public sphere recognizable in the terms that Habermas uses to describe the English public sphere of the nineteenth century. The fall of the Qing in 1911 lubricated this process.

The May 4 movement

On 4 May 1919 student demonstrations forced the government not to sign the Versailles Peace Treaty. This was a manifestation of public opinion in itself quite remarkable. But the event had cultural as well as political significance, indeed the expression May 4 movement has connotations of radical reformism in every aspect of society and of neophilia and disdain for the past which is only now being interrogated as the conventional wisdom of modern China.

One particular aspect of it mattered a great deal to journalists. Whereas before people had taken to the streets to demand that their country stand up to the foreigners but only a few intellectuals had wanted language reform, afterwards using the vernacular became the touchstone of your patriotism and desire for change. Until then, the vernacular (*baihua*) was used in popular tracts, novels and anything which ill educated people deployed; people with pretensions to culture used the literary language ('classical Chinese', *wenyen*) in everything from letters to documents to poetry; yet most people could not make much of *wenyen*, let alone compose it; *wenyen* was to them as Latin to a fourteenth-century European peasant. Together with the widespread rejection of Confucianism as a failed ideology, language reform reorientated the Chinese towards a common future, an increasingly similar outlook, the May Fourth outlook.

The student demonstrations of 4 May 1919 which forced the government not to sign the Versailles Peace Treaty were the catalyst for a further radicalization of the Chinese media. At the same time very many more joined the Nationalist Party. Not only students, but schoolchildren joined patriotic clubs and began to read newspapers, the readership of which was vastly increased by the rapid replacement of the literary language by the vernacular. Marxism, anarchism, syndicalism and other new ideas were under consideration. At least four hundred more periodicals were launched in the months following, among which was the little-known *Xiang River Review*, the founder-editor of which was the self-educated son of a farmer, Mao Zedong. Intellectual journalists and pundits Hu Shi and Chen Duxiu, co-editors of *New Youth*, were the cynosures. Chen Duxiu was in the Liang mould:

> He preached 'science and democracy' as the basis for renewed national strength. He launched a head-on attack on Confucianism, dismissing it as irrelevant to the modern world. Above all, he brusquely dismissed the central dilemma which faced China, the choice between preserving her culture and preserving her existence as a nation. 'Where are the Babylonians today?' asked Chen. 'What good is their culture to them now?'
>
> (Gray 1990: 198)

The excitement of the educated young of the 1920s for new ideas and for journalism is well conveyed in Ba Jin's novel *The Family*, originally published in 1933.[10] In it, the young protagonists are constantly referring to political theories and western literature and are more wrapped up in the newspapers they are trying to publish,[11] modelled on those of the May 4 exemplars, both as writers and as organizers, than in anything else, even their love lives and family troubles (Ba 1956: Chapter 29). In fact they are so taken by the thrill of imported ideas and new theories that they tend to be quite out of touch with the majority of their fellow Chinese. Both those features of Ba's novel are prescient. Although the *impact* of the May 4 journalists was great – large numbers of Chinese had an idea of what was going on – it is likely that their ideas failed to be *influential* beyond their own social class. It can be seen as an acknowledgement of just how little influence beyond a restricted class those May 4 proselytizers had had, when, in the 1960s, Jiang Qing would seek to fashion a mass, revolutionary culture to replace the 'feudal' one which apparently still existed (even after land reform and class struggle). Escapist literature and 'fun' papers of very traditional genres were still the majority taste in the early 1960s (Lee 1985).

The 'Golden Period'

One journalist interviewed suggested that, 'before Liberation in 1949 the media were merely tools of the capitalist classes'; another that only now was Chinese journalism raising itself to the standards of the 1930s. The former is a view associated with CCP loyalists and the latter with their critics, for the expression 'Golden Period' appears in a *History of Journalism* (Zeng 1989) and other works published on Taiwan. However, it should be possible to recognize both the vigour of the 1920s and 1930s and the limitations then upon journalists.

The overthrow of the monarchy in the *Xinghai*, or 1911, revolution came at a time when there was already a communicating public which drew in a greater number and variety of people than China had ever before known, a public opinion which was a creation of journalists and a widely held but inchoately developed belief that democracy and science together would somehow return China to its rightful place among the greatest of the earth. In the chaos following the 1911 Revolution, China was, in effect, partitioned up into spheres of influence of, on the one hand officers ('warlords') whose political leanings varied from restorationism through sympathy for democracy to sheer banditry, and on the other hand foreign powers. In many areas the press was sufficiently free to advance competing theories of China's predicament and future, often very radical, and to further the evolution of public opinion. Public opinion came to accept as orthodoxy, in the years following 4 May 1919, the disgust with China's past and the neophilia which gripped those who came to be the exemplars of the 'May 4 movement', including activists of both Nationalist Party and CCP.[12]

The vigour of the Chinese press can be attested to by its direct and immediate influence on politics. Not only was the May 4 incident itself in a sense the result of a journalistic scoop, but revelations by investigative reporters of the Nishihara Loans scandal and later of Russia's secret Karakhan Declaration both had consequences for China. Chinese and western observers agree:

> In this decade the level of debate was high. Nanjing's fitful and inconsistent censorship and its erratic attacks on journalists did not prevent the growth of an intelligent, responsible, courageous, and critical press. Indeed, in spite of all the restrictions imposed (or half imposed) by Nanjing,[13] China possibly enjoyed more intellectual freedom then than ever before or since.
>
> (Gray 1990: 245)

Zeng reserves his approval for a slightly later period than Gray:

> From the time of the Northern Expedition onwards, the Chinese mass media normalized its development and strode into its golden period.
>
> (Zeng 1989: 317)

That Northern Expedition to unify the country under the Nationalist government (1925–7) was backed up by an alliance of business, industrial labourers and intellectuals imbued with the May 4 *outlook*. The impetus for it can be attributed at least in part to the press, and in part to the propaganda and organization of both KMT and CCP working through the media. Nevertheless some Chinese journalists today look back to this period as one of 'freedom' compared with post-1949 Chinese journalism:[14]

> Many people realise now that journalism in China was very free before 1949 and that china has its own tradition of free journalism.
>
> (Li Zhengmao)

During the 1920s and 1930s there were political newspapers with fixed subscription incomes arranged through the Party but it was the private ones, or *yinglixing*, that 'stood in the market place' and demonstrated the vigour of which the Chinese press was capable. They were able to 'serve society and business and earn the trust and support of readers' (Zeng 1989: 351) because commercialization gave them the means, the Japanese invasion the motivation and technical developments in production and distribution the opportunity. They also won concessions from the government: in 1930 Regulations for the Protection of Press Freedom were enacted.

By 1935 there were 910 newspapers and by 1947, 1,781 (Chang 1969: 18), yet in the mid-1930s the earlier relative tolerance of the Nationalist Party faded. The ebbing of the power of the warlords allowed the Nationalist Party to turn its attention to the rival CCP; it became paranoid, afraid of any questioning of its own creed of anti-imperialist, 'national socialism' or of its practical failures.[15] Chinese politics polarized those who had once been allies in a national cause.

During the Anti-Japanese War, editors in the Nationalist-controlled cities of Chengdu, Chungking and Kunming continually resisted censorship (Lee-Hsia 1974: 151–155) and were generally able to exercise some freedom within the parameters of the patriotic consensus; in 1949, when the CCP took power, this would end.

Conclusion

We might say that the aims of Thomas Barnes (1785–1841) and Liang Qichao (1873–1929), to take two of the most exalted editor-journalists in the anglophone and Chinese worlds, were similar, allowing for the very different circumstances of their two empires. Both wanted journalism which was rational and responsible, which would promote their respective countries in the world and which would promote reform within them. However, their relationships to politics were quite different. Liang was often a fugitive, dependent on the vagaries of the power struggles at court and among the regimes succeeding the Qing Dynasty. Barnes was a respected exponent of public opinion, listened to, however grudgingly, by power holders. In England, by the mid-nineteenth century, the conditions had been created for the appearance of a concept of journalism which has been a model ever since and whose relationship to the polity has been often both aspiration and archetype. Journalism rapidly developed some professional norms, its own techniques and a variety of genres. Moreover, it fed upon the increasing rationalism of intellectual discourse in the period and upon that scientific approach of finding truth from facts which came with the Enlightenment; in doing so it advanced the idea of objectivity, or at least political detachment. As with the great popular novelists, the investigative journalists married rational observation with moral empathy and made exploitation and abuse an ever more likely topic of analysis, discussion and inquiry.

As to China, there is an indigenous tradition of observation of and comment upon current affairs; this tradition combined with the circumstances of western encroachment to give a particular status and role to journalism; the manner in which the literati apprehended the West nourished an extreme sense of mission among Chinese journalists. From an anglophone perspective, however, what they failed to do was to provide a justification for the profession of journalism independent of the great patriotic enterprise, the kind of legitimizing of its role in polity and society which journalism developed in the anglophone countries. This was impossible, first, on account of the philosophical assumptions from which the creators and justifiers of the Chinese journalistic tradition worked. The idea that conflict is valuable and opposition necessary; the notion of compromises in which all lose that all may gain something better; these were foreign to them.[16] The task of life was to return to the Great Harmony[17] which is the natural state of affairs, in which all differences are subsumed into the Great Unity;[18] this was their strength in that it gave them confidence and a common purpose but also their weakness in that it made it difficult for them to see deficiencies in the Chinese social system and to see the need for institutional development.[19]

Second, it was impossible on account of the political conditions in which the media worked. These were conditions of armed factionalism and intimidation, violence and savage conflict. These conditions no longer pertain today and, moreover, ideology has to an extent been superseded by profit as the criterion of truth. Whether Chinese journalism is returning to old traditions or constructing new ones is a theme of the next chapter.

8   The journalist as tribune

As the state has reduced its absolute control over media content, Chinese journalists have been thinking about their own functions, about what it means to be a 'professional'. Although some freedom of thought and action is associated with the concept of professionalism, so too are service to the state and the transmission of orthodoxy. The admission of 'impartiality' as a fundamental ethic of the professional journalist is limited by the context, in a society where it is partiality that is expected, and prized.

It can be argued that Chinese journalism has some of the attributes of professionalism as identified in the West, but lacks others. In place of those missing, journalism performs certain other functions which demonstrate the particularity of its role in the Chinese polity. It carries out comparable functions in a different way and it represents authority in a manner which is out of keeping with anglophone assumptions about professionalism.

Why 'professionalism' is an issue

During the 1980s there was much enthusiasm among Chinese journalists for the idea that journalists have an essential role in society independent of the executive and that they need professional status if they are to carry it out. They were trying to distance themselves from politics, from the kind of situation Porter, a British journalist who worked in the Foreign Affairs Department of the New China News Agency (NCNA), describes. 'The Agency', he writes:

> reported almost exclusively good news, to the extent that many outsiders would consider a significant proportion of its material not to be news at all. There was a tendency to be didactic and to deliver homilies, even in news coverage intended for external release. . . . the general preference was for a pedestrian observation over one that might have some insight. On some occasions the facts of the matter at hand were quite plainly misrepresented.

Political considerations were responsible for important lacunae in the coverage of events, and fundamental shifts in policy over the years meant that what was painted white at one stage must be represented as black at another.

(Porter 1992: 7–8)

Since then, journalists have hardly stopped debating how they can distance themselves from politics and attain some independent standing. This is reflected in such comments as these, by a think-tank staffer who was involved with popularizing the policies of President Jiang Zemin:

We need laws to protect journalists, so that they can serve the people according to professional standards and not be interfered with by officials.

(Zhang Ximin)

Journalists of all ages and types are concerned about their professional status, in that they want protection so that they may work to norms and in ways they and their fellow-professionals deem appropriate. They have declared for wanting to be relieved of political inference rather as many anglophone journalists may want to reduce the commercial pressures upon them:

China's journalists should be a real profession, not dominated by the government or the Party. Then they can serve the country and the masses better.

(Xie Yizhi)

What is this 'profession'? Professionalism can be looked at in a number of different ways and it is not clear, from talking to Chinese journalists, what they mean by the term, translated from *chuanye*, although it is likely that they are influenced by the generous characterization of journalists made by Weber in *Politics as a Vocation*,[1] or by assumptions about journalists culled from an acquaintance with American myths, and from the 'May 4' idea of the journalist as activist, patriot and modernizer,[2] discussed in Chapter 7.

In the anglophone countries, before the 1980s, it was assumed that professions were distinguished from other occupations by a number of traits (Millerson 1984). Although nobody agreed with any precision as to what these might be, the most commonly cited such traits were the possession of skills based on theory, agreed educational qualifications, mutual competence testing, adherence to codes of conduct and social responsibility. By 'social responsibility' it was meant that professionals are not entirely self-interested but perform some tasks out of social altruism. Others have seen professions as being interest groups effecting a monopoly in the market (Larson 1977), groups trying to define and control their own work (Friedson 1994) and groups at a particular stage of anglophone development trying to wrest control of their own work from external determination (Johnson 1972). Abbott's (1988) view of professionalization as the business of establishing dominance over the resolution of socially constructed problems, and controlling membership through entrance competition and knowledge tests, has been influential.

In the nineteenth century, elite English journalists took on certain characteristics which seemed to suggest that they were on the way to establishing professional status in the loose sense in which this is understood to refer, for example, to teachers and academics. They thought themselves impartial, they showed that they had the professional skill to identify evidence and the knowledge to investigate as well as the skills of exposition upon which their employment was based. Moreover they claimed altruism or social responsibility, and detachment. In the first half of the nineteenth century *The Times* developed such independence of political influence that it could claim to be reporting impartially, or at least without conscious deference to the interests of the powerful.

The development of professional norms in England and China took place in different contexts. Detachment was not celebrated by Chinese journalists even though the commercial environment of the 1920s Shanghai may not have been very different from that of 1860s London. The political environment most definitely was different, pushing journalists into being activists of the reform camp, such that detachment must have seemed an irrelevance.

This does not mean that they did not wish to develop a concept of professionalism appropriate to their perception of Chinese circumstances. The idea of social responsibility was adapted, after 1949, to the new circumstances of nationalization of the media and ideological control. A different idea of professionalism came about.[3]

The public and the private functions of journalism

In interviews (de Burgh 2001), as in surveys (Chen 1998), most journalists mention as their prime responsibility that of connecting government and citizenry, although exactly how individual journalists formulate the relationship varies. Their practices in the achievement of this task are different from those of western journalists, particularly in the fact that they have a separation of public and private duties, most clearly demonstrated in the treatment of reader feedback and in the existence of the Restricted Circulation Publications[4] (RCPs):

> In China, except during the Cultural Revolution, the masses have always written their criticisms to the newspapers. This shows how important the media are, because they are the interface between people and government.
>
> According to westerners' outlook criticism is only criticism if you get at the president or prime minister. That's not our way. In the exceptional case that the highest authority has erred, then there are conditions under which the media will report; in general they will use [the RCP system] to resolve the matter.
>
> (Wang Qianghua)

The functions of journalists came to be divided into public and hidden, or the external and the internal. In their public functions they provided such information as was deemed useful and necessary by the party, to the readership. At many periods in the last fifty years, readership has been compulsory for large numbers of people who were to read the papers in order to discover what was expected of them and as an earnest of their seriousness about their work. Editors were enjoined to ensure that 80 per cent of that reported would be positive (Hu 1985). After all, the newspapers promote public policy and realize the 'Mass Line'. The 'Mass Line' was defined as 'from the leaders to the masses from the masses to the leaders' and this meant that the media should also be a mechanism for understanding these masses. Except during the Cultural Revolution and in particular since the early 1980s, journalists therefore evaluated readers' feedback expressed through letters to the newsroom and acted upon it where it was deemed appropriate.[5]

Until recently in China the media provided the only possible avenue to redress of grievances for many people and they made use of it by writing to the newspaper or, increasingly, broadcast programmes, hoping that even if it were not published, their complaint would receive attention from the army of staff responsible for taking note of, checking and attempting to get action on their complaints.[6] Unfortunately the work unit to which the journalists would refer the complaint was often that which was being complained about; it would be asked to prepare a response. If the journalists were not satisfied then they would refer the matter to a higher level (Chu 1983: 56), but whether this resolved the matter depended on the interrelationships of the various officials involved as much as the matter itself.

The other internal function of journalism is Restricted Circulation Publications. In 1992, a Taiwan delegate to the National People's Congress, Huang Shunxing, complained that the legislature refused permission to journalists to conduct interviews. When one did approach him for an interview, he found that the reporter was from a genre of publication of which he had never heard, *Internal Reference*. When he learned that the journalist was reporting from a publication with a closed, VIP, circulation, he refused an interview, with fury, on the principle that such publications were undemocratic and that what he had to say was for everyone or no one (Dai 1994: 112).

Internal Reference or *Internal Situation* are published by all the top media, especially New China News Agency and *The People's Daily*, and usually marked with warnings such as 'confidential' or 'secret' although much of it is easily available to quite minor officials, university teachers and the like so that to imagine that it is all very secret is wrong.[7] There are categories restricted to, for example, the politburo or to officials of various ranks, these are like the briefing sheets issued by the information officers of western governments' ministries, except that in the West they tend to be written by specialist information officials or contracted academics, whereas in China they may be from elite media journalists. Some are distributed at the point of production, others (such as that produced by *Liberation Daily*) go to the central government for distribution by special couriers (Hsiao 1995: 82).

Restricted Circulation Publications such as *Internal Reference* have been important to the CCP since before 1949. There are those, such as *Reference News*, which
convey to the recipients the views of the foreign media on current issues, and
upon China (Rudolph 1984) and those which publish investigations of possible
abuses or crises and publish them in the appropriate category such that action
may be taken by the authorities. Other content of the domestic RCPs consists
of relatively unmediated accounts of events and trends which strike journalists
and editors as significant, fulfilling parameters set out in regulations published in
the 1980s:

> The state of thinking of cadres [officials] and masses, every change in social
> direction, and reflections and proposals from every quarter on the Party's
> line and general and specific policies – which has value as reference but is
> not suitable for public reporting – must be supplied to the leadership organs
> and related departments through the active and responsible writing up of
> internal reference materials.
>
> (Grant 1988: 55)

Journalists can consider this task to be more important than their public roles
since government policy may be made or modified in response to the way in
which they investigate situations or present trends.

Reporters say they spend around 30 per cent of their time on RCPs and
70 per cent on their public work, but their duty goes beyond the identification
and writing up of a phenomenon. If it is construed as negative then the writer
must draw it to the attention of the level higher than that at which the phenomenon under investigation is identified. At that level it is decided whether to
further the investigation. In some cases the journalist does not submit the report
to the RCP until the forewarned authorities have been able at least to propose
how they will deal with the questions raised although this, as we see below with
the case of reporter Wang Lili, is often a matter of bargaining.

In the earliest case that I know of as having come to public attention, the
Po Hai incident of 1979, journalists' reports were suppressed for a very long
time:

> On November 25, 1979, an offshore oil rig in Po Hai Bay was dashed [sic]
> while it was being towed during a storm. The incident resulted in the deaths
> of 72 people and loss or damage to considerable property. In our judge-
> ment, this would be news. Something went wrong and the responsible cadres
> should be criticised. However, it took more than eight months for the Chinese
> press to report and criticize this incident. The delay had nothing to do with
> the Chinese journalists' competence. Nor did it have to do with cover-up by
> the news source. In fact, reporters had been dispatched to the scene. Still,
> nothing had been reported until July 22, 1980, when the *People's Daily* and
> the *Workers Daily* broke the ice. The incident, involving deaths, damages,
> and the petroleum ministry, was simply too important for the journalists

to decide upon. Without specific instructions from the Party Central, the journalists were immobilized.

(Chu 1983: 55)

Various examples are available of the application of RCPs. At the highest level, it appears that, for example, Chairman Mao was well aware of the mass starvation caused by his Great Leap policies, even as the public media ignored their ill effects. In 1989, shortly before the massacre of 4 June, the leaders had available to them reports, on the demoralization of students and their anger at corruption in the Party, which they could have acted upon (Hsiao 1995: 85). A former senior Chinese official now in the West gives examples of how some leaders were misled by partial or exaggerated RCP reports in 1986. He believes that Deng Xiaoping was led to expel three prominent intellectuals from the Party thanks to a biased RCP and that he made his momentous decisions to sack Hu Yaobang in 1987 and then to condemn mourning for Hu as counter-revolutionary because he was swayed by partial RCPs (Yan 1995: 13).

Thus what many anglophone journalists, and indeed Chinese journalists, would regard as the most interesting and valuable material may, even today when investigative and sensational journalism is returning to the Chinese media, be kept 'internal' and only released, if at all, when it has been reflected upon. While the exact mechanisms may have changed in recent years, and material that in the past would never been made public is now exploited by journalists for their public work, the concept remains the same, based as it is on the idea that the main objective of the journalist is to help the government make and implement successful policies, and perhaps explains the relative disinterest in timeliness. It may be that it is the commercial, rather than the cultural, context which makes for this difference between anglophone and Chinese journalists, in which case we may expect Chinese journalism to change as commercial imperatives become sharper. It may also be the case that the traditional Chinese reluctance to air conflicts until resolution has been attempted (Bond 1999) will be given up in the process of making the media more sensational.

The transmission of orthodoxy

It has often been remarked that Chinese officials, and the Chinese media, use what are clearly standardized expressions to describe people, countries and circumstances. These expressions change from time to time (for example, refugees around the Dalai Llama of Tibet will one day be the 'renegade Dalai clique' and another day something more polite) and when they change they change in the mouths of every official and in every media outlet. On the subject of Tibet, one study reveals that the language of colonialist media is similar no matter whether it be in Chinese or English. The Tibetans are represented as backward and needing 'massa's guidance' for their own good, as well as, sometimes, his knout (Kolas 1998). Other instances have been examined (see Fang 1994, Bernstein and Munro 1998).

In China this is not a consummation achieved by osmosis[8] but the result of directives by Party offices, in particular the CCP Central Propaganda Department, the NCNA and the Propaganda Department of the PLA General Political Department. One of their principal jobs is to supply the appropriate formulations in regular circulars or in the newsletters for journalists, such as *Newspaper Trends*.

While in the UK a rival media outlet can ignore what the BBC considers suitable or avoid following the government recommendations, in China this is not so.[9] Often a particular official acts as the link between the Party Central Committee and the editors and senior journalists of *The People's Daily* and provides very detailed comments on specified articles. Individual members of the politburo read and approve editorials, intervening against their own politburo colleagues, too, if they attempt to express themselves in formulations which are different from that of the main powerholder.[10]

In 1978 the CCP reissued Hu Qiaomu's record of his comments and corrections with the evident intention of providing guidance for the future and this quarter-century-old fiat is an important text for aspirant journalists in universities today. His strictures as to how and which foreign countries were to be cited in articles, as to the way in which the naughty children of high officials were to be portrayed or whether certain facts were to be attributed to a few cities or all cities, these and many other issues are dealt with.

Public scrutiny

Today Chinese journalists will tell you that they are guided by the concept, or ideal, of 'yulun jiandu'. Although usually translated as 'supervision' this loses some of the meaning. Here is a Chinese journalist's explanation of the concept:

> 'Yulun jiandu' has spurred on the economic reform, the political reform, the development of culture and science. There are three aspects to 'yulun jiandu'. They are
>
> • Keep functionaries in order by exposing wrongdoing and corruption. Many cadres have been criticized by the media.
> • Proposing ideas which improve government policies. There are successful examples in law, especially law of bankruptcy and law of copyright, all of which came about as a result of media opening up of the subject leading to discussions among parliamentary representatives.
> • Reflecting and interpreting social phenomena and social problems such as women problems, the black market, gambling, drugs, peasant travails, unemployment.
>
> (Lu Cihui)

In other words, 'yulun jiandu' means acting like a watchdog, keeping an eye upon society and drawing attention to what the authorities may have missed.

It is loosely translatable as 'public scrutiny' and reference to it has become a conventional explanation for the role of the journalist, even where the meaning remains hazy.

Thus when a Chinese journalist characterizes journalists as professional, undertaking those tasks that are considered appropriate in a manner that is respected by their peers, s/he is likely as not thinking of the journalist as mediator between people and government in a different sense than would spring to mind to an anglophone, and moreover as the proud transmitter of orthodoxy in a way with which few western journalists would empathize.

Social conformity as a barrier to professionalism

Political diktat is not the only means by which topics are put on society's agenda or excluded from discussion, or by which the terms for discussion are set. Arguably more powerful and constitutive of the criteria is the wider cultural framing. It frames the development of institutions and journalism is no exception. Without over-essentializing, it can be argued that there are distinctive features of how Chinese behave which can be attributed to early socialization and educational style (Wilson 1974, Bond 1996, Bond 1999) and these condition the activities of journalists as they may other members of the same society. These reflections were stimulated by the claims of two interviewees:

> Mr Chen [managing editor of *Liberation Daily*] was very angry with me when I said I was leaving; he told me he had treated me like a son but I had not treated him like a father. I felt very ashamed of myself. If I had wanted to return to China I would have also been afraid of making Mr Chen angry, but I wanted to make a future for myself in the West.
>
> (Kang Keming)[11]

> When I said I wanted to leave the Journalism Department [of Fudan University] and study here for my Ph.D., Professor [Z] would not give me permission. He said that I belong to the Department and I must come back. So when I heard he was coming to England and even coming to my university [Cardiff] I was afraid. I ask you please not to tell him where I am.
>
> (Chen Long)

Approaches to authority and to relations with others are different from those encountered in anglophone societies and condition work in many different ways. Authority is expected to be paternal in style, mirroring family relationships, and obedience is due regardless of the behaviour of those in authority. Only this can explain the willingness of innumerable Chinese CCP activists and officials to continue to serve loyally leaders who have treated them atrociously. As a saying goes, often repeated by Chinese in this connection, 'does a child find its mother too ugly?'.

Psychologists argue that products of the typical Chinese family form are particularly dependent and, when family or community lacks respected and established leadership, may feel deeply insecure. They 'feel a need for idealized authority yet can never find one that satisfies' (Pye 1968: 6) and often this leads them to try to create situations of total predictability and control. This approach is reinforced at different stages and in different institutions throughout life. In Chinese higher education, as elsewhere, students learn the socially approved skills: in China these include deference to authority to the extent of reproducing the teacher's ideas. You do not step out of line without risk (Bond 1991: 31).

The first relevant outcome of these circumstances is that the anglophone tolerance of complementary or even competing authorities within the same society, and of situations by which individuals can have different roles according to circumstances, is very foreign. How this is manifested in the environment of the Chinese newsroom is noted in Porter (1992: 16). Wang Gongwu remarks in an essay on Chinese politics that, in the 1940s, competition between Nationalist Party and CCP was for the establishment of the new orthodoxy; nobody doubted but that absolutism must come, only who would win the power to impose it (Wang 1991). When Chinese do break free from convention they are very remarkable, as Buruma notes in his vignettes of Chinese dissidents in *Bad Elements* (2002).

The second outcome is that Chinese can find it difficult to handle relationships outside the family (Bond 1996). They have, after all, had it drummed into them from their earliest moments not to make emotional commitments outside the family and therefore, where the blood family is not available, attempt to create pseudo families with the same hierarchical structures and absolute loyalties, for example in workplace or college.

Senior people tend to have built up networks or pseudo families over many years. These give them not only influence but also prestige in a society in which the capacity to create ties of obligation and interdependence is highly valued (Yang 1994). Recent psychology research has indicated that Chinese do not merely strive for connections as a way of countering the insecurity of Chinese politics or lack of impartial institutions but they see themselves as necessarily interconnected and in relations of inferiority and superiority with others in ways that are quite foreign to anglophones (Bond 1999). In such a situation it is not surprising that skills valued in anglophone *métiers*, particularly by journalists, such as creativity and argument, are not particularly respected in China. 'Learning by Nellie' is regarded not merely as prudent but as ethical and responsible.

> When I first came to Zhejiang Television station I simply followed around my mentor. So I learned how to do everything and now we have a very good relationship. Whenever he asks me to do something he knows I'll do it just as he does.
>
> (Kang Wei)

These general tendencies have further implications. The relationship can be more important than the business for which the relationship is the ostensible reason, to the extent that relationships matter more than truth or efficacy; indeed, hierarchy *is* truth. The need for dogma, as establishing absolute authority, is a another implication. One more is the failure fully to comprehend the need for change beyond personal rectification, so evident in President Jiang Zemin's approach to institutionalized corruption. He, as with other Chinese leaders before him, has sought a solution for ills such as peculation, nepotism, factionalism, officials' fear of enterprise, administrative negligence or high-handedness in calls for moral cleansing, repentance, 'back to basics' and so forth rather than in attempting to establish systems which will help people behave in the approved manner. When Qiao Shi, a senior leader, or Zhang Ximin,[12] a policy adviser, and other reformers argue for systems rather than homilies they are pitting themselves against a heavy weight of tradition.[13]

Government

Since 1989, the weakened moral authority of the party, the increasing power of the big institutions and regions vis-à-vis the centre and the emergence of new interests have changed the relations of power and the way in which it is expressed. The centre is not all-powerful, but haggles with regional, industrial and institutional groupings (Cheung 1994).

Such developments need to be understood within the framework of Chinese social psychology. The emergence of media conglomerates, for example, is a function of the ways economic development is being permitted to manifest itself, i.e., under controlled conditions whereby factions loyal to the leaders can command key sectors; it is a function not only of the political developments noted by several contributors to Hamrin and Zhao (1995) but also of these wider cultural conditions:

> Today we are developing media conglomerates. This gives the newspapers and television more independence and more power in the market compared to other industries.
>
> (Chen Zedong)

There are attractions for those in lowly positions, too. The bigger the unit to which you can attach yourself, the better, as it can bargain for you, protect you and enhance your life in many ways. Chinese workers, to succeed in their careers or to have any influence over their own work, must follow their patron and the patron's faction: loyalty is the ultimate value, not truth or efficacy. Journalists therefore are placed in a dilemma particular to the Chinese context here described: they have notions of professional competence but are tied out of gratitude and tradition to their units and patrons within them, and this tendency is being reinforced in the accelerating commercial climate.

As to change and the penetration of new ideas, it is not the case that those below cannot influence those above, but that they can only do so by first being part of the faction of those to be influenced and by being deferential, attributing success to the senior. The implications of these various observations taken together are that journalists will continue to work in factions but the factions will increasingly be localized in provinces and institutions. Thus when opposition or counter-orthodoxy does take place it may manifest itself in factional guise. I will now draw upon three examples to show how the media operate together with faction politics.

The case of the World Economic Herald (WEH)

> Every journalist who wants to spread new ideas remembers the story of the World Economic Herald. Qin Benli did not understand the limits.
>
> (Cao Xin)

Editor Qin Benli was a well-established party member and executive editor of Shanghai's *Wenhui Daily*. In 1980 he founded a new newspaper using the correct procedures but managing to achieve relative autonomy in how he organized, staffed and financed the new venture. Having done this he and the team he had collected around him published articles promoting reform, often very controversial.

Attempts were made by the left, in 1983, 1986 and 1988, to have the paper closed, but it was saved through the protection of, for example, Party General Secretary Zhao Ziyang and Deng Xiaoping (Yang 1995: 186–187). In April 1989, as the tension rose not only in Peking but all over the country where student demonstrations were being mounted, *WEH* published articles sympathetic to the students. It had gone too far. In effect it was Jiang Zemin (then Mayor of Shanghai) who dismissed editor Qin Benli. He Baogang has argued (1997: 32) that the case demonstrated clearly the limits of the kind of autonomy available in the developing Chinese civil society, since although *WEH* had held that it was independent of state finance or hierarchies, the state nevertheless closed it down. Today there are experiments afoot, with a new 'semi-private' newspaper now being launched in Peking, but the supposed owners cannot be sure that, if they find themselves in trouble with the centre at some point, their fate will not be that of the *WEH*.

The case of the Three Gorges

On 28 February 1989, the journalist Dai Qing, well connected to the ruling factions,[14] along with associated journalists and academic experts held a press conference to release a book called *Yangtze! Yangtze!* It was a compilation of articles and reports that they had been unable to get published by their employers and amounted to an indictment of the manner in which decision-making over the largest ever Chinese construction project (the Three Gorges Dam) had proceeded as well as questioning its value and its effect on the environment.

The gestation of the book was as follows: in 1986 a report on the Yangtze Dam Project by qualified scientists and engineers was submitted to the Central

Committee. It recommended that the project be put on hold. However 'no widely circulated, non specialist newspapers had objectively reported the findings of their study' (Dai 1989: 6). Dai attended a meeting of the Chinese People's Consultative Conference at which the report was being released and found that the story she then wrote was spiked. When she took this up with the editor she was told that there was a 'spirit' abroad which permitted only positive reporting of the project. She tried various magazines to get publication but failed at every attempt; after trawling many potential publishers, she eventually found a provincial one.

In the months following the publication of the book, government agencies retracted their commitment to the project. However, in June 1989 the Tiananmen massacre took place and the left wing returned to power as the progressives were blamed. In October her book was banned and Dai imprisoned for nearly a year. In April 1992 the NPC reinstated the project. What had happened in the meantime?

To impose this grandiose project the processes of consensus building, developed in the 1980s, were undermined. Those whose consent was looked for were kept ignorant or fed with partial information using techniques familiar to western public relations practitioners; engineers were protected from exposure to questions (Dai 1989: xvi); procedural rules of the NPC were used to prevent the distribution of information and the manipulation of data in the manner to which UK citizens have become accustomed.[15] Notwithstanding all this one-third of NPC delegates either opposed or abstained on the issue, an unprecedented opposition, perhaps related to the fact that a dozen newspapers, including *The People's Daily* and *The Guangming Daily* had managed to carry reports of the book's publication.

Focal Point: Behind Official Openness

An interviewee who had worked for several years as a reporter on *Focal Point* referred to a report *Behind Official Openness*, the synopsis of which is to be found in one of CCTV's publications (CCTV 1998a: 136–144). She then described what really happened in the making of the programme:

> Through my own contacts I found that officials had been cheating peasants in the North East by manipulating the price of grain to the disadvantage of the peasant farmers. We got together all the evidence and my boss was very supportive. We thought we would be able to screen it but the Party authorities in the North East got wind of it and used their contacts at the top level to lean on Sun Yushang [the head of CCTV at the time] who stopped the programme being transmitted. We complained bitterly and there were many meetings about this subject, with our boss fighting for the right to transmit. The Party authorities then did their own investigation, agreed with us and applied disciplinary procedures to the officials in the North East who had been corrupt. It was then agreed between CCTV, Party Centre and the

Provincial authorities that the programme would be transmitted but that it would show that the situation had been put right and the corrupt officials punished.

(Zao Hungwen)[16]

These three examples indicate the limits upon journalists' professionalism even as great changes are taking place, with opinions on even such sensitive subjects as economic and foreign policies argued in the press, as radio explores areas of life never before exposed to scrutiny and as television investigates (some) official malpractice. The journalist can perform an essential function in a society in which corruption or bureaucrats' incompetence or fear may prevent the exposure of issues, although the performance is kept within limits. Despite the limits, the journalist gets satisfaction from being an intelligence gatherer and from knowing that s/he contributes to public policy, a satisfaction surely not dissimilar to that which may be felt by the national journalist in England when s/he learns that the issues s/he identified will be taken up by the politicians.

The issue of 'corruption'

Professionalism is also conditioned by 'corruption', an epiphenomenon of the social culture and of the political system, of which the principal currency is favours.

A friend of mine was having problems owing to the re-zoning of land. He had paid the price suitable to the building of poor people's housing for the local government and now he needed the land re-zoned so that he could build luxury apartments for sale. This meant an increase in the land value of about 1,000 per cent. He came to me and asked me to help him meet the local mayor. I was able to help him. I did this by arranging to do a profile of the mayor for my newspaper [*Liberation Daily*, one of China's leading newspapers]. On the day I went to see the Mayor[17] he was very welcoming so it was easy for me to say 'By the way, I have a friend who needs to ask your advice on a zoning matter'. The mayor said 'Of course I'd like to help any friend of yours, just tell him to come and see me'. 'Oh he's waiting outside in his car right now' I said 'so it might be convenient if he came in right away'. 'No problem' said the Mayor, so the developer comes up and we fix everything there and then. I got about two years' salary out of that.

(Kang Keming)

The pressures of family or pseudo-family obligation in Chinese society are so great as to make nepotism, favouritism and what in the anglophone countries would be termed 'corruption' hard to resist. The early Communist 'cadres',[18] such as the idealistic parents of Jung Chang, author of *Wild Swans*, were thought incorruptible and this was part of their popular appeal; however, as a substitute for institutional checks and balances, revolutionaries with mission were to prove inadequate. The CCP destroyed many means of communication and transaction, public spirited organizations and institutions and these were given the final death blow by the Cultural Revolution (1965–75).[19] That period also saw destroyed the channel put in place by the CCP as the alternative, the missionary cadre; in its aftermath the ideology was discredited such that it was impossible to revitalize it and there has been a general reversion to culturally more typical behaviour, albeit given a new intensity by the lack of traditional alternative modes of mediation (Yang 1994). In 1993, 6,740 cases of embezzlement and bribery by CCP functionaries, each exceeding 10,000 Yuan, were prosecuted. There were also 1,748 identified cases of the illegal use of public funds of over 50,000 Yuan (Hao 1997: 184) Both revelations are of very much greater numbers than any previous publicizing of corruption and demonstrate the concern of the government.

Wu Haimin (Wu 1996) and Zhao Yuezhi (Zhao 1998) have drawn attention to corruption among journalists, which they see as bedevilling the Chinese media. Favouritism is rife, and in new forms. Not only are the claims of business published almost unchecked in the vast amount of media that now covers enterprise and economic development of one sort or another, but in virtually all the media business can buy itself editorial by one of a number of methods which they detail. Journalists are easily frightened or corrupted by business and as a result few sceptical stories are ever seen, and topics of great public interest such as the despoliation of the environment are touched upon too seldom. Chary at any time of offending the influential and perhaps frustrated by their inability to play the watchdog role that they have learned at university is theirs, journalists turn their energies to exploiting the willingness of business to pay them and invent new ways of lining their pockets. Not surprisingly, poor areas of China or difficult subjects can be neglected and the emphasis in much of the media is on promoting products, from film stars to forklift trucks to cosmetics.

Today, those who want to strengthen the independence of the media, so that it may scrutinize the politicians better, pin their hopes on getting the government to allow privately owned media, just at a time when their western counterparts, as we noted in Chapter 1, are becoming convinced that private ownership of the media can be almost as restrictive and anti-democratic as state ownership (Philo and Miller 2000). Whether this would solve the problem of corruption is open to question.

Attempts to devise a regulatory framework

An important condition of the emergence of a professional status is the ability to procure legislation which then helps define and establish the rights and duties of the profession. Proponents of journalistic independence are aware of this and regret the fact that 'there are no primary laws in China that govern the telecommunications, Internet, broadcasting, press or publishing industries' (Perry and Seldon 2000: 26). However, journalists have exploited opportunities provided by the (1987) Civil Code to try to establish their rights and responsibilities and have tried to go further:

In order to establish the rule of law in journalism, Chinese journalists, lawyers, judges, deputies from the People's Congress, academic researchers and educators have been making efforts since the early eighties in two areas: (1) to explore the possibility of having national press laws to protect the news media from abuse from the executive and the Party, and (2) to enact a civil law to protect citizens, businesses, and organizations from libel by individuals in organizations, including the press.

(Zhang 1999)

In the 1980s a press law was mooted which, its advocates claimed, would distinguish legality from professional ethics. It has never come to anything and we can surmise that at least one reason is that the very idea contradicts the old CCP axiom that journalism should be 'the throat and tongue' of the Party. Like many other changes which could be seen to be introducing western concepts, it surely is opposed by those forces leery of market economics and cultural liberalization. They have tradition on their side; for thousands of years authority has had accepted its right to stipulate truth and its right to educate. Nevertheless, a media law is still talked of as if it were an essential (Huang Hu 1997, Li 1998, Zhang 1999).

There has been a rapid increase in the number of libel cases brought under the Civil Code in which broadcasters and journalists have been defendants. There are also recent cases of journalists being punished and their publications suppressed, cases which highlight the precarious nature of tolerance even today; topics which are acceptable one minute are not the next. For example, Canton's *New Weekly* was given a four-month suspension for mentioning the 1989 Tiananmen massacre in December 1998, while *Shenzhen Pictorial Journal* was banned indefinitely for similar sins in January 1999; Peking monthly *Fangfa* was suspended abruptly on 12 March 1999 for no obvious reason except that it had established a reputation as a frank medium of discussion about political and economic reform. On 1 January 2001 there were at least twelve journalists in prison. They included an art critic and reporter for unofficial media as well as an NCNA reporter punished for publishing his investigation of the failure of an irrigation project. Furthermore, the editor of *Weekend South* was dismissed that month when he wrote a defence of persecuted journalists (Prisma 2001: 201).

In this climate it is not surprising that journalists would like to have a framework of legality within which to operate and the fact that the chairman of the NPC Media Legislation Working Group is also editor of the (self-supporting) magazine *Law and Democracy*, a vehicle for examining abuses, may indicate that the issue is being kept alive thanks to some factional support.

Conclusion

Journalism has nowhere, even in the USA, managed to establish itself as a profession with the same success as medicine or law – yet. In anglophone countries, this is probably for a number of easily imagined reasons: there is no readily identifiable 'core activity' (Tunstall 1970); journalists work for a multitude of utterly different types of organizations and with very different job descriptions. They use skills specific to particular market segments and technological environments and tend to identify with them rather than with the profession as a whole, for example the *East Anglian* farming correspondent and *Euro Trash* producer, the *Tablet* feature-writer and the *Trent FM* reporter. Employers have more power over journalists than the equivalent employers of other professionals; within the organizations in which they work journalists are separated according to speciality and have little in common although they are increasingly similar in educational and social background.

However, some elements of professionalism are acknowledged. The right to protect sources seems now entrenched in anglophone countries. Splichal and Sparks (1994) consider that journalists generally are becoming more professionalized because of the increasingly specialized nature of their education and professional knowledge plus greater assertion of their professional autonomy and ethics.

When accountancy was attempting to establish itself as a profession the move was widely derided since accountancy was not seen as being able to satisfy the conditions deemed essential. Macdonald states as essential the ability to: control admission to, and training for, practice; demarcate jurisdiction within which they alone may practise; impose own rules of ethics or practice on one another; defend and enhance their status (Macdonald 1995: 228). These are all things Chinese journalists are trying to do.

However if, as Everett C. Hughes argued, the interesting matter is not the definition of a profession but the posing of the question 'what are the circumstances in which people in an occupation attempt to turn it into a profession and themselves into professional people?' (Macdonald 1995: 6), then it can be argued that journalists can be seen to be gaining ground. Indeed it may be that those circumstances are now appearing in China.

Civil society

In recent years there has been much discussion, both in China and abroad, as to whether China is developing the kind of civil society that is often regarded as a prerequisite not only for democracy but also for stable economic development; the hope is that such a development will condition the power of the state and make possible the growth of democratic institutions (Gold 1990; Nathan 1990). What they have in mind was discussed in Chapter 1. Sociologists are keen to identify the emergence of 'semi-autonomous bodies' as evidence of burgeoning diversity; the lack of them is held to hinder the emergence of democratic politics (He 1997: 1).

This is not a new debate, but was suspended during the long totalitarian period and has resumed off and on since the 1980s. Historians of modern China have blamed the failure of Nationalist China upon its inability to develop civil institutions and in turn blamed that failure upon the kind of social psychological or cultural factors discussed above.[20] Accused is the 'authority dependency pattern' by which an individual acquires a sense of personal worth or individual attainments from a realization of his relative position, or status in a tiered society (Eastman 1975: 288). There is a preference for clinging to what is strong rather than setting up independently (Hsu 1963) and the inability to stomach criticism,[21] seeing it as not 'legitimate difference of opinion' but 'a rejection of authority', makes it very difficult for institutions to grow up which might be construed as wanting to share power. Recent studies in anthropology suggest that over the last 20 years these characteristics have been modified. Scholars are coming to understand concepts of 'family' and 'relationships' in new ways (Yan 2003, Yan 1996). Furthermore, recent political developments in Taiwan suggest that these aspects of Chinese society are by no means immutable.

Nevertheless, our expectations for Chinese journalists should be tempered to accord with these considerations, even if their own are not. For professionalization is understood in different ways by journalists in China and in England. Whereas in England it may be assumed that professionalism equals independence from outsiders deciding your criteria, it is also more and more recognized that professionals are constrained by pressures from employers and by their own working culture. Professionalism is not, in other words, a universal standard.

The Chinese journalists' sense of professionalism is different, yet they share characteristics of professionalism identified by western sociologists; for example, they satisfy Macdonald's conditions as they do those of Millerson and Larson. Johnson sees professions as groups at a particular stage of development trying to wrest control of their work from external domination. Chinese journalists appear to be trying to do that; where they absolutely fit the bill is in their sense of social responsibility or altruism.

9 Becoming a journalist

What are the motivations for becoming a journalist and how are they influenced by beliefs about journalism? What goes through the mind of a young man or woman who is thinking of trying to become a journalist?

Having decided to try to become journalists, the aspirants must come to terms with the formal discourses of journalism which dominate the professional establishment and the universities. They must also equip themselves with the skills and attitudes that their employers consider necessary.

Imagining yourself a journalist

Why does anyone become a journalist? The motivations of individuals need not necessarily have any bearing upon the social significance of their chosen professions, but it is at least possible that the motivations claimed reflect social perceptions of those professions, or perhaps myths which, inhaled from the ether, condition the decision to aim for journalism. So the question is worth putting; it is striking how similar are the replies. This one is representative:

> I'd always wanted this career from when I was very young. I reckoned it was a good life, meeting loads of people, getting around in society . . . There is unlimited potential to make contacts . . . I'm not very studious but . . . I really like ferreting around for information, finding out secrets. I'm fascinated by everything in the social world around me . . . Ever since I started have I loved my work.
>
> (Li Feishi)

This statement by **Li Feishi** is striking in two ways. Firstly, because it makes no reference whatsoever to the heavyweight reasons for being a journalist which are part of the customary discourse of journalism in a society in which politics is everywhere overt; second, it is so similar to the kind of reasons for wanting to be a journalist advanced by Li's contemporaries in England. Moreover, the assumptions underlying it tell us much about him, about what he thinks of himself and about what he thinks of journalism and the nature of journalistic work.

Although academic observers of journalism are very exercised by the powers and responsibilities of the profession, it is not these heavyweight aspects of their work that occur to anglophone journalists when they are asked to reflect upon their reasons for choosing the profession. According to one study of British journalists (Henningham and Delano 1998: 146) they were attracted by the excitement that the occupation seemed to offer; very few indeed had any intrinsic interest in news or current affairs.

A study of English regional television reporters, a narrower group, found the same (de Burgh 1998). Very few had 'always' wanted to be journalists. Overwhelmingly they took up journalism because it was more 'fun' than whatever else might be available; in teens or early twenties they had noticed that journalists got around, met lots of different types of people, were paid to observe and enjoyed constant variety. Only one, older, journalist said that he came into journalism in part because he wanted to defend 'those who need us'.[1] As to what they liked about the job today, all identified similar aspects of the job that they like, formulated in slightly different ways:

'it's immensely glamorous'
'every day is different'
'its exciting, a fun way to earn a living'
'I like the pace, the deadlines, the adrenalin coursing through'
'the competitiveness – trying to be first'.

(de Burgh 1998)

Li Feishi's colleagues were very similar. A younger one, a law graduate, is seemingly less interested in the contacts, more in the sheer variety:

Law seemed very restrictive to me as a career because I wanted to get around. It was the freedom of journalism that attracted me . . . I can see a lot of what's going on; one day I'm among the peasants, the next in a factory or a university. Most people can't please themselves in looking at this or that thing. My work lets me interview interesting people . . . excuse me [mobile phone rings].

(Wu Weishi)

The curriculum vitae

If we look at the curriculum vitae (CV) of journalists we can see that what started as the reason for wanting to become a journalist – the love of novelty and 'ferreting things out' – becomes the source of self-respect once you have done so. You claim that your efforts influence the wider world through the impact they have on your audience. The CV of a well-established English TV journalist declares:

I have made a large number of current affairs films and documentaries ... these range from an investigation into far-right political group *Combat 18* to a film about the killing of a Devon farmer by an élite police firearms squad ... my programme about the Louise Woodward case [an English expatriate nanny accused of murder] included the first interview with her. My programme on the paedophile Sidney Cooke led to further charges being brought against him in January 1999 and my latest programme, transmitted in March, uncovered sharp practice on the part of surveyors and pulled in an abnormally high audience against tough opposition.

I was responsible for *Stir Fry*, a half-hour programme in which a celebrity chef tries to cook for 200 prisoners on a tiny budget of £1.37 per prisoner per day and several editions of *Clear My Name*, broadcast live from Oxford Prison. *Clear My Name* set out to highlight cases of potential victims of miscarriages of justice and to appeal to the public to help them demonstrate their innocence. *The Whitechapel Murders*, an investigation for Channel 4's Secret History strand revealed the original police suspect for the Jack the Ripper murders. *The Hay Poisoner* a personal re-assessment of the evidence against Herbert Rowse Armstrong, the only solicitor ever to be hanged in Britain, is another popular history programme. It was transmitted as part of the *Short Stories* strand on Channel 4.

(Steve Haywood CV)

On the CVs of some Chinese journalists, the emphasis is upon just how busy they have been:

I have visited above 30 provinces for interviews and organised a lot of important news reports about nationally significant events.

Or how important they are:

I was sent to report many big events, interview many famous people ... Now I was among the chief journalists and other more important tasks were given to me such as the 2002 World Cup. And now we have a branch in Shanghai, one of the most developed big cities in China, our newspaper has decided to send me to Shanghai as the Chief Journalist there. More challenges are waiting for me, I feel happy and also passionate.

While those who provide references for them emphasize their passion for work:

During the past nine years, Mr X has produced and presented nearly 5,000 hours' live programmes and has been involved in large scale outdoor live broadcast activities over 100 times. The interviewees of his include top officials, musicians, artists and ordinary people. Over 30 programmes of his have been awarded [prizes] since 1996, leaving other colleagues far behind. Moreover, Mr X's devotion to his job was reflected by his hard work during a mission to Tibet, where 'plateau effect' from the over 4,500 meters Qinghai-Tibet Plateau caused him serious physical discomfort. In disregard of that, he wrote eight special reports within two weeks, which had a tremendous impact upon the audience.

Others provide long lists of awards:

1996 awarded 2nd prize for National Excellence in economic reports
1996 awarded 1st prize in Jinan Excellence in TV Awards
1997 awarded 2nd prize in Jinan Excellence in TV Awards
1997 awarded 2nd prize in Shandong Television Awards
1998 awarded 2nd prize in Shandong Television Awards
1998 awarded 3rd prize in Jinan Broadcasting Excellent Thesis Awards
2000 awarded 1st prize in Shandong Television Awards.[2]

Kang Keming has gone far on the *Liberation Daily* with his nose for news:

Since I was promoted to work for economic news, I have published nearly 200 articles in a year, a dozen of which have enhanced awareness of the local authorities in their environmental efforts, especially in the field of garbage recycling . . . two of my reports were commended and selected as a case in policy making by Vice-Premiers Qing Lilan and Guo Wubang, among which, those dealing with the reduction of spindles in textile investment and the reformed taxation of gasoline for automobiles effectively influenced the related policies . . .

(Kang Keming CV)

However, having a nose, or wanting to have a nose, is not sufficient to get you the chance to use it; in all countries today, applicants to work as journalists are more likely to be graduates than a generation ago. In England 49 per cent of journalists have a degree and a further 20 per cent have attended or are attending a tertiary educational institution (Henningham and Delano 1998). The proportion in other anglophone countries is rather higher. In China the young aspirant aims for a degree too.[3] A high percentage, – 86 per cent – pass through some kind of higher education, of whom 44 per cent attend a university (Chen *et al.* 1998: 21). In a country in which a tiny minority of the population goes to university and the competition is so strong that special allocations have to be made for applicants from universities' home cities lest they be swamped by the peasant youngsters with their perpetually higher marks,[4] you cannot get to read journalism without good grades in the school leaving certificate. Although Li (who has a journalism degree from Fudan) says he's 'not very studious', he surely drew heavily upon his claimed liking for 'ferreting out' in fighting his way into his chosen career: determination and academic ability are necessary if you are to get into the kind of university which will provide you, not only with the appropriate qualification, but also with those introductions to the profession which will make your career possible.

Li mentions 'contact making', a reference which might be passed over in an English context even though in recent years 'networking' has increasingly become openly acknowledged as a vital skill for a careerist. However, in China it is likely enough one of the most valuable aspects of the job where the where-withal to please, or displease, powerful potential patrons in business, politics or any other field is a commodity of value. Yang (1994), among others, has written extensively on the functions of networks of connections in Chinese society where formal structures of recruitment, lobbying and decision-making of every kind are much weaker than the informal personalized groupings behind them. Journalists in China, as elsewhere, are society's ultimate networkers, but those who, in a society which is particularly suspicious and closed,[5] having the professional right and kudos to open doors otherwise forbidding, have a mighty power.

Formal and informal discourses

Where did Li Feishi get the idea that journalism is like that? Certainly not from his formal courses at university which emphasize the heavyweight role of the profession ad nauseam. Yet everything he knows about journalism predisposes him to know that being a journalist is being a gadfly! There is a discrepancy between the 'function in society' and what he sees himself actually doing. For what do journalists actually do all day? As he said in reply to a different question 'talk to people, find stories, pull them into shape'.

There are at least two discourses around journalistic activity. If you glance through university textbooks such as Yuan's *Guide to Journalism Practice* (1997) or commentaries like Sang's *The Study of News Reports* (1996) you find the formal discourse. This 'frames' journalism as an institution of society and journalists as functionaries with highly prescribed roles to perform. With the help of these texts, the aspirant journalists learn the framing and what they have to achieve for their organizations or at least what they must say they will achieve for them.

What we see Li enunciating is the informal discourse of journalism, describing the predisposition which recruits to journalism are likely to take into that activity. They won't refer to it in their essays, but it will surely be the subtext of their job applications and, as such, is one, perhaps rather significant, contributor to the discursive framing which plays a part in the creation of the journalist. If all the talk and writing about journalism can be treated more or less as a 'broad text' then this informal discourse of journalism is at least as relevant to the explanation of journalism as are the formal discourses to which we will be referring at length later.

Hay (1996) says that texts

> effectively construct an empty storyboard which recruits readers as *dramatis personae* upon an expansive stage created within the text itself. [This storyboard comprises] a basic set of characters, plot relationships, minimal relevant aspects of context and a variety of interdiscursive cues, intended associations and connotations.

We are invited, as 'active decoders' to identify with a particular 'preferred' subject position, i.e., we take on board the approved manner of being a journalist. He goes on: 'we actively position ourselves as subjects within the narrative . . . we are constituted as subjects through the text, as we are simultaneously subjected to it' (Hay 1996: 262).

Taking Hay's cue we might say that Li chose an occupation which allowed him to express his own personality because he recognized its correlation with the informal discourse of journalism around him. It is a discourse of journalism which, in England, does not contrast as radically with the formal discourse as in China. For example in England advertisements for journalists often reflect that informal sense of what a journalist is:

> Must be hungry, ambitious senior. Stunning news patch. Great place to live. Good opportunities for promotion . . . we're looking for a whizz kid . . . must be enthusiastic and hardworking . . . Experience in layout and Quark Xpress an advantage.
>
> (*UK Press Gazette* 2 October 1995)

> Could you be our Christmas cracker? The perfect present for our production tea would be a bright, enthusiastic sub-editor with a flair for design and a passion for words. The Norwich Evening News is a bright and breezy tabloid which fights for its community and produces the stories that really count. Its up to you to convince us that you're the ideal candidate. Oh – and Norwich is a great place too . . .
>
> (*UK Press Gazette* 22 November 2002: 20)

> You will be a top class motivator and know how to spot a top class story.
>
> (*UK Press Gazette* 2 October 1995)

> We need someone who can keep their finger on Poole's pulse and cover everything from page one to parish pump.
>
> (*UK Press Gazette* 11 March 1996)

> Young thrusters can apply. Prove you can handle the words and we might let you look at the pictures.
>
> (*UK Press Gazette* 15 January 1996)

As well as the more formal position:

> You will need to demonstrate . . . wide familiarity with the relevant target areas and in-depth current understanding of their news and current affairs, history, politics, social issues and culture, as well as the changing needs of the audience; an extensive knowledge of the media situation . . . a very good knowledge of international current affairs . . . the ability to generate original

ideas and to turn these ideas into lively output ... a good broadcasting voice ...

(*Guardian* 6 June 2000)

In China it has until recently been rare to advertise for journalists, with most positions having been filled by recommendation as in Mediterranean Europe. However, advertising has taken off in the last few years. Here are some examples:

Essential qualifications for this post are:

1   Devotion to the Party; of very high political awareness; excellent professional ethics; high levels of professional competence.
2   First degree or higher; a journalism qualification; 3 years or more professional experience as a reporter on a city paper; 3 or more commendations.
3   Physically fit; under 40; of either gender.

(*The Chinese Journalist* January 2000)

Under 25. Males over 1.68 metres tall, females over 1.63 metres. Good looking.
Minimum qualifications are a degree in Chinese Literature, Journalism or very similar.
Excellent foundation in written Chinese. Modest demeanour and highly competent as a communicator.

(*Diaozuo Daily* 12 May 2000)

Basic requirements:
Solid competence in political theory. A risk taking approach. Genuine love of hard work. At least 2 years experience in the middle ranks of reporting or editing. With significant networking ability.

(www.chinahr.com for *New China* 13 June 2002)

Required:
1   Politically qualified; with a correct understanding of Party policy; trail blazing; honest and upright; with a fierce sense of responsibility; physically fit; with a powerful analytical and synthesizing ability.
2   At least a first degree, majoring in journalism, economics or law; currently in a middle ranking reporter position; with 3 or more years of experience at provincial or city level newspapers; under 30.

(*The Chinese Journalist* July 2001)

Ostensibly, without formal qualifications you cannot get a job as a journalist. Whatever the teenage Li recognized about the informal discourse of journalism, he knew he had to find the (formally) correct educational programme which would equip him for it. But his motivations were more in keeping with aspects of the trade which are not publicly acknowledged. As another colleague says:

> With this job there's continuous self-discovery, you are forever changing and developing your skills and getting new experiences.
>
> (Xia Yi)

The journalism establishment

In England the gatekeepers of the profession of journalism have until recently been the National Council for the Training of Journalists and the Broadcast Journalism and Periodicals Training Councils,[6] although employers decide for themselves whether to pay attention to their recommendations. These organizations have validated courses, which may or may not be within universities. University departments of journalism, however, do not of necessity have close relationships with the media at a senior level, in fact senior journalists have often expressed contempt for university courses in media and journalism.

It is in the role of the university departments of journalism that we see a further clear distinction between England and China.

> Of course I know the people [who teach journalism] there. We are all one big family. My Chinese literature teacher [lecturer] still gives me advice.
>
> (Tung Xiannian)

In China it is appropriate to lump together media school academics, media managers and journalists as 'media people' and to regard the accounts of academics as being at one with practitioners in a way that would not be the case in England. This is because they work together in rather closer relationships than their English equivalents. Many[7] practising journalists now have graduated[8] from media schools where they have undergone a rigorous curriculum which usually includes a grounding in Chinese literature and history as well as Marxist and Maoist thought.

> Many people now in important government positions studied at Fudan School of Journalism. This is why so many people apply to study there.
>
> (Liu Chao)

The young reporter's laconic remark shows us that it may not be the content of the courses that people think about as much as the network an institution provides. It also confirms that the relationship between politics and the media world is different from those in the anglophone countries and is probably itself a topic worthy of study. It is well known that senior journalists in the national media such as *The People's Daily* and New China News Agency obtain executive positions in party and government in Peking. Something similar seems to pertain in the provinces. The Deputy Mayor of Shanghai, a national political figure, was formerly of the Journalism Department of Fudan University; the recent Dean's last job was as a senior government official in Anhui Province.

How media personnel have their position reinforced was clear at the Seventieth Anniversary Celebration Meeting of Fudan University School of Journalism and the 6th National Conference of Communications Research which followed it. Present were, as might be expected, the cream of journalism academics concerned with the electronic media, including Internet. In addition there was a large number of media personnel including the chief executives of, among other things *Liberation Daily*, Shanghai Television and *Wenhui Daily*, senior executives of the New China News Agency, *The People's Daily*, *Guangming Daily* and many others; as the celebratory meeting went on the announcer read out the names of the 'top leaders' who kept arriving, together with messages of solidarity from those who sent their apologies.

Apart from the obvious point that the Fudan School and its Dean wished to emphasize the importance of the School and its excellent political connections to all those present, the immediate significance of all this only came home during the speeches, especially the final one by Gong Xueping, Deputy Mayor of Shanghai. Gong's speech was preceded by that of Professor Chen Guilan, Dean, Fudan School of Journalism, and those of senior leaders from the National Journalists' Association, Propaganda Department, Peking Committee of the Chinese Communist Party [CCP], *Canton Daily* (the CEO of which presented an enormous cheque, of 1bn RMB, for bursaries), *Peking Daily*, the CCP Branch of *Liberation Daily*, Shanghai CCP Propaganda Department, the Wenhui-Xinming Press Group, Shanghai Television, the Fudan University CCP Branch, Alumni, the Fudan staff and the Fudan students, and the Propaganda Department of the Shanghai CCP.

The final speech was given by Gong Xueping, 'Honorary Dean of the Journalism School of Fudan University and Vice General Secretary of the Shanghai CCP', Shanghai's Deputy Mayor. While the speakers preceding limited themselves to platitudes, he departed from his set text often; he presented himself as someone who well understood the aspirations and frustrations of journalists and academic journalists and was on their side, yet in the process probably left many rather bemused. He declared that the task of the reporters was to report anything, to respond to the needs and demands of ordinary people and cover matters they care about from poor housing to corruption to pollution. However, he argued that there was not much point in making general accusations against a government which was struggling to cope with huge problems and he gave the example of water:

> Don't tell people that only 40 per cent of the water of this city is fit to drink [he did not make clear if this was off the cuff or an official statistic!] but go out and find the factories, the individuals, the communities who are polluting the water and expose them.

In other words, get at the manifestations but not the system, a sceptic might interpret. From an administrator's point of view, the reporter who does this is a help rather than a pain; they are on the same side, all for better water. Mr Gong also discoursed at length upon the nature of truth, suggesting that the vaunted impartiality of, for example, the BBC, was not so impartial when you considered some particular examples. Truth, he opined, can be subjective; it depends from what angle you look at it. 'Truth serves purposes so do not be taken in', summarizes his message.

While appearing to be unambiguous and forthright and, indeed, being tailored to please his audience by its advocacy of journalism as a key mechanism by which China might be modernized, the speech was in fact quite contradictory. It was noticeable less for any clear guidelines than for the sight of a politician courting the constituency both with gifts – he called upon the media executives present to emulate *Canton Daily* and give money to Fudan's Department of Journalism – and with flattery; and the whole event and his presence at it was loaded with political innuendo. For example the, today almost unheard, word 'comrade' was used every moment; references to Marxism, Mao Thought and Deng Theory were plentiful and the intimate relationship between the media and politics was the common premise. Finally, the hectoring tone of the political speeches was not only curious to the foreigners present but considered rather out of order by at least some visiting Chinese academics who thought it most inappropriate for a university, a throwback to the 'bad old days' when politics dominated everything. The students seemed less sceptical; at least they applauded Gong enthusiastically.

In addition to their relationship with the politicians, journalism teachers also mix with academics and intellectuals and may well have a different approach to life from students who are attracted by the 'action-man' idea of journalism. Teachers are at least as likely to be researchers into journalism history as they are teachers of skills, giving them a perspective rooted in culture and history. Moreover, they are established, senior or junior, in jobs which, even today, give total security and prestige, whereas the aspirants have yet to get in and establish themselves. Since one of the reasons the interviewees gave for wanting to be a journalist was related to 'action, doing' and another to 'public affairs, proximity to power' it is not surprising that young journalism students do not necessarily share the scepticism of their teachers.

Studying journalism today

Lee (2000a: 14) has categorized Chinese journalists from official statistics and studies. Excluding the most junior and contract workers there are about 87,000 full-time journalists employed by 3,600 outlets. Half are employed in print and half in broadcast media, two-thirds are male and most in their mid-thirties, 8 out of 10 have university education of whom one-third have studied journalism.

Although by no means all Chinese journalists go through university departments of journalism, the higher reaches of journalism, the principal state media and the professional associations which were until recently the exclusive arbiters of standards and still have all the prestige and much of the power, are dominated by their graduates (He 1998).

> If you really want to succeed, you ought to study in a journalism department.
>
> (Tung Xiannian)

> I want people with imagination, zest and courage. These kind of people are more likely to come from literature or arts departments than from the social sciences. However, those from journalism studies departments do have the basic knowledge.
>
> (Chen Zedong)

Interviewees were at pains to emphasize that they regarded journalism education is an important but neglected topic. The knowledge and skills with which journalists start their working lives may influence the way they construct and reproduce events for their audiences for the rest of their careers. How they see their social role may be determined not only by their industrial and technological environment but also by their education.

Although in Europe there are individual courses that are held in high regard, in general journalism education is thought of with suspicion in both the profession and the academy.[9] There is confusion over the difference between media studies and the study of journalism. There is no agreed approach, let alone body of knowledge or skills that are common; for example, the curricula of Spanish and UK courses could hardly be more different (Stephenson and Mory 1990). The lack of even common principles may help to account for the confusion over the rights and duties of journalists that characterizes much discussion of issues such as privacy, freedom of information and investigative journalism. This is the case in an environment of hugely increasing numbers of media channels, changes in the skills and knowledge required of journalists, globalization and new challenges to journalists' ingenuity. Such changes affect Chinese journalists, but the formation which they have undergone inclines them to different reactions.

Compared with Europe, journalism education has a long history in China, influenced by the importance ascribed to the mass media by the early reformers, by the example of the universities in the USA and by the Bolshevik origins of both Nationalist and Communist parties. The Peking University Journalism Society was founded in 1918; one of the initiators was a graduate in journalism from Michigan. It held classes, organized visits to newsrooms and gave students opportunities for practical training through work on a weekly publication (Chang 1989: 232). Although it closed in 1920, the same year saw a journalism department established at St John's University in Shanghai; in 1924 at Yenching University in Peking and in 1929 at Fudan University, Shanghai. The Department of Journalism of Chengchih University, originally the Nationalist Party Academy, was founded in 1935. It transferred to Taiwan in 1949. Before that date all had close connections with US departments of journalism.

The pre-eminent schools of journalism in the PRC today are those of Fudan University in Shanghai and Renmin University, although Tsinghua, China's outstanding scientific university, has recently set up an ambitious Department of Media and Communications as part of its extension into the social sciences. Renmin, in Peking, was founded in 1955 but from 1958 incorporated within it Yenching's department of journalism, founded 1924. In 1959, independent of the university system, the Peking School of Journalism was set up; in 1996 this was incorporated within the (National) Peking Broadcasting Institute which had been established in 1959 to train technical, managerial and presentation staff. These organizations, and their achievements, were virtually obliterated during the Cultural Revolution and, when English journalists worked at New China News Agency in 1979, they reported that skills and motivations were abysmal (Porter 1992: 11–12).

In recent years there has been prodigious expansion in journalism education, such that institutions struggle to cope and the China National Association for Journalism Education struggles to keep track.[10] Today there are three categories of institution. The first, of which there are 232, are those established by either the Ministry of Education or the Provincial Departments of Education; they are generally within universities, although there are some other homes such as the Academy of Sciences, School of International Relations and the Army Political Academy. Most of their students are four-year *benkesheng*[11] undergraduates and they have master and doctoral students too; their degrees must follow one of four pathways, journalism, broadcasting, commercial media or publishing and editing. The second kind are Ministry of Education validated distance-learning[12] colleges or courses, around 119 of these; most of their students are three-year *zhuankesheng*, with a very few *benkesheng* but definitely no postgraduates. The third type are private, quality approved, schools which charge high fees and are controlled as to what qualifications they may award.

Detailed information on student numbers is only available for 1999, and for the fifty-five institutions[13] which have provided their data to the Chinese Association for Journalism Education. Nevertheless, the numbers are instructive. At the moment of census, August 1999, there were 2,869 studying for postgraduate qualifications and 15,849 studying for undergraduate degrees. The total number of those who had received first degree or postgraduate degree qualifications since the re-establishment of university courses was 67,428. Few of these Departments of Journalism were operational until the mid-1990s (Zhongguo Xinwen Jiaoyu Xuehui (ZXJX) 2001).

The chairman of the Journalism Education Association and, until recently, dean of journalism at Renmin University, says that the expansion of journalism education is a high priority for the government. 'We cannot move fast enough' he says, 'so many youngsters want to study with us'. Certainly his students were extremely enthusiastic and intensely interested in the media; at sessions with a visiting foreign journalist,[14] among the topics which they raised (often citing European examples which demonstrated familiarity with issues of journalism elsewhere) were journalists and privacy, freedom of information, cultural imperialism, the social responsibility of journalism, the independence of producers in news/current affairs, biased reporting of China, reporting of human rights matters and the effects of digitalization on the work of reporters.

There are many more applicants to places in journalism departments. They are selected on the basis of grades scored at the final secondary-school examinations that take place in July each year in one of three strands of examination, the science specialists, humanities specialists and social science specialists. Of the latter, a very high proportion want to study journalism. Each university department sets the lowest mark below which they will not consider applicants and journalism departments have been able regularly to raise their level such that it is almost always higher than other humanities and social science departments. Moreover popular city destinations such as Peking and Shanghai can set higher entry criteria.[15]

There are not enough places even for many of those who have achieved high marks in their secondary exams, so that the competition is fierce. 'We are an important minority' laughed a group of Fudan girls seeking information about studying for their MA in the UK. There tend to be many more girls than boys attempting to enter journalism school, although there is a reluctance on the part of the broadcasting organizations to recruit females (Chen, Chongshan *et al.* 1998, Lu Weidong).

One-half of the students are financially supported by the Ministry of Education and 50 per cent by the provincial governments such that Renmin has one or two from each province. Students in China are a privileged class. They all live on campus supplied with shops, laundries, restaurants, libraries and other facilities to make study as easy as possible. Thus, rather as English undergraduates before the great expansion of higher education, students in China know and are reminded daily that they are a fortunate minority. When later a journalist refers to his or her responsibilities and to the fact that s/he is perceived as an official it is clear that these identities have their roots in the early inculcation of student journalists: they are a minority of a minority and moreover, those who have, in some manner, a voice.

The curriculum

As to the curriculum, regular undergraduate students study for four years, in seven semesters, with approximately thirty hours' classwork per week. The eighth semester is a placement in a media organization which takes place in the third year. The placements are chosen in consultation with the student and often will offer him or her a first job upon graduating.

Theory and practice are combined more than in the very vocational anglophone departments of journalism. Aside from a common grounding which will usually include philosophy, history and literature and other modules more immediately related to current media, they go on in the third year to select one of usually two or three pathways, typically broadcast journalism, print journalism or commercial journalism (advertising/PR) yet these distinctions do not appear to diminish the sense of solidarity among students, graduates and teachers.[16]

At postgraduate level, with Master degrees usually requiring three years' study and a significant dissertation, there are two main streams, journalism and broadcasting. Within either of the streams, studies are pursued in one of several fields (*fangxiang*), for example theory of journalism, history of journalism, media management (He 2002). At Renmin courses specific to Master students include political theory, research methodology, public opinion, current affairs reports and comparative studies of socialist and capitalist news. Research fields from within which MA students tend to select dissertation topics include the reporting of China by foreign journalists, history of the early Chinese press, the Portuguese media in China, the careers and impact of the 'Three S's' (Snow, Smedley and Strong)[17] upon foreign perceptions of the Chinese revolution and *Pravda*'s early years. These topics seem conservative in the sense of restricting scholarship to ancient or politically safe themes. However, as the variety of academic papers given at the 6th National Communications Conference in 1999 demonstrated, academics are increasingly in touch with the themes of research which have interested western scholars over the past forty years, and are tentatively applying this knowledge within the parameters of what is acceptable in China.

Journalists are prepared for work within an ideologically orthodox, perhaps doctrinaire, institution. They receive an academic basis which will often extend to western history, literature and philosophy as well as classics, foreign languages and a broad knowledge of the world outside China. However, by the very nature of their work and their mixing with other humanities and social science students they are exposed to the most radical ideas and intellectual currents available. These are not always helpful:

> Our teachers would tell us in our final year: 'now you must work at forgetting everything you have learned at journalism school'!
>
> (Li Zhengmao)

From the outset of their careers, therefore, they have to cope with dissonance. Consciousness of their privileged position may make this easier to bear.

The job and its power

When you decide that you are aiming to be a journalist and set yourself the task of meeting the academic standards of the gatekeepers in the academy, it may well be that you are motivated by the feeling that your own particular qualities will be nourished by and valued in this occupation of 'ferreting around' as Li Feishi called it. However, as we have seen in Chapter 3, you are surely also aware that the competition is great because journalists have power, or at least that power is ascribed to journalism.

> In the eyes of ordinary people I am powerful, I can speak for them. Thus when I am interviewing a politician I represent the audience. But I must be

careful, I am not representing myself. When I speak to the general public I represent power.

(Liu Chao)

The official discourse of journalism emphasizes this power and the fact that it is exercised on behalf of the Party, and the conventional phrase to describe it crops up again and again:

Journalism is a high status occupation. We are the *throat and tongue of the Party*.

(Jiang Weihua)

A former teacher explained why he had decided to change occupation in mid-career:

Journalism was not a popular choice in 1988, but at about that time the social status of teachers had begun to plummet after the 1985 reforms. I felt that journalism would regain its past high status because they are regarded as representatives of the government . . .

(Tang Musan)

Tang is reminding us that since 1949 there has been a very clear conception of the journalist, a Maoist one which originated in, and barely developed from, the ideas of Lenin. Even today, when the environment is so different from the nineteenth-century one in which Lenin's ideas were developed, journalism students are required to bow to it, even as they are made aware of other interpretations. It probably makes the concept easier to respect, that it seems close to the traditional Chinese one of the good official, at which we look in the next chapter. Students and thoughtful journalists are aware of other interpretations of the roles of the media.

Perceptions and proclivities

Academics too are cautiously rethinking the roles of journalists. According to Lee Chin-chuan, after Hu Qiaomu laid the foundations for today's journalism education by backing academic study of the subject just after the Cultural Revolution, the greatest impetus for developing media studies came from the translation of Siebert's 1956 classic *The Four Theories of the Press*. This book was first translated into Chinese in the heady days of the mid-1980s and had an immediate impact,[18] doubtless because its analysis of what journalism was about contrasted so sharply with what Chinese journalists had been taught in the preceding decades.

Although *popular* opinion in England sometimes appears to lean towards the 'hypodermic' characterization of the media, such that wicked powers are ascribed to journalists whose communications 'inject' us with decadence (according to the right) and greed (the left), academic views of their *agency* (power of action) are much less clear-cut, as we noted in Chapter 1.[19] These views have trickled down to journalists themselves. They often prefer it to be believed that they merely reflect society and have no 'effects'. Whatever view they take, there is a seriousness in discussion of the media which derives from a sense that what the media do is important, if only in creating 'climates of consent' rather than changing opinion. Revulsion against journalistic sensationalism is expressed as often as it is insisted that the freedom of journalists to report is an important social freedom.

In China, on the other hand, the fact that the hypodermic model of the media is the official one has discredited it such that there appears to be widespread nonchalance about their effects. Beneath the statements of the journalists interviewed there is indeed a sense that the media perform important functions in opening people's eyes to new ideas but also the view that people are sufficiently inoculated against indoctrination as to render the media not dangerous. Thus, while the convention in England is to be concerned about the potential the media have for harm (either by perverting the public or by representing the exploiters)[20] the convention in China is to assume that there is nothing to fear.

> Journalists in China have a very important part to play in the development of our country. They have to modernize people's thinking and introduce them to new businesses and products.
>
> (Wen Weiping)

The media are seen as not problematic, i.e., stimulating economic development but having little or no political or cultural impact. That journalists can be in the business of expanding or contracting moral boundaries as well as mere knowledge is not a topic which comes up; this lack is reflected in the instrumental approach to the kind of education, or professional formation, that journalists need.[21] They believe that the most important qualities for such a journalist are energy, enthusiasm, quick thinking, an ability to grasp the here and now. Asked what are the characteristics and abilities required of modern journalists, reporters typically listed qualities such as 'very sharp, disciplined, creative' (Ou Lin). Those that they need to cultivate include 'logical thinking, adaptability, high level of theoretical (i.e., party dogma), specialist competencies (in economics, science, education for example), analytical skills' (Deng Huo).

Although Li Cihui expressed respect for academic knowledge, he rated other qualities highly:

> To be a good journalist you need a solid knowledge base, especially sociology, history and economics. That is a key condition. There must be a good academic base. You also need to have other strings to your bow; I myself like sport, radio, film. Even that is not enough. To be a successful TV reporter you also need a certain ingenuity, resourcefulness, what we in Peking dialect call inspiration (*ling qi'r*) to make things popular. It is the kind of mind that, given one idea can find three ways of realizing it . . . that kind of initiative is very much in demand.

Tang Musan regretted that there were no Chinese role models available (implicitly from a pre-Communist period):

> Young journalists are not to follow the old tradition of arranging news according to political priorities but to focus upon what people need ... Little importance is given to journalism history in the curricula, people are ignorant of pre 1949 journalists so there is no possibility of them being emulated.

Liu Chao wanted to see certain attitudes in place. Graduates should come equipped with 'an impartial approach, spirited ambition, sense of duty, work experience'. A young reporter appeared ambivalent as to whether academic study was worthwhile:

> The basis you get at university is of no practical use – it's a basis which helps you to put everything in context and to be analytical [but] the essence of journalism is to be active, to cover a great deal rather shallowly, not to ponder deeply.

> (Kang Wei)

An older reporter said that, from his perspective:

> Young reporters have an urge to express their personal views, to take part in society and to be in the thick of things. That is why they became journalists.
> (Qian Long)

In sum, those who enter journalism do so because their individual proclivities lead them towards a profession seen as providing fun and constant stimulation; they undergo a very serious formation which may or may not influence their attitudes; they assimilate the idea that they will be part of the establishment; they obtain good contacts by having fought their way into educational institutions which provide such contacts and, if they succeed in getting on, they find themselves in a profession offering a freedom unknown to their compatriots in other fields as well as a status for which others might work many years to achieve. That is only part of the picture though. The Maoist vision of their chosen profession imposes upon them the need to conform to the norms of the profession, to speak the formal discourse as well as to adhere to the informal.

In the next chapter we will look at them once they are well established in the profession, asking: who do they think they are?

10 Who do they think they are?

Once they are in the profession, how do they see themselves? We can speculate that the withdrawal of state control from certain aspects of the media and the vast expansion of that media would reduce the commitment of Chinese journalists to the totalitarian, Maoist, interpretation of their professional role. We can imagine that commercialization of the media and liberalization of content, as the media become more responsive to the market, might have journalists become more solicitous of the customers than of the political masters. We could guess that both trends would fuse with increasing influences from western, particularly anglophone, media in driving journalists to see themselves in the 'watchdog' and 'critical' roles perceived as being archetypically 'western'.[1]

When questioned, what qualities do they attribute to the professional journalist? What roles do they think journalists perform in society? What do they regard as 'good journalism'?

What is a journalist?

According to Chen Zedong of the Peking Broadcasting Academy, there have been five great changes in the Chinese media in the last five years: quantity, economic independence, autonomy, serving the audience, and relationship to the polity. By 'autonomy', Chen means that the media have taken upon themselves the task of scrutinizing society 'to decide themselves what kind of news is the most important, what is most attractive to viewers, and what can contribute most to social development'. This is echoed by Lu Cihui, the deputy editor of a current affairs programme:

> Our task is to identify the latest news facts and social phenomena and to reflect them in our recording of them. Of course, we have our own objectives, one of which is to be close to the citizenry. If there is a topic in which the citizenry have shown no interest, yet you cover it, then you will create a

social effect. There are some matters that are known to the audience but not reflected upon or thought out by them. . . . We go into depth on these topics and demonstrate our views, perhaps providing revelation.

All journalists talk of their relationship with the audience. According to Li Feishi of Oriental TV:

Chinese and western audiences approach television in different ways, because China is a country 'in development'. The Chinese audience wants, first, truth, and second, responsiveness to their interests. It is political reports and social reports that interest me most, because I believe our job is to serve the public and to help the public understand [public] matters and their contexts and background.

An idealistic tone was given to the same basic idea by the younger regional television journalists. For example, Kang Wei said: 'You are a reporter because you have a sense of justice. Because you want to, first, expose evil, and second, give information'. Xia Yi also commented: 'Journalists tell people those things they don't know and provide a deeper understanding of those things they do'.

Similar ideas can be expressed in different ways and given a different emphasis: 'The job of a journalist is to process the news for the people and to supervise the government. Yes, the government must be supervised', said Chen Muli. What Chen meant by that was slightly less challenging than it sounds: 'Residents in an area cannot get their gas supplies properly attended to, so they come to television reporters. It's that simple'.

The question of where they stood between people and government was a vexing one to Tang Musan:

Journalists are the mediators between people and government. Their tasks are the communication of news and scrutiny. The responsibilities of the journalists are to making a news programme that keeps the interest of the people – but not all stations are the same. Impartiality is very necessary but the absolute is impossible. We can only do our best. If something is controversial, we get it said by others. We don't say it.

Despite the history of activism in politics that we identified earlier, when the idea that journalists should be 'social activists' was put to senior print journalist Wen Weiping, he was very forthright: 'Certainly not. "Social activists" are very different from "journalists". A reporter should try to report impartially whereas a social activist has some aims. Journalists report opinions and facts'. Emphasizing the active aspect of journalism, the older reporter said about his profession:

When you teach in a school, you teach few. As a reporter you teach many and at all levels. . . . A reporter works because he has a sense of justice, because he wants to do justice and to cry out about it. . . . There are many qualifications to the work of a reporter. For example, if an ordinary person asks for help from a reporter, the latter has to judge 'is this just helping an individual, or is it a wider issue of significance to many?' Then he has to argue it with his colleagues.

Another senior journalist, Liu Chao, supported Wen's views: 'The reporter has a special role as *the throat and mouth of the Party*', said Liu, 'but should serve the people first. Since you represent the Party in their eyes you are not free to speak as you might wish'. As we have seen, Liu views himself as being powerful, a broker of information representing one side to the other.

So did he think of the journalist as a 'social activist'? Liu answered: 'There is not really a contradiction between the social activist and the impartial journalist'. He thinks that a journalist is 'to work on behalf of the citizenry', and this makes a journalist a social activist, because 'your aims are activist'. However, as a journalist, Liu believes that 'in the way you deal with topics you must be impartial'.

All interviewees agreed, explicitly or implicitly, that people have high expectations of journalists. As Xia Yi put it: 'Journalists have a high social position; at least people attribute to us a high status, although to ourselves we don't seem to have that.' To summarize, the interviewees appear strongly to incline to a social responsibility, even paternal, view of their role. It may help us to understand this if we look at the responses to other questions: can you tell me about any heroes? Which journalists do you most admire? Before doing so, however, we should look at some contemporary studies.

The Global Journalist *study*

From 1995 to 1997, scholars undertook a substantial postal survey of Chinese journalists. From their questionnaires to 5,800 Chinese journalists, Chen and his colleagues (Chen *et al.*, 1998: 26) discovered how they viewed their work:

Our respondents chose the dissemination of news quickly and accurately ('information role') as the most important [task], with 79 per cent of the sample naming it as 'very important'. The next most important role, endorsed by 72 per cent of the sample, requires the media to provide analysis and interpretation of major social issues, which may be called the 'correlation role' according to Lazarsfeld and Merton (1948). The 'mouthpiece role' came in third, with 64 per cent considering the dissemination and explanation of governmental regulations and CCP policies to be very important. A slightly smaller number of respondents supported the 'watchdog role' by looking over either the government (61 per cent) or the negative sectors of society (60 per cent).

The least popular role among the Chinese journalists surveyed is entertainment, endorsed by 19 per cent of the sample. The 'public forum role' offering a free marketplace of ideas to ordinary citizens, also lacks widespread support, as less than a quarter (24 per cent) viewed it as very important. Contrary to the strong support for the mouthpiece role, only one out of three respondents supported the 'indoctrination role' in promoting Communist role models. The journalists' preference of mouthpiece over indoctrination role is consistent with our previous studies (e.g. Zhu 1990) in which Chinese audiences were found to be responsive to media messages about governmental polices but resistant to campaigns promoting Communist ideology.

Chen and the team concluded that 'future research needs to compare the perceived and the practised journalistic professionalism by Chinese journalists' (Chen *et al.* 1998: 29), a contribution to which is made in Chapter 12. Lee (2000a) has examined Chen's study in the light of a contemporary one carried out from within China and considers that they profess high-minded but unrealistic ideals. He comments:

> A scrutiny of both national surveys discloses the emergence of a mixed and ambiguous normative conception about the role of journalism in the 1990s. . . . Since they rebuff Western norms of separating facts from values or presenting balanced views on controversial issues, they vow to find out right and wrong before they report. But, then, 'right and wrong' from what or whose vantage points? Their answers are vague.

The key point made by Lee, which helps explain my interviewees' responses, is that their expressed goals 'remain highly abstract'. He is referring to the watchdog or supervisory role believed in by 60 per cent of Chen's respondents. Interviewees in my own study were asked to describe reports of which they were proud, what makes for a successful report and whether reports influence the authorities. Universally, they cited work that is 'investigative'.

Chinese journalists define investigative journalism

Across the generations and regardless of the medium within which they work, Chinese journalists do at present have a passion for that journalism which scrutinizes authority and delves into the failings of society. They call it investigative journalism[2] and they admire it even if they themselves do not practise it. Asked to describe the journalism they most admired, all of 39 interviewees cited an investigative programme, or a print publication best known for its investigations, as their 'models'. They believe in 'reports that put things right', programmes that 'reflect what people really think and care about' and are 'controversial'. As to those famous vehicles of investigative journalism, *Weekend South*, *Tell it like it is* and *Focal Point*,[3] 'every journalist wants to work with them, every journalist wants to be like their journalists' (de Burgh 2001: 183). When they make these comments, to what kinds of journalism are they referring?

According to Chen Muli:

> The best programmes are those which report a problem first (there's much competition) and those which provide information of immediate use to the people. People don't think much of you if you don't take their side. The job of a journalist is to process the news for the people and to scrutinize the government; yes, the government must be scrutinized.

And there is a definite yen for the underbelly of society:

> Corruption. Unhealthy social phenomena, disasters. Catastrophes. They like to see corruption dealt with, very much. They like things told in story form.
>
> (Tang Musan)

One of the hottest current topics is 'the environment'. On page 42 we saw that reporter Fang Chih was particularly proud of a report on the industrial pollution of the Dadu River. One of Fang's colleagues at Zhejiang TV told of another major environment story, investigating the destruction of officially protected species:

> Elephants in Yunnan were killed by peasants because they had invaded their crops . . . the programme investigated and found that the peasants were desperately poor and therefore one could feel sympathy for them, even if they had killed an endangered species; the programme went further though and found that the original feeding grounds of the elephants had been polluted.
>
> (Xia Yi)

Also dissected are social issues. On one programme a juvenile criminal's life, and treatment at the hands of the authorities, was subjected to the most detailed examination as he went from prison to parole. Yet another criticized the failure of authorities to deal with runaways:

> On teenage children who ran away from home because of family troubles . . . how the local authorities tried to deal with them – we opened this up as a national, rather than a personal issue. We showed that it was not just a Peking or a Shanghai or a Hunan issue but something much larger which all could address together. The whole society got a shock, discussion programmes, newspapers, everywhere people talked about that.
>
> (Ou Lin)

The most striking current affairs story seen dealt with the sale of a baby by its father, described on page 43. The local authorities were held up to criticism.

Those responsible for dealing with problems are reluctant to have their, or their associates', shortcomings aired. However, officials can be manipulated:

> I made a series on exploitation of 'maids' in Shanghai households. After the first one it was taken off air as it was too daring. But I got onto the mayor and persuaded him to override the detractors so that the series was put back on.
>
> (Li Zhengmao)

The authorities are particularly called into question, as they have been in Britain ever since the *Rough Justice* and *Trial and Error* series started, by programmes dealing with miscarriages of justice:

> Last night we did a programme about a lawyer and university professor who had been charged with accepting bribes but, after 100 days of investigation was found not guilty . . . Our report also discussed the repercussions of the case in law circles.
>
> (Li Feishi)

When these reporters veer into official malpractice they are on risky terrain. However, Fang drew attention to the fact that he had also managed to get righted an injustice involving overpayments. He had discovered that the cost of installation of telephone lines in a certain area of the province was nearly double that elsewhere. In his film he is seen questioning officials and putting them on the spot. 'Who authorized the rise and why?' The officials respond that it was all a great mistake (!) and are obliged by the reporter to attend a confrontation with the consumers. At the filmed meeting the officials are contrite and a solution is found in the form of a rebate to all concerned and we see the cash payout to the happy victors. We are told that the telephone office was fined 5,000rmb, indicating that the story was all put to bed a long time before transmission. In this instance Fang appears to have been dealing with officials who were quite lowly and quite exposed. However, as we saw above, when Zao Hungwen researched a report on the exploitation of Shandong farmers by corrupt officials she was dealing with people at a very high level and found her way blocked:

> Through my own contacts I found that officials had been cheating peasants in the North East by manipulating the price of grain to the disadvantage of the peasant farmers. We got together all the evidence and my boss was very supportive. We thought we would be able to screen it but the Party authorities in the North East got wind of it and used their contacts at the top level to lean on Sun Yushang [the head of CCTV at the time] who stopped the programme being transmitted. We complained bitterly and there were many meetings about this subject, with our boss fighting for the right to transmit. [Hearing about it from us,] the Party authorities then did their own investigation, agreed with us and applied disciplinary procedures to the officials in

the North East who had been corrupt. It was then agreed between CCTV, Party Centre and the Provincial authorities that the programme would be transmitted but that it would show that the situation had been put right and the corrupt officials punished.

(Zao Hungwen)[4]

Reports sometimes touch upon puissant or wealthy people who in the very recent past were untouchable although it is said that 'such targets can only be addressed if it suits the highest echelons' (Fang Chih). For example, there was an investigation of poor or false diagnoses and muddle in the Luoyang Health Service. We saw the reporter marching to and fro to get embarrassed excuses from doctors and administrators – we saw several victims and heard their stories. Finally the reporter got to the high official responsible and interrogated him quite roughly. On another occasion, a senior industrial manager who had killed bicyclists while driving his car and then got his corporation to bribe witnesses and the police for a cover-up was exposed. Police have been filmed beating up a camera crew which had been filming them accepting bribes; developers with good connections who illegally developed public land have been exposed; milk price fluctuations in Shanghai have been analysed to understand who profits; local government corruption, construction safety, official malpractice in home purchase, the quality of education in some areas; student poverty and the effects of environmental pollution; all these have been covered, and many more.

From such illustrations we understand what Chinese journalists mean when they talk of 'investigative journalism'. Although the term is disputed everywhere, perhaps nowhere more so than the UK, there is begrudged common ground that, to be termed 'investigative', journalism usually involves extensive research by one or more journalists to uncover matters which affect the citizenry of the society in which the journalist lives and of which the society generally does not approve but is unaware.[5] The Chinese journalists, just like the anglophone equivalents, are proud of 'revelation' about issues such as corruption on which they know the audience will side with them. Sometimes journalists are entrepreneurial in that they try to get the citizenry to care about matters of which they did not care; this might be the case with the environmental issues in China, or 'difficult'[6] subjects in the West such as the exploitation of foreign labour by western companies. The methods they use may be documentary research, espionage, subterfuge and sting. They are often controversial and expensive.

Garnham (2000: 84–5) has identified three ways of defining 'the specialists in symbolic production whom I will call intellectuals'. There is the definition of them as those whose power derives from what is sometimes called cultural capital; as those with a special position in the processing of information and finally as those representing 'a critical, emancipatory tradition appealing to universal values'. In anglophone society investigative journalists are described as the conscience of society, pointing out what is wrong in terms acceptable to that society, demanding that we care about it and commit to changing the situation (Protess *et al.* 1991), such that they illustrate Garnham's third definition of intellectuals.

In drama as in conversation, investigative journalists are depicted as fearless loners, the adversary of the powerful and those in authority over us when such authorities have let us down. As understood in anglophone countries – and to some extent in other European countries – it is a concept firmly based in the liberal vision of society as being for the benefit of its democratic members and in the discourse of individual responsibility and the individual conscience. Other kinds of journalists are interpreters of events and disseminators or information; *investigative* journalists are the *adversaries* in Weaver's taxonomy (1998). There are echoes of this in the way Chinese investigative journalists refer to themselves. A senior reporter from Shanghai explained some examples of his TV work in terms which suggested that he is very pleased at being able to subvert or out-smart officialdom:

> The second is my report of Shanghai's most devastating fire accident in more than 40 years . . . I took the risk of being punished for airing the story before getting the official approval, and my report was the quickest and most complete one among all the media coverage of the accident . . . the third is my report of a major regulation of the Chinese stock market imposed by the government, which produced significant impact on local people. When I was doing this news story, there were also strong official indications . . . that local people [should] not touch upon this issue to avoid any possible risk of local turmoil.[7]

Investigative journalism as parable

In a study of reports from *Focal Point*, Hua Xu finds that they have 'taken on the characteristics of tabloid journalism' identified by Briller (1993):

> we see many magazine shows model themselves after the morality play, in which the characters, presented as embodiment of good or evil, serve as tools of moral lessons. In many of these programs, there is a corrupted official devouring public funds; a local cadre bullying villagers; a wicked merchant cheating customers; or a devoted daughter supporting sick parents; or an abused wife getting rescued . . . it seems that television, as an embodiment of justice, has acquired the power of watching over the indecent and assuming a standard of right and wrong, thus to a certain extent manages to provide the masses with a means of accountability in an age of disillusion and ideological crisis in China.
>
> (Hua 2000: 19)

Hua's study suggests that investigative journalism is ritual in the familiar sense of a set of recurring rule-governed practices, of symbolic significance for a particular society. In performing this ritual, the investigative journalist also promotes certain myths about society, relations of power and citizenship, images of China and its constituent parts and of course the 'northern narrative'[8] as an all-embracing explanation of China's current predicament and future position. Some illustrations: environment stories tell us that good Chinese do not pollute; stories which, typically, exclude peasants, women and the young from being anything more than scenery, reinforce the belief that males over 40 matter more; prominence given to competent Mandarin speakers marginalizes the hundreds of millions who are not, and so forth. These are messages which are perhaps more enduring than the facts of the particular story being told.

To say this is not necessarily to negate the critical function of a story which shows corrupt officials getting their come-uppance; nor does it render worthless the idea, hinted at earlier, that journalists see themselves as, and to some extent are, using the rhetoric of revelation and exposure, sensationalism and prurience, to establish a consensus of what is acceptable or not.[9] The audience is being constructed as engaged, patriotic and moral on terms laid down by the mediators. However, there is a process of interaction: the world is framed, ordered and named by the mediators, but even as the inquiries of the investigative journalists legitimate certain attitudes and behaviours so they stimulate response.

The process changes or reinforces aspects of national identity in the manner described by Scannell, writing of the British context.[10] It introduces new expectations of what it is to be Chinese, a businessman or woman, an official, a citizen. Some people are excluded: those who do not speak good Mandarin; the marginalized; non-Chinese inhabitants of the PRC; unfortunates. Chinese current affairs TV, doubtless like its equivalents elsewhere, ritually condenses abstract ideas and reformulates them as 'facts' or 'actuality', creating models in the process.

The journalists they mention

When Chinese journalists today are asked which journalists they admire, the replies are various, perhaps according to the generation of the respondent and/or the circumstances of the conversation. Aside from mentioning some names on which no information is available, presumably 'local heroes', those journalists spoken to in more formal settings, who also chanced to be older, mentioned modern names such as Hu Jiwei (1916–), or, cast back into history, Shao Piaoping (1886–1926), Tsou Taofen (1889–1926), and early journalist-radicals such as Liang Qichao (1873–1929) and the founders of *New Youth*.

Shao and Tsou have much in common: they were persecuted journalists of the Nationalist period, who founded influential newspapers and have been incorporated posthumously into the Communist pantheon. Tsou appears to have been a proponent of civil rights who denounced abuses by the Nationalist Party and called for press freedoms well before he associated with the CCP (Wang 1997). Shao was a courageous investigative journalist who also worked hard to promote professionalism through his lectures at Peking University and textbooks. According to Li (1984), Shao 'believed in a free and independent press, with a public interest as its highest consideration. He argued that reporters should act as "a king without a crown" or a "fair minded judge" who took no sides.

"Truthfulness is the backbone of news, while human interest serves as flesh and blood", he wrote'. Interviewee Kang Keming also extolled Shao in such terms, and attempted to explain the expression 'king without a crown' as describing someone who has a position of power with neither glory nor responsibility.

In recent years, these names have all reappeared as models to emulate, so it is not surprising that they are called to mind. Whether they are admired because they stood up to government or because they stood up to the Nationalist government is a significant distinction. While this was rather unclear, it appears that it was the style of journalism, together with the fact that they were among the few names of past journalists they knew of, which made them suitable for citing! Another figure that is more controversial today and not obviously attractive to modern-minded journalists is Deng Tuo. Deng is nevertheless an interesting case which illustrates various points about Chinese journalism and which has also been the subject of some fine scholarship.

Deng Tuo

Deng Tuo was the first editor of *The People's Daily* after the CCP victory of 1949 and a founder of the All China Association of Journalists. After losing his editorship in 1966 he became Secretary for Culture and Education in the Peking Municipal Party Committee, which, among its other responsibilities, controlled the Peking-based universities. He was thus both journalist and administrator although he probably considered himself first and foremost a scholar, having published original literary and historical researches as well as essays, innumerable press articles and speeches. While one commentator has characterized Deng Tuo as a fighter who dared criticize Mao Zedong's capricious leadership (Leys 1971), his American biographer Cheek (1997) sees him as a conventional, if inspired and singularly able, intellectual. To him, Deng was a servant of the state in the Chinese tradition, adapting himself to a modern medium of service, namely journalism.

Thus his idea of the journalist was more complex than that of most of his fellow journalists abroad. The roles included that of the old scholar-gentry, viz culture bearer, transmitting and mediating knowledge and values and offering a context within which and with which the issues of the moment could be discussed and problems solved. The journalist was to be a pedagogue, striving to raise the cultural level of his compatriots. He was also to uphold orthodoxy. Being a propagator of orthodoxy is rather far from what most anglophone journalists believe in today, although it is possible that before the Second World War, they too would have taken pride in a similar role. In Britain, both leading politics scholars (Kedourie and Mango 1988) and senior editors (Page 1998: 46) have recently questioned whether critical or investigative journalism is indeed what journalists should be about.

Deng was an integral part of the system which, in time, he was to criticize. He always advocated supervision of the executive by 'the masses' and saw one of the important roles of the media as the vehicle by which this supervision should be effected. He also believed that journalists themselves must speak truth to power and did so in 'veiled criticisms' in *The People's Daily* in 1957 after the disaster of the Great Leap Forward (Cheek 1997: 172). Mao took offence and insulted and humiliated him, a precursor of the kind of treatment that would be the lot of all Mao's opponents in the mid-1960s.[11]

Nevertheless, in March 1961, Deng began to publish a series of essays in the *Peking Evening News* called 'Evening chats at Yanshan', followed in October by 'Notes from a three family village', mentioned on page 57, for their significance in the genesis of the Cultural Revolution. These grew out of investigation into local conditions and revealed that the policy of 'People's Communes' was causing the most appalling dislocation and misery in the countryside. Deng and his supporters were asserting their right to be more than cogs in the Great Helmsman's machinery (Cheek 1997: 267).

Retribution was so savage during the Cultural Revolution that Deng took his own life in May 1966 rather than suffer the abuses being vented on others, and perhaps in the hope of saving his family and associates.[12] In 1979 he was rehabilitated posthumously and all his works were thereafter republished as well as many hagiographic articles. He has been held up for emulation by journals aimed at young journalists.[13] Yet whether Deng is a plausible model for today's journalists is open to question. His was probably the last generation to have a high level of classical culture; the relationship of the intellectual to the state has changed and there is a cynicism about the Party which Deng would have found shocking.

Zhou Zuoren

Younger journalists were, if anything, even more hesitant to name fellow professionals as admirable. Only one gave a name from a past generation and, since it was that of Zhou Zuoren, the interviewer assumed the reference to be ironical. Zhou, a writer not immediately associated with current conceptions of journalism, was editor of *Tatler* until 1927 (Pollard 1973: 333). But he is remembered more as a writer of erudite essays, as the scholarly brother of China's 'greatest modern writer', Lu Xun, and as someone who became more and more aloof from the concerns of the activists of his generation and, eventually, a collaborator in the loathed Japanese occupation.

What can we make of a journalist in his twenties citing this man, whose very name was anathema in the PRC until recently and whose works have only just been republished, as an admired journalist? It may be connected with the fact that not long before there had been a big article about Zhou in a literary magazine.

By contrast with the urge to modernity, rejection of Chinese tradition and abstractionism of the May 4 outlook, he proposed that China should look within itself for sources of change and development. He rejected what he regarded as the assumption of many of his contemporaries, that Chinese civilization was inferior; his alternative to the dominant discourse was not another kind of nationalism such as today appeals to some of the 'neo-conservative' intellectuals. Zhou rejected both the totalizing, nationalistic ideologies of the Nationalists and the CCP, which he probably regarded as almost interchangeable. Daruvala (2000: 219–220) states that Zhou is associated with 'a criticism of the notion that there is a homogenous definition of what it is to be Chinese and a rejection of the demand that self cultivation must benefit the state'. He opposed 'education on national humiliation' which became a staple of both Nationalist and CCP schooling and can be argued to have had a poisonous effect upon China's relations with other peoples. His construction of Chinese civilization was one made up of diverse localities, traditions and individuals, welcoming to outside influences, with its own resources for self-criticism. He rejected the assumption that the present is always superior to the past, the western to the Chinese.

In this connection it is relevant that the interviewee who cited Zhou also made the remark that journalists from his area (Shaoxing)[14] were limited in their range of expression by being obliged to voice reports and write articles in Mandarin, in effect their second language. Although he drew the line at agreeing that other Chinese languages ('dialects') should be made official, he nevertheless implicitly drew attention to the injustice of the totalizing tendency[15] and demonstrated that his localist views of culture coincided with those of Zhou. He might not go as far as Friedman (1995) who suggests that the homogenizing thrust of the CCP has disintegrated and that many, if not most, people outside the CCP now reject the centralizing cultural tendencies just as they do the 'northern narrative'.[16] Be that as it may, the initial assumption of the writer when confronted by the name of Zhou Zuoren as a 'model journalist' that the interviewee was being ironical was almost certainly wrong. He was cited because he stands for an alternative, and a very radical one too.

Two other names were also mentioned, and without irony. Citation of Dai Qing, associated particularly with criticism of the Three Gorges Project (see p. 115), was not qualified; however, Liu Binyan (1927–) seemed to be disparaged.[17]

Liu Binyan

Liu is involved in a New York-based organization for promoting press freedom and human rights in China, and is usually referred to in the West as a 'heroic investigative journalist'. Under the patronage of his editor Hu Yaobang,[18] Liu first published exposures of bureaucratic incompetence in 1956, as well as a now famous story about RCPs and how the life of a young journalist is blighted by the fact that though she investigates honestly she finds always that her work is only used in RCPs and ends up ignored in some obscure filing cabinet. In *News from Inside the Paper*, reporter Huang wants to reveal the reality of a coal mine but is pressured to depict it in a manner approved by the Party, far from the reality she observes. Huang's application to join the CCP is judged according to her willingness to conform, so that her urge to be truthful will prevent her from obtaining membership of the CCP. Another typical tale tells of a man who fakes being deaf and dumb so that he does not have to participate in any meetings or worry about any official work. The moral of the story is that only those who close themselves off from all around them can survive in such a society.

Criticized by the left, Liu was expelled from the Party in 1957 and sent to labour reform in the countryside, returning to his original employer, *China Youth Daily*, only to be arrested in 1969 as a 'rightist' (Goldfein 1989). Rehabilitated in 1979 and given a post on *The People's Daily*, he wrote his most arresting work, *Between Men and Monsters*, which exposed in detail a case in which an enterprising woman had come to involve in corruption a vast network of managers, businesses and officials right up to national level. These are scandals comparable to those unearthed by Lincoln Steffens in the USA at the turn of the century (Ekirch 1974: 92) and by Ray Fitzwalter in the UK of the 1970s (Fitzwalter 1981) and it is interesting to compare the treatments. Whereas the anglophone journalists are factual in the approved social science manner of their times, Liu resorts to fiction, or at least faction, to point to abuses.

In 1985, Liu appeared to have gone too far when he published *The Second Kind of Loyalty*, the story of a minor official who, moved by his allegiance to the Party, unceasingly denounced corruption in its ranks, a contrast with the Party's model of blind obedience, Lei Feng. This story infuriated influential people and Liu was forbidden to write for *The People's Daily* for a period. Discussion of him polarized and his appearances became controversial, with the intellectuals on the whole admiring him. Liu was associated with dissidents for the first time in March 1989 when he signed the petition for the release of Wei Jingshen, who had been imprisoned by direct personal command of Deng Xiaoping. Out of the country at the time of the Tiananmen massacre, he was placed on a wanted list by the government, did not return and later joined those dissidents who had fled, in denouncing the government. His experience provokes some reflections, first on his œuvre and its methods, second, on what he represents.

Journalists are not often judged by their œuvre in anglophone countries since with a few exceptions, the components of their achievement are quickly forgotten. They tend to be remembered for the books they later wrote or as the editors they became. Anglophone journalists comparable to Liu in this sense might be Phillip Knightley, John Pilger and Seymour Hersch. Although Knightley is associated with his recent books he is also known for his œuvre in that the stories he worked on were so important, and still tell us so much about the societies he worked in, that they have remained topical, 'Thalidomide' and 'Vestey' in particular (de Burgh 2000: 50, 205).

Liu Binyan could not write his investigations in the evidential mode allowed to the anglophone. He wrote them as fictionalized reports, or, as Liu would have them 'social realism' or 'reportage literature' not too far from what Wolfe, Mailer and Capote aimed for in the 1960s. His stories demonstrate the failure of idealism, the ease with which the systems can be subverted, how the high-minded are sidelined or persecuted and the perverting influence of ideology.

On the face of it we might imagine that Liu would be the nearest to a hero that modern journalists exercised by freedom and rights could have. When questioned on their attitude to him, respondents referred to him as 'old-fashioned' or 'a Party member'. They assign to him a belief in the Party that they consider he has never outgrown (although perhaps he now has) and which they, feeling superior in doing so, have rejected. Duke has suggested that his limitation has been that he never criticized the system as a whole or drew the conclusion that seems implicit in his work, that the main obstacle to progress is the CCP itself (Duke 1985: 122). Perhaps it is this, possibly unfair and outdated judgement,[19] which diminishes Liu in the eyes of a type of journalist who is sceptical of authority's good intentions or competence.

To try to understand his ideals, it is now appropriate to examine the references made to two historical figures, Qu Yuan and Hai Ru.

The journalist as the good official

> We don't know any heroes! Well, its just my opinion, but I think that journalists very much admire Qu Yuan. Maybe they think they are Qu Yuan! Do you know Qu Yuan? He was an official who told the truth to the Emperor.
>
> (Tang Musan)

It sometimes appears as if foreign ignorance and CCP propaganda have conspired to present imperial China as a totalitarian society with neither light nor shade. In fact CCP rule constitutes a despotic departure from a system much more benign than usually credited, even when it lacked some of the institutions and liberties which are now thought of as essential elements of a civilized polity (see Leys 1983).

In traditional society, in place of representation, the *petition* was an institutionalized channel for the expression of dissent and by the time of the Sung (960–1280) petitioning, by students in particular, had become traditional. There was a unit of government concerned to investigate and take action over abuses, often identified through petitions, called the Censorate. It was the Censor's task to make administration conform to moral precept without fear or favour and, in the stories and saws that were the common currency of all Chinese, there are many cases of upright scholars, who were not necessarily designated censors, acting in this role.

No less than other countries China has mythical figures who in some manner express certain values of the culture and that of the 'Thomas More' figure who stands for service to absolute values at the risk of his own self interest is a particularly emotive one.[20] Since there was no immunity guaranteed for this role, the critic's success or even survival depended upon the whim of those in power who might, or might not, honour the code which justified criticism on the grounds of respect for, and obedience to, the real interests of the hierarch, as described in the canons:

> If a man has a good friend to resist him in doing bad actions, he will have his reputation preserved; so if a father has a son to resist his wrong commands,

he will be saved from committing serious faults. When the command is wrong, a son should resist his father, and a minister should resist his august master. The maxim is: 'resist when wrongly commanded'. Hence how can he be called filial who obeys his father when he is commanded to do wrong?

(*The Canon of Filial Piety*, Section XV)[21]

Such sentiments were part of the warp and woof of the life of most Chinese until very recent times. The historical Qu Yuan, the figure mentioned by Liu Chao, employed his poetry for remonstrance. He lived in the Kingdom of Chu 338–278 BC. His example has been cited from as early as the Han Dynasty (206 BC–AD 220) to the CCP–Nationalist polemics of the 1930s. In the Sung Dynasty

Officials frequently criticized the Emperor for issuing orders bypassing the Prime Office, which had the authority to check all imperial orders for improprieties and impracticalities. In one protest against this irregular practice, a memorial written by Liu Fu around 1270, the emperor was sternly told that 'The affairs of the Empire ought to be carried out together with the empire; the ruler cannot regard them as his private concern'.

(Metzger 1977: 182–184)

It was a 1960s controversy over the correct interpretation of how the Ming Dynasty (1368–1644) official Hai Rui had related to his Emperor that would spark off the Cultural Revolution (see page 57). During the early Qing (1644–1911) many literati proved their loyalty to a moral authority higher than that of those who composed the government by rejecting office under the new dynasty and remaining constant to the overthrown Ming. This was notwithstanding the fact that the Qing adopted all Confucian roles, rituals and examinations, which might be thought would placate the orthodox. As a young man Mao Zedong was to join a study group devoted to eulogizing a loyalist scholar who had lived a life of resistance to imperial authority out of fealty to the Ming.

In other words, the impartial official who speaks, without fear or favour, for the moral order is a stock figure in the Chinese world order. There is Judge Bao Qingtian of the Sung Dynasty, legendary for his even-handedness and Judge Di (upon whom Robert van Gulik based his *Judge Dee* mystery novels) noted for the scrupulousness of his investigations. The memory of Shang Yang (*c.* 361–338 BC) moved Prime Minister Zhu Rongji to tears in 1996 when he attended a play about him. Shang Yang was a great administrator of the Warring States period. Not in the same mould as the popular hero-officials, he is more of a model for prime ministers than for journalists. He served the Qin by centralizing power and eliminating the privileges of the nobility and is attributed with the desire to establish the rule of law over that of faction or favourite. He fell foul of the ruler on account of that very impartial strictness which had first been his attraction and symbolizes the statesman who serves the long-term interests of China rather than the fleeting policies of her temporary custodians.

China also has its equivalents to the Andreas Hofer / Salvatore Giuliano / Robin Hood popular hero of the European tradition.[22] Storytellers in China have always liked tales of the noble-minded and courageous men who are forced to step outside the established order to fight unjust officials. Romantic tales of this kind are the core of some of the most famous Chinese historical novels and operas, such as *The Water Margin* and *The Romance of the Three Kingdoms*. It has often been noticed that Mao Zedong was inspired by these two sagas.

Qu Yuan

Of all the dissidents made heroes the most popular is Qu Yuan, particularly Chinese in his yearnings to be 'part of the establishment' and despite the fact that he is different in class to the swashbucklers. His myth is suffused throughout popular as well as high culture. From the Dragon Boat races to foodstuffs throughout China, references to him in popular culture can hardly be escaped. What does he represent?

The historical information is limited. During the Warring States period (403– 221 BC) Qu Yuan (338–278 BC) was an official who fell foul of court intrigues, was forced to retire from public life despite and because of his high sense of duty and, passionately committed to the mission he was prevented from carrying out, eventually killed himself in despair. The Chinese have empathized with him ever since.

Notwithstanding the dearth of historical facts, there are countless books, poems, paintings and theatrical works in the high-culture tradition dealing with Qu Yuan as well as innumerable manifestations of his story in popular culture. Literati of later periods, who felt their own predicaments most expressed by the myth, reinterpreted it with emphases differing according to the age and the need. However, the constant themes are that misfortunes are bound to attend the conscientious public servant (Schneider 1980: 5) and that regret is the lot of the man debarred from serving his chosen master. In the first thousand years of the myth, it was usually the 'loyalty' which was the most prominent characteristic. By the Ming period it was the 'ardour' or enthusiasm of the man which was inspiring; he was being seen as an uncompromising spirit dedicated to absolute values regardless of mere mundane success.[23] He can be distinguished from other kinds of resisters. There are the poets who refused office lest they compromise their principles, such as Li Po; there is Yueh Fei who died in 1141 because he opposed a policy he thought would harm his state; there are those who would have no truck with the Manchus out of loyalty to the Ming. Qu Yuan shares with them a steadfastness to values and he is the most universally seen as symbolic of principled public service.

Early in the twentieth century, while other semi-mythic figures were rejected by reformist intellectuals in their attempts to 'modernize thinking', Qu Yuan was not. European romanticism was influential, following translations of Goethe and Byron,[24] and Qu Yuan was reinvented as a 'moral individual struggling within the immoral society'. This Qu Yuan was attractive to Liang Qichao, to the founders of the CCP Chen Duxiu and Li Dachao and to the foremost fiction writer Lu Xun (Schneider 1980 Chapter 3). He became interpreted as iconoclast and revolutionary, particularly after another of the leading writers and scholars of the period, Guo Moruo, staged his play *Ch'u Yuan* (Guo [1942] 1978). Guo made him an associate of the common people and a moral leader excluded from power rather than a 'loyal minister'. He has him say:

> I can look upon death without flinching. Which of us is right and which is wrong, which loyal and which treacherous, will be judged by future genera-tions. What you have plotted against is not me but our kingdom, all China!
>
> (Guo [1942] 1978: 44)

When journalists suggest that they are standing up for principles, for the people, this is the cynosure they may have in mind. In the anglophone myth, exemplified by Gray Grantham in *The Pelican Brief* (Grisham 1998), the journalist is among others a lone wolf, fighting evil with his conscience alone. Despite the romantic gloss given to Qu, he is not really an outsider, but remains a Mandarin. His dramatist, the radical young Guo Mojuo, became the old politician and dignit-ary who surely saw himself as re-establishing authority and orthodoxy.[25] The difference is great.

The journalist's journalist

The Chinese journalist's image of the journalist appears to be made up of a mixture of ideas and myths. There is the discourse of the intrepid investigator of rights and wrongs, the 'Tintin' journalist, often regarded as 'American' or 'Anglo-Saxon'. Then there is the ideal of the good public servant who risks his all in his duty to the Chinese state and thereby joins the pantheon of the righteous, with Qu Yuan at the pinnacle. Expressions used by interviewees of no matter what gender, age or seniority, appear to reflect the power of this ideal. Between humdrum daily life and these archetypes are some human-size models, journal-ists who clearly tried to be faithful in accordance with their ideals and suffered for them – Deng Tuo, Liu Binyan, Dai Qing. However, most journalists live in the world as it is constructed for them by their political masters, and probably jog along as best they can, accepting the perks of the job, fitting in with the spin doctors and propagandists, ducking the risky opportunities to anger the bosses but still imagining themselves to belong to the congregation of the faithful.

Barmé (1999) shows how the Chinese intellectual today is co-opted by the state because of his or her usefulness in pointing out problems, sketching possible futures and providing the ideas of which the ruling officials are so bereft. But the fact of co-option does not necessarily negate the subversive function. According to one TV producer, she sees the programme on which she works *Tell it like it is*[26] as attacking conformism. She seeks to 'train people into thinking as individuals' to encourage people 'to speak out, tell the truth and express their opinions' (Gordon 2000: 17).

Others go further:

> the main duty of the media in China should [be to] draw more attention
> to frustrations, not only in education, entertainment and information, but
> extinguishing corruption, establishing public confidence in the government
> and turning democracy into reality. It is a revolution, and the motivator of
> this storm is the public.
>
> (Kang Keming)

A century or more ago Chinese journalism began to develop as a response to the
collapse of traditional China and the challenge of the West. Journalists tended to
be activists and used the press as one medium among others, such as teaching or
literature, to alert compatriots to new ideas, new dangers, new opportunities.[27]
So Kang's apparently radical manifesto is squarely within that tradition.

Journalism and public policy

Asked whether journalism today has any influence upon government and government policies the Chinese journalists' answers, taken overall, were ambiguous
and perhaps reflect their unsettled position in the polity. However there was in
one or two cases a desire to deny any clear influence, in exactly the manner of
BBC current affairs journalists.[28]

> Journalism should not have a direct influence upon government. We are not
> a law enforcement agency, an executive. We are merely providing public
> scrutiny; we find the appeal in a topic. It's possible that as a result of our
> alighting upon that topic a good solution will result such as a new regulation
> or law. This may occur, but it's not our responsibility to make it so. After a
> report with which we have created awareness of some improper phenom-
> enon this may attract attention from both audience and government such
> that the matter is dealt with.
>   It is not our function to solve problems but to cast an impartial eye over
> problems. Nor is it our function to get you to go and solve the problem,
> there are appropriate agencies for that.
>
> (Lu Cihui)

Li Feishi is more concrete:

> We do not have specific programmes on, say, housing policy, but if after a
> government policy comes into effect, people have doubts or an interest in
> exploring aspects, then we do it. We cover every area of interest or rel-
> evance to ordinary people. We have the responsibility of looking at all
> matters touching ordinary people.

On page 111, we examined the concept of 'public scrutiny' or *yulunjiandu*, which
seems to encapsulate the idea of social responsibility. In the past Party and state

decided what was bad or good; today journalists, in their scrutiny, appear to believe that they are applying their own professional norms or even 'universal' moral laws.

> Actions contrary to ethics should be dealt with and make good programmes. For example, a family in which the parents do not treat the children or an old person in accordance with ethics . . . in accordance with the precepts of the Confucian Canon of Filial Piety [should be reported]. That is an important topic.
>
> (Tang Musan)

The equivalent elsewhere might be a reporter on regional television who argues that news stories should be about breaches of the Ten Commandments.

In the national arena, one very senior journalist made another rather startling claim. He, on his own responsibility, made a moral decision whose results equate with that of Watergate in the USA. The interesting aspect of the claim is less its plausibility than the fact that it was made:

> I was at the *Guangming Daily*[29] and I published an article, or rather I organized its publication. [It argued that] the sole criterion of truth should be practice. We shouldn't care who had an idea, only whether it works. Now I was general editor and I had not had Chairman Hua's endorsement for this article even though it implicitly criticized the *Two Whatevers* [policy, i.e., whatever Chairman Mao did, or said, was right] and proposed the empirical criterion. It opened up a great debate as to whether the criterion of truth should be practice or authority. The situation got complex; Hua criticized *Guangming Daily*, didn't want to allow the debate, but Deng Xiaoping was very supportive. He wasn't in power, he'd been sacked by Mao, but the upshot of the whole affair was that Hua fell. Now this case is not exactly like Nixon's Watergate and yet [the fall of Chairman Hua] was precipitated by my *Guangming Daily* article which aroused Hua's opposition and stimulated Deng's support.
>
> (Wang Qianghua)

In sum, the journalists may see themselves as a kind of moral police to society, making decisions as to where are the boundaries they must patrol – and what should be on the agenda.

11 Making news: a case study

This chapter is a case study reporting an examination of Chinese regional television news packages to find out what congruence there might be between the declared beliefs of the reporters about their work, and the reports they produce each day.

Chinese television reporters from Hangzhou were interviewed, and a month of their news product examined. From the interviews it emerged that they see themselves as scrutinizing government, representing the people to the government and vice versa. From the analysis of their product it appeared that they are mere transmitters of the political line of the government and of the cultural prejudices of their masters. In being so contradictory they reflect an ambivalence in Chinese society as a whole, where market individualism coexists with political author-itarianism. These journalists believe they have social responsibilities but, to an outside observer, cannot fulfil them while making news. Examining their product in the light of their declarations points up the great gulf which separates their aspirations from their practices.

The reasons for the case study

How news is constituted and what cultural and political significance it has is a well-established theme of enquiry. There are, however, relatively few studies of non-anglophone countries. This chapter reports an examination of regional television news packages from Hangzhou to find out what congruence there might be between the declared beliefs of the reporters about their work, and the reports they produce each day. Do the reports reflect their concerns? If not, why not and what do they reflect? What can the analysis of these reports tell us about television journalism in China today? Can we learn anything more general about Chinese society from them?

Here we concentrate exclusively on those components of the news programme which journalists refer to as *packages*, though on transmission they are called *reports*. This is an almost universal subgenre which in England takes the form of a personally authored report of between one and ten minutes long, commonly one minute thirty. As a way of examining television journalists and their work, alighting upon the package as a discrete unit of study is suitable because the text is individually authored (the reporter's name is announced); it forms a very important element of the whole news programme; it is a recognized construction, success at which is a touchstone of a reporters' ability; it is of manageable size and has its own identifiable grammar.

After reporters' explanations[1] of their work had been heard, the product was recorded and examined in that light, following a method which had been piloted in Birmingham, England. The study of English regional television news was originally conceived simply as a pilot, but its findings are included here because the distinctness and cultural influences upon the Chinese journalists are identified more clearly when compared with a familiar equivalent. Indeed the import of the Chinese study, in terms of the very different focus of each news organization and the differently expressed attitudes to work as journalists, is not fully revealed unless the Birmingham findings are seen first; also, the application of the method in Birmingham prepares the reader for implementation in Hangzhou. On the whole, journalists regard their task as the reporting of reality, innocent of the scepticism with which such claims are viewed by academics who see their apprehension of reality as being heavily conditioned by many factors, visible and invisible and largely beyond their control.[2] At the other extreme, from journalists' naive explanations, news has been described as 'myth' (Bird 1988) and Zelizer (1993) describes news as 'stories told and retold' because they have cultural meanings that transcend the particular events of which they are reports.

> One of the most productive ways to see news is to consider it as myth, a standpoint that dissolves the distinction between entertainment and information. By this we do not mean to say that individual news stories are like myth and folklore. . . . Bascom (1954) in a classic statement on the functions of folklore, writes that it serves as education, as a validation of culture, as wish fulfilment, and as a force for conformity, while Malinowski (1974) considered myth to be a 'charter' for human culture. Through myth and folklore, members of a culture learn values, definitions of right and wrong, and sometimes can experience vicarious thrills – not all through individual tales, but through a body of lore.
>
> (Bird in Berkowitz 1997: 333–350)

This study follows a tradition of inquiry which has attempted to get beyond those limitations which sociologists have identified, and to understand the cultural framing within which they happen and from which news criteria emerge, an orientation which tends to see media as 'ritual' rather than 'transmission' (Carey 1975, 1998).

Many scholars[3] have contributed to our understanding of the cultural implications of news. Ettema and Glasser (1988) in a series of stimulating reflections upon journalism in the USA, also argued that (investigative journalists in particular) are telling stories to fit moral types. They write

> The task is accomplished by cueing the audience's response to these characters through the emplotting of events as recognizably moralistic stories and, more specifically, through the skilful use of such story elements as point of view, ironic detail and ritual denial.
>
> (Ettema and Glasser 1988)

Silverstone (1992: 22) asked the key question, as to what is the relationship, if any, between television's stories and the stories told in myths and folklore? The scope of this study is, more narrowly, to understand how television news reporters classify stories and to identify what kinds of general social myths these classifications might represent. When the term myth is used, it is employed in Barthes's sense, as a concept or 'chain of concepts widely accepted throughout a culture, by which its members conceptualize or understand a particular topic or part of their social experience' (O'Sullivan 1994: 286).

As to the subjects, most studies to date have dealt with journalists of a metropolitan elite (Tuchman 1972, Gans 1979, Schlesinger 1987, Porter 1992, Tunstall 1993). An equivalent in China might be the newsroom of China Central Television in Peking or the writers of *The People's Daily*. Although these journalists are influential, and possibly trend-setting, they are not typical.[4] Most Chinese journalists, like most UK journalists, work in regional and local television stations and are subject to commercial and local pressures which mark them out from the journalists of the metropolitan elite. I therefore decided to study the work of regional television reporters.

With a population of 1.72 million, Hangzhou is capital to a province of over 44 million.[5] It is one of China's richest agricultural areas and the media of Hangzhou are wealthy and various. At least forty television channels can be received and there are ten transmitting stations in the city, many of which are received throughout the province. One of the two principal television stations is Zhejiang television, housed in a large complex in the centre of the city, along with Qianjiang television. They are both funded by commercial advertisements and sponsorship. They are extremely well equipped with the latest digital technology.

The pilot was conducted in Birmingham, which has a population of 1 million and is the second largest city of the UK as well as capital of the industrial West Midlands. It has been an industrial centre since the sixteenth century. Central Broadcasting is based there but its franchise covers a quarter of England with a population of nearly 9 million.[6] The conditions of the franchise require that Central supply certain types of programmes, in particular regional programmes and news, although the core schedule, as with other television regions, is provided by the Network Centre to which Central is a substantial contributor of programmes. Central competes locally with the West Midlands BBC, limited cable penetration and with satellite subscription channels.

The pilot

Among the questions asked of journalists in Birmingham was 'what makes a good story?' and 'for what kind of story are you looking?' It was soon clear that it was not the subject for which they were looking – whether politics, economics, sport, local affairs, consumer – so much as a particular *type* of story. They were then asked to recall the best stories.

The journalists remembered very few triumphs and almost no failures. It's as if they lived only for the day – a parody of the news journalist which is almost too much of a stereotype! Those stories they remember as good have certain characteristics (apart from memorability), which are that they are 'visually exciting', 'unusual', something which 'makes 'em sit up' and have 'plenty of action'.

When asked for examples of 'really good' stories only one interviewee – the controller – answered instantly. Aside from the features editor, who suggested some of his own recent ones, the others had to think quite hard; most found it difficult to remember any before the current week (indeed three of the nine stories cited – out of all the thousand odd stories a year – were from that week); three offered none, even after much prevarication. Nobody suggested that any distinction need be made between 'hard' and 'soft' in assessing a story's 'goodness'. Those that were mentioned were:

1   Rebuilding a family after tragedy
    'A couple which lost all 4 children in house fire ... 3/4 years later it emerged *via* [reporter] Sandy Barton who gained mum's trust having got to know them well that mum now couldn't have children ... she adopted a baby ... we told the story and then viewers sent in money for IVF treatment ... we broke the story today that they'd had twins. The story had everything: hard news; overcoming tragedy; warm-hearted viewers; struggle against all odds.'

2   Second Handsworth riots – it was very exciting [Handsworth is a district of the city which suffered fierce inter-ethnic violence]

3   The Rackhams slasher attack [Rackhams is a well-known shop in which an assault took place shortly before the interviews]
    'It was terrific – why is it a good story? It was just before Xmas; random attack; amok with knife; attacking blonde women; good eyewitnesses; pix of arrest; human drama and we've captured it!'

4   M40 [a motorway between London and the Midlands] children minibus accident
    'Whole programme devoted to it, we handled it really well – school praised us for not intruding'.

5   'A story about a shark being moved – the pictures were very good'.

6   'The cat on crutches – a wonderful story'.

7   'When the police started using Rottweilers ... we got a sweet blonde girl to come in and stroke the police Rottweiler' [this was one of this week's stories; the reference to Rottweilers, a breed of savage dog, refers

to a contemporary debate as to whether the breed should be prohibited after several cases of Rottweilers savaging children]

8   'What's an example of a good story? Now take the [girl accused of murdering her boyfriend, now on trial] story, that's good because she's such a f***ing slapper ... she looks the part so everybody makes prejudicial assumptions about her ... they'll say its obvious she's guilty ... she's the one in the corner of the pub having a fag and a gin at 11.30 in the morning, she just looks the part, guilty as f*** ... so its obviously a picture story ... good fun, strip off the voice and you just know what's going on ... dyed blonde hair, dazed by drugs ... she's in real trouble ... whether she's found guilty or innocent she's going to sell her story ... its got crime dokko-drama written all over it ...'

9   The Controller of News was the only interviewee who instantly supplied an example – the story of the rescue of a lost yachtsman [Bullimore]. He said 'it had everything: man alone; search; fading hopes; joyous resolution'.

Story classifications emerging from the interviews

On the whole the journalists interviewed found it difficult to classify stories, or to accept the probe that they might subconsciously look for certain elements in an event that might lend themselves to a particular kind of story. However, after initial resistance they did, almost all, propose a number of story types. They were stories which have the 'aah! factor' or make the viewer say 'wow!'; that are 'quirky'; that are 'fun'; that show a 'little man battling against odds'; that 'tug at the heart, or heartstrings'; that evoke human sympathy; that show 'the people versus the big boys'; that demonstrate that 'all is well'. Favourite topics include health ('everyone thinks they might get ill'); disaster (but its alright, the 'authorities are tackling it'); progress or new inventions and developments; the other ('aren't those foreigners quaint'); enterprising unfortunates; revisiting the scene of a tragedy; 'wickedness come to judgement' and 'untoward events'.

These categories are very similar to those identified in other studies, for example Langer (1998). I have refined them down into a smaller number of types as it seemed there is overlap. They are listed below with a brief explanation drawn from the conversations with the journalists.

'Wow! stories' (aka 'Aha! stories' or 'skateboarding ducks')

This deals with something you couldn't dream up if you tried, it's so weird. It is definitely a 'down at the pub' story.

'Heartstrings'

This makes you feel empathy – sometimes with animals as well as people.

'What fun people we are'

Reminds us that we are good at enjoying life, that life is full of jolly characters, despite all the heartache.

'Our kind of folk'

Reminds us of our own identity, characteristics. May also include 'heritage' stories for even if the galleries and the National Trust palaces are only distantly relevant to the audience they are nevertheless among those things which define us as English or Midlanders or Brummies (Birmingham people).

'Adversity overcome'

An escape from danger: the boy wrongly imprisoned; the woman who fought to have a child . . . finally they have made it. Shows how pluck, determination and love win through in the end.

'Fight for rights'

The big people are always trying to put us down – but we get off our butts and fight back, don't we? Community action fits here.

'All is well; mankind advances'

Terrible things happen, but thanks to the public spirit of those in authority, the ingenuity of our technical people and boffins and the heroism of our (young) guardians, we need not fear. Our belief in progress is reaffirmed.

'Wrongdoers cannot escape; the law is our trusty shield'

Court stories are there to reassure us that good, the community, will triumph and that (despite the Birmingham 6 or the Bridgwater 3 – celebrated cases of the miscarriage of justice) there is justice. Bent coppers will always be found out in the end. Crime stories, where the crimes are not solved, are used in the same way because authority is invariably seen handling the matter methodically and reassuringly.

Many, perhaps most, stories fall into more than one category. Moreover, while the initial event, the raw material, is seen to promise desired elements (e.g., 'heartstrings') the treatment of the story will determine exactly which elements are to be most emphasized. Thus a story about a dog which had been maltreated could have been angled on catching the culprits who abused pets and would have therefore been predominantly a 'wrongdoers cannot escape' kind of story; in the event it was a 'heartstrings' because it was useful as such.

In sum, the stories can be classified and the classifications derived from the journalists themselves. The impetus at Central is to put human interest stories first because they are 'what people want' and 'more memorable'. The journalists believe that this is their function and that the criteria by which they must be judged are simply those of 'good practice' and 'bad practice' in carrying out these professional tasks.

The journalists, having themselves classified the types of story for which they were looking, with the help of the interviewer, the next task was to look at the news they produced to see whether the classifications could be applied, without undue distortion. They could. Of a week's product, a total of 45 packages, the biggest single category was 'All is well', which included 11 stories.

Table 11.1 Story types classified

Type (signified)	Number of incidences	Ranking
All is well	11	1
Our kind of folk	7	2
Wow!	6	3=
Fight for rights	6	3=
Heartstrings	5	4
Adversity overcome	4	5=
What fun	4	5=
Wrongdoers/law	3	6

Note: Some stories fit into more than one category; some fit into none.

Governing themes or myths ('signification')[7]

Interpreting the story classification, attempting to connect it with a signification in the manner of Barthes (1972), is necessarily subjective and open to dispute; however, when the similar product of two different cultures is looked at together, the different significations really do leap out.

Myth of progress

The most prominent myth, despite the fact that the English are often thought of as harking backwards to past glories, is the myth of progress. It can be explained in this way: although there are accidents and although there is dark in society, thanks to the public spiritedness of those in authority we need not fear. Moreover the scientific and technical people are solving everything and making everything better.

Myth of distinction

The second myth might be called the myth of distinction. Every society defines itself by certain, doubtless changeable, characteristics, and has a myth about being distinct from other societies. There is a kind of television story, just as there are kinds of behaviour and conversation, which mark out that identity, reminds us who 'our kind of folk' are. Thus a story about a great Chinese artist reminds Chinese viewers of their identity and one about the Birmingham art gallery does the same for English people (from Birmingham). This role is even more clear in Chinese thanks to the use of expressions such as 'our country', 'we Chinese' and 'foreigners' (literally: 'outsiders') repeatedly through such reports. However, although the English do not use such expressions very often, there appear to be more of these kinds of packages in the English sample.

Myth of individualism

The myth of individualism seems to pervade the stories which have been classified as 'fight for rights' and 'adversity overcome'. This myth tells us that we live in a society where we can achieve a lot if we struggle. Entrepreneurs are not much in evidence, but individuals, who have struggled against all odds to have their plight recognized or to overcome a disadvantage, are.

Myth of common humanity

'Heartstrings' and 'what fun' are categories which serve to remind us of our common humanity – which reflect a myth that what we share is more than what divides us. We are all alike really, rubbing along despite life's difficulties, and we can take pleasure in bits of fun to bring us together.

Myth of benign authority

Finally we have the myth of benign authority or public spirit. Crimes happen, even crimes by people in authority. But in the end we can take comfort from the fact that the system works. Authorities handle these matters reassuringly. The implication seems to be: aren't we lucky we are not like foreigners? It may be the case that this is particularly a regional television, rather than a national television, phenomenon.

The Hangzhou study

In China the examination of news reports was also preceded by interviews which, among other things, attempted to establish what journalists were looking for in a story. However, the Chinese television reporters who were interviewed consider that they have very little discretion in the selection of stories. They all veered away from discussing the news almost immediately and talked about the kind of stories which (it became clear) were only rarely included in the news, although they might well be included in current affairs magazines.

Had the researcher simply reported what the journalists told him they looked for and produced, without actually viewing their product, he would have had a completely wrong understanding of the daily work of television news reporters.

At this point it is necessary to note that there are two main types of work undertaken by television journalists in China today, the news[8] programmes and '*shendu baodao*' which can be translated as 'current affairs' in the English sense or 'in-depth reports' more literally. Journalists, it appeared, avoided acknowledging their input into straight news because they felt that the work with which they wished to be associated was better represented by current affairs. Many stations now have current affairs programmes which offer documentary features and investigative stories and it was these investigative stories that they wished to tell the interviewer about.[9]

When pressed to discuss the best stories, the journalists classified them as revealing difficulties such as corruption: 'viewers like to see corruption dealt with, very much', 'unhealthy social phenomena', disasters and 'catastrophes'; stories which 'show how problems are solved', which 'provide information of immediate use (e.g. – 'road construction in a vicinity and when it will start and finish'); stories with attractive pictures, which are informative, thought provoking and explanatory of the essence and the processes of society; stories which show 'how economic development is working' and which demonstrate 'help from one community to another'.

These categories are expressed differently from the English journalists, who appear to be seeking more explicitly for a certain impact rather than for coverage of particular topics. No English journalist said, for example, that s/he was looking to cover economic development. This might have been the case twenty years ago, though that is another question.

Examples (paraphrases from the interviews)

1   Residents in an area cannot get their gas supplies properly attended to, so they come to us, we make a report and the problem is solved.
2   Things that people care about . . . like interest rates and whether they are going up or down.
3   The story inside the news. For example, 'the Qianzheng Bridge was badly constructed. I reported on this and found that people wanted to know the whole saga of the investigation and court proceedings and the sequel, what punishment was meted out'.
4   The story of illegally prepared pork. 'People not only wanted to know of the event itself, but what the government was going to do about it.'
5   Issue of new banknotes; opening of a new park – these kind of items tend to come from the organizations responsible for them, they get sent in. But 'more and more most of our news probably derives from punters calling in'.

6 'My best ever story I did last year. From one of the letters that came into the newsroom I heard that a woman, incorrectly diagnosed by a fraudulent doctor as having a sexual disease, committed suicide. This brought out into the open that there were many unlicensed doctors being prosecuted in various parts of the province and this became an important running story. I was able to spin this out for ten more days and to be given nearly 15 minutes each day as the top-running story. For example – first day introduction, second day I went to the hospital to interview patients, third day to the prosecution office, fourth day to the accused to get them to tell me about their organization, etc'.

7 The Provincial Governor goes to visit big new company making an investment in our province. 'When we film this we show that the Governor is supporting this business and that he is working hard.'

8 'It is necessary to show that we are progressing in economic development because otherwise people will lose heart. When new figures are available to show that our cotton goods production is higher than a certain advanced country, then we tell the people.'

9 'Recently there were terrible floods in Wenzhou so many students from Hangzhou went to help.'

10 'You have seen that there are many announcements about the Falungong on our news programme. Well this is an example of a government announcement.'

11 'I like doing documentaries. I presented every one of a 160-part series on the History of Zhejiang.'

12 The Henan [province] bribery case. 'Although the programme was made after the police arrests it minutely researched the social factors surrounding it and the mistakes of the government and social institutions. It interviewed the accused after sentence. It analysed and discussed the systemic problems that had given rise to the criminality.'

Story classifications emerging from the programmes

When the journalists had identified and classified the types of story which they tended to cover, the next task was to look at the news which they actually produce for broadcast to see whether these classifications could be applied, without undue distortion. For the Chinese sample of news a much longer period of time, and hence a greater number of news stories, were collected, across twenty-five days.[10]

The difficulty here was that, by contrast with Birmingham, it was very much less simple to apply the journalists' classifications to their product. It was necessary to create new classifications to cover the variety. For example, reports of economic developments took up the most time on Chinese television yet this was the last of the topics mentioned by the reporters; other major classifications such as 'what senior leaders do' and 'meetings' were not mentioned by the reporters (except in one case, and disparagingly). Thus the classification drawn from the reporters' own declarations would have been as set out below:

1   Revealing difficulties such as corruption.
2   How problems are solved.
3   Information of immediate use.
4   Inside stories of problems: that's what really happened!
5   Revelation of malfeasance: got the rotters!
6   Disasters: life's a tragedy but we'll sort it.
7   Help from one community to another.
8   Economic development: ever upwards for the Chinese!

When the actual news programmes were examined to establish the incidence, and significance of, the packages could be classified according to the reporters' statements. From Tables 11.2 and 11.3 it is possible to compare the significance placed upon topics by reporters with the actual incidence of those topics and the time devoted to them (the 'editorial value').

Table 11.2 Did the programmes reflect reporters' values?

Reporter value	Topic (the shaded topics did not register in the reporter interviews)	Incidence	Editorial value
1	Revealing difficulties such as corruption	1[11]	14
2	How problems are solved	29	3
3	Information of immediate use	0	0
4	Inside stories of problems: that's what really happened!	0	0
5	Revelation of malfeasance: got the rotters	?[12]	?
6	Disasters: life's a tragedy but we'll sort it	?	?
7	Help from one community to another	5	13=
8	Economic development: ever upward for the Chinese!	66	1
0	Government announcements[13]	36	2
0	Meetings showing policy being agreed	27	4
0	What the senior leaders do	22	5
0	Arts, culture	17	6
0	Conservation/environment	15	7
0	Education	14	8
0	Others	14	9
0	The CCP and its history	11	10
0	Sports	10	11
0	Military	7	12
0	Good officials	5	13=

Table 11.3 The actual value given to topics by the programmes in terms of incidence (number of packages) of type (the signified)

Editorial value	Topic (the shaded topics did not register in the reporter interviews)	Incidence	Reporter value
1	Economic development: ever upward for the Chinese!	66	8
2	Government announcements[14]	36	0
3	How problems are solved	29	2
4	Meetings showing policy being agreed	27	0
5	What the senior leaders do	22	0
6	Arts, culture	17	0
7	Conservation/environment	15	0
8	Education	14	0
9	Others	14	0
10	The CCP and its history	11	0
11	Sports	10	0
12	Military	7	0
13	Good officials	5	0
14	Revealing difficulties such as corruption	1	1
0	Information of immediate use	0	3
0	Inside stories of problems: that's what really happened!	0	4
?	Revelation of malfeasance: got the rotters	?	5
?	Disasters: life's a tragedy but we'll sort it	?	6
0	Help from one community to another	5	7

The first impression received is that the news programme is primarily a communication about economic development, since more packages deal with that topic than with any other. For sixty-six packages the viewers are informed of successful economic advances: improvements in production, heartening trade statistics and the establishment of new enterprises. Only rarely, and fleetingly, are the individual entrepreneurs featured.

Twenty-seven of the packages in which leaders appear are also records of meetings, records which appear intended to display unity and cooperation among officials. Twenty-two packages show senior leaders in action. Thus 49 packages promote the decision-makers. However, if you consider that categories 2, 4 and 5 all consist of instructions from, or doings of, high leaders, screened for 85 out of the 278 packages in the news, and that each news programme can contain more than 3 packages in these categories, then the communication appears to be at least as equally about leadership as about economic development.

Reports show official after official in 'important' activities, usually meetings; high leaders inspect developments and greet foreigners who bring trade and investment. They congratulate low-level leaders from time to time. In general there is a narrative in which authority figures are dutiful slaves of the public weal. When they are not seen in action, their instructions are received mediated by presenters or captions, instructions which are introduced as the decisions of this or that high leaders' council.

Problem-solving is shown in 29 packages and the Chinese Communist Party (CCP) is presented as saviour of the nation in 11 major features, over 3 in each week, although these figures may be distorted by the period in question (see Tables 11.2 and 11.3).

Conservation and the environment, now a matter of official concern, are covered in 15 packages. The treatment generally emphasizes respect for the heritage and need to protect it, as do those 17 packages dealing with culture and the arts.

Of the remaining stories, those on education either focus on thorny questions of examinations or are special features in preparation for Teachers' Day; 5 good officials are praised and 1 naughty one exposed; there are 7 packages on the military in preparation for Army Day.

It might well be argued that the news is simply a function of a political system and the way the Propaganda Department[15] operates, considering news simply as the provision of information decided as appropriate to the audience. This could account for the relatively small amount of negative news, its uncompromising seriousness and the emphasis upon the benign activities of the leadership and the successes in economic development. Some observers consider (e.g., Friedman 1995) that Chinese viewers are completely cynical about this news, proving that it has no cultural resonance whatsoever.[16]

However, there does emerge a limited number of themes, which resonate with cultural myths identified by other scholars in other areas.

Governing themes or myths (signification)

The myth of hierarchy and leadership

Scholars of Chinese social psychology (Bond 1999), of management (Redding 1990), of bureaucracy (Weber in Beetham 1974) and of family life (Ho 1989) have all argued that Chinese are more inclined than anglophones to accept hierarchy as natural, to expect paternalism and to attribute competence to leaders. It should therefore not be surprising that journalism devotes a very large amount of its time to the doings and pronouncements of these leaders.

The myth of the CCP as saviour

Friedman (1995) and other scholars have characterized the CCP story of how it saved China from both foreign imperialism and internal traitors, and how it remains the only possible salvation for all Chinese people everywhere, as the 'northern narrative'. They critique it as only one of the possible ways of interpreting modern Chinese history and of predicting the Chinese future. Thus they have placed the narrative in a wider cultural perspective, diminishing claims made for its authority. It is not surprising that this particular myth is prominent since it cannot be publicly challenged in China.

The myths of cooperation, unanimity and absence of conflict

The same scholars who have described the propensity to hierarchy in Chinese society have also pointed to the belief that unanimity is possible, desirable and to be presented as if true. This is a society which values interpersonal and inter-unit harmony and does not value open confrontation.

Thus we can say that the importance given to the coverage of meetings – which are 'not televisual'[17] and regarded by anglophone reporters as to be avoided at all costs (actually Chinese reporters say they don't like covering them either) – chimes with the myth of unity. For at these meetings, unanimity is invariably one of the main messages, presumably along with the presentation of the topic itself and of the leaders.

Moreover the solution of problems comes into the same category. Hardly an accident or problem is seen without its solution; this is not completely unlike England, except that the emphasis seems slightly different. We do not see the solutions in England, but we are usually promised them, so that we can relax. While this is also the case in Chinese stories, there appears to be a greater propensity to transmit stories only once the solutions have been worked out and are in operation.

The myth of salvation through wealth

It appears to be an unspoken belief underpinning the vast amount of programming covering different aspects of economic development – and on the whole in a dull way, supplying statistics over mediocre footage, without any attempt at human interest – that economic development is the most important thing in the world. Since the content of many of the other stories, of meetings and high leader activity for example, is also connected to economic development, we can see that this myth suffuses most of the news. That it is an important myth in today's China will not be a surprise. This is also an important myth in England, but English news is not pervaded by it. One possible reason for this, is that it is eclipsed by the stronger myth, that of the individual, which has every issue and every event presented in individual human interest terms, diluting other messages.

Comparing Chinese and English journalists

News reports were selected as proxies for professional practices because of the significance they have for journalists as proof of their competence within the profession and as the evidence of their skill to the audience. The Hangzhou news reports examined are not as varied or as complex structurally as many of those in the Birmingham newsroom. The Birmingham reporters are straining to create the kind of news story of which NBC boss Frank Reuven would approve:

Every news story should, without sacrifice of probity or responsibility, display the attributes of fiction, of drama. It should have structure and conflict, problem and dénouement, rising action and falling action, a beginning, a middle and an end. These are not only the essentials of drama, they are the essentials of narrative.

(Frank Reuven, President of NBC News Division, in Stam 1983: 31)

By contrast, many of the Chinese reports are still one dimensional, 'flat' description over 'moving wallpaper'. Nevertheless, these topics have been chosen, consciously or unreflectingly, in preference to others and have been retold in a particular manner which has resonance for those conceived as the audience. Silverstone (1992: 17) writes that 'When we watch television we are watching a series of messages that both order our experience and define its categories, but which do so in ways that transcend the historical conditions of that experience'.

To further interpret the stories and to identify any relationship they may have to cultural myths, let us consider the allocation of time: of 500 minutes of Chinese packages, 108 minutes told us that economic development mattered most; 90 minutes instructed us on obedience to the government; 76 minutes showed our leaders in unanimous worthy activity; 54 minutes showed how history justified the present government and that there was no possible alternative; 32 minutes showed problems being solved by authority. The remaining 140 minutes dealt with a range of topics, rarely covering a topic for more than one minute.

Another distinctive feature of the Hangzhou news is that those who spoke were almost exclusively males over 40. Interviews with people lacking official position were few and hardly any women were asked to comment, although many of the reporters are themselves young women. Overall therefore, the narrative is one in which older males manage life authoritatively, ensuring ever-improving economic development in a world where every problem is already being solved by the leadership.

The English are also progressing, but, if the programmes are a guide, they do not think very much about the economy. England has some bright technical people who are making sure that the country stays in the forefront of technology. One impression which emerges from the programmes is that this is one of the things which makes England distinct, another is the warm good nature of so many of the English.

Unlike their Chinese counterparts, the Birmingham journalists don't bother to put on screen many pictures of their city or regional politicians greeting visitors. But they see a lot of people – ordinary 'people like us' – being asked their opinion about this or that. It is as if the reporters were assuring us that 'it's people who rule, after all, with a little help from those bright scientists and the police and fire services'!

Above all, the Birmingham journalists consider that what their viewers like news to tell them is what successful individualists 'we' are. 'If there is a problem, then an Englishman or woman can solve it, especially if it's to do with a disabled child or a lost cat. Honesty and hard work will get one there in the end!'; these are the predominant sentiments.

The very distinct social context in which the Chinese journalists operate has been alluded to in the interpretation of the myths, above, as has the political context, but the historical experience must not be ignored. For over thirty years China has officially believed that all society and its economy can satisfactorily be regulated according to a central plan, and the governing classes, with whom journalists are intimately connected, have sought to believe this, abolishing centuries old markets, associations and other institutions of knowledge and product exchange in the attempt to get reality to conform to the belief. It is not surprising that people imbued with the official ideology retain a predilection to attribute all to a plan.

There is another aspect of social context which may explain the lack of business representation in the television news. Until recently, business people were lowest in the social hierarchy. Here Communist class definition coincided fruitfully with traditional elite prejudices. Journalists, as I have suggested already, still see themselves as members of the ruling class in terms which are both Communist and classical. Some resistance to foregrounding entrepreneurs and market traders is not surprising.

As to the extraordinary dissonance between what the Chinese reporters declare to be their concerns and what they do (see Tables 11.2 and 11.3), they are so proud of their social role as investigators of social problems and scrutineers of authority that they forget that in their everyday work they appear in reality to be reflecting that which authority wants them to reflect, whether out of confusion or conformity. This coordinates well with observations from another angle, an analysis of the findings of some substantial quantitative research into the attitudes of Chinese journalists:[18]

> They perceive their own role as going far beyond informing people to 'lead public opinion' and to 'exercise public opinion 'public scrutiny' on the government'. These goals – as stated in the surveys and other writings – remain highly abstract without articulating the modus operandi for realising them or for resolving possible role conflicts (for example, the Party versus the people). Finally, most journalists surveyed resolutely disapprove acts of corruption and the practice of 'paid journalism' contrary to what seems to be ample evidence of widespread corruption.
>
> (Lee 2000a)

Chinese regional television news rarely challenges or investigates, but, in the interviews, the reporters appear to believe that they are doing just that whereas instead they beat the drum for economic progress, passing on the statistics provided by government departments and large companies and promote the image of the leadership and the myth of the CCP as the essential dynamo of China. Indeed the range of news content is not substantially different from that identified by other researchers twenty years previously, notably by Porter in his report of NCNA news selection and operation (Porter 1992 Appendices A and B). One of the most distinct features is the absence of strategic rituals of detachment and evidence.

From this examination of both Hangzhou and Birmingham, it could be argued that the news is not just about news. It is about dressing up new events so that they fit old beliefs. It is about reminding us who we are and what we believe in. The parliamentary system and the Party monopoly do influence the news, but they are only part of the story themselves, part of the cultural construction in which we live.

In Chapter 1 we saw that in the UK in recent years much concern has been expressed about the dumbing down of news and how this connects with increasing collusion between government information providers and harassed or lazy journalists, something considered dangerous to democracy. One finding of the present study has been the lack of interest of the English journalists in their 'higher' role, a lack of concern well reflected in their product. One editor even gloried in it.[19] In this they may be quite distinct from metropolitan, elite journalists who do appear to believe that they have a 'higher' calling.[20]

What can we make of the contrast between the ideals of the Chinese and the cynicism of the English (excluding the editor) in Birmingham? The Hangzhou journalists' ideals are much more akin to those of elite English journalists interviewed elsewhere (de Burgh 2000 Chapters 1–3) than to their supposed equivalents in English Regional TV. Why? Is it that the Chinese are more politicized, more enthusiastically patriotic, more educated or more naive? Lee (2000a) pointed out the gulf between Chinese journalists' aspirations and the reality of their work. Perhaps English journalists tailor their aspirations to what they actually do, whereas Chinese journalists, with the Liang Qichao inheritance, of the involvement of journalism with the patriotic cause, and with the mental model of the hero official, do not. Perhaps there is less division of attitudes in China between elite and provincial, a situation with which Mediterranean Europeans more easily identify than anglophones.

Although the Chinese journalists whose product was examined and who were examined on their product were regional television journalists, representatives of that metropolitan elite were also interviewed for the wider study of which this forms a part (de Burgh 2001). There was no difference in attitude between the two. It may be speculated upon as to whether the variation between the Chinese and English in this tells us about distinctions of social class in English society, or whether other factors are at play.

The Chinese journalists are ambivalent. On the one hand, they see themselves as scrutinizing government, representing the people to the government and vice versa. On the other hand they are mere transmitters of the political line of the government and the cultural prejudices of their masters. Examining their product in the light of their declarations points up the great gulf which separates their aspirations from their practices.

12 Conclusion: beliefs and practices, myths and realities

In this book we have surveyed the present state of the Chinese media; looked at the recent history and compared it to the earlier years of the development of journalism; looked at the ways journalists see their occupation and their product; through a case study, we have found some contradictions between the idea they have of themselves and the limitations prescribed by the state.

From an anglophone perspective, several points emerge as being of interest. The first is that journalists have different functions and roles in different societies, and that these are fashioned by the 'culture', that nebulous complex of tradition, social psychology and domestic habit which conditions a given unit of people, and differentiates them from others.

Second, there are nevertheless certain practices of journalism that are increasingly common everywhere, even when they are, as in the case of investigative journalism, conditioned by the home culture.

Third, commercialization may bring benefits and opportunities but it carries risks and does damage. Even while expanding horizons and expectations, commercial media can also impose their own limitations.

An image

One of the most startling sights to greet any anglophone visitor to China must surely be the petition. You are about to enter the high, guarded, portals of the provincial television station. Either on the opposite side of the street, or cluttered around the gateposts or both, you see dark-skinned creatures, old and young, sometimes with families; there are women suckling babies, crippled grandmothers beside scared urchins and defeated-looking and hungry men with sores. They are kneeling on the pavement and kowtowing, abasing themselves in the manner which so revolted eighteenth-century English emissaries to the Manchu court. The petitioners bow often, holding out clasped hands, spreading their arms wide or waving documents, the compositions of some village scribes, imploring attention. Their eyes gaze up at the great marble-faced palace before them, ignoring the armed police and the TV announcers with tight skirts and Gucci handbags who trip in and out. If they see a big limousine they rise, like a gaggle of disturbed geese, and rush towards it arms outstretched and crying out in incomprehensible dialects, in Tibetan, in Lolo . . . the limousine sweeps past.

The image of the petition is one which we must hold in our minds as we attempt to understand the Chinese journalist. In the course of this book a number of ideas has featured. One is the idea that journalists have social roles which correspond to the requirements of the societies in which they live, in that although there may be comparable aspects of being a journalist – just as there are comparable aspects of being a bureaucrat, an army officer or a fire-fighter – it is more illuminating to examine the differences than it is to celebrate the universals. Thus the image of the petition is so startlingly at variance with anything which might be seen in an anglophone country that it may serve as symbolic of the gulf which separates the two journalisms, notwithstanding all claims by Chinese modernizers or anglophone exponents of globalization.

The historical antecedents of the petition have been sketched earlier. Today they remind us that journalists are seen as being people of power, in the state if not of it, notwithstanding the commercialization of the media and all the other developments which have been described in the preceding chapters. It brings to mind some words of Stuart Hall's, who wrote that there is:

> a fundamental a-symmetry . . . between those who shape events, participate actively in them, those who have skilled and expert knowledge about events, and those who have 'privileged access' to events and participants in order to report on and communicate about them: and, on the other hand, the great majorities and minorities of the 'mass audience', who do not directly participate in events (even when they are directly affected by them), who have no expert knowledge about them, and who have no privileged right of access to information and personnel.
>
> (Hall 1973: 11)

He was writing about England. Chinese journalists are not merely interdependent with the politicians, they are identified with the state, an identification which appears not to preclude other ties.

From the interviews it can be seen that, by and large, the journalists saw themselves as representing the interests of the people, although some also still adhered to the Maoist view of the media as mouthpiece of the Party, without necessarily perceiving any contradiction between the two views. Representation of the interests of the people was achieved by providing accurate and timely information, by being in touch with people's concerns and by exposing the wrongdoing of officials or exploiters. Journalists were immensely proud of the genre of investigative journalism that has developed over the past few years; although asked to restrict their comments to news,[1] they rarely managed to do so, much preferring to draw attention to such journalism as could be interpreted as reflecting '*yulunjiandu*'. In so far as it was possible to judge, concepts of the journalist as 'tribune' drew more upon Chinese traditional myths of the 'hero official' than upon imported ideas of what journalism is about. Although there was pride at the way in which journalism was now able to be more responsive to the needs of the citizenry rather than only reflective of Party orders, the relationship with the state, now distinguished to some extent from the Party, supersedes the relationship with 'the people', no matter how often 'the people' are invoked. If it is agreed that the idolizing of 'the people' under Maoism was merely the cover for the powerful to do what they liked with the country and all in it, why should we imagine that present-day use of the term, to imply that things have changed and reporters now work for the people rather than the Party, should reflect reality any more than under Maoism; should demonstrate any greater intention to listen to, or represent the interests of, ordinary people, than that of the predecessors?

The key relationship is with politics, not necessarily for the reasons usually advanced by political scientists, namely that the Party imposes orthodoxy and that ideological factions vie to be the exponents and interpreters of that orthodoxy, but because Chinese society operates through power factions. In Chapter 9 we noted some proclivities of Chinese social psychology which make the anglophone concept of the journalist – perhaps even the anglophone concept of the individual – exotic.[2] We have tried to indicate the weight of tradition, to which Communism contributed and which it has imaginatively adapted.

Journalists and political factions

In 1967 Mao Zedong recalled that after the Great Leap Forward he 'could not even publish articles defending his own position' (Leys 1981: 32). In order to launch his 'Cultural Revolution' he had been obliged to ally himself with marginal radicals in the Shanghai media who were prepared to put forward his proposal for a radical shake-up which would bring him back into power.[3]

The commonplace assumption that the media are always necessarily the creatures of the Propaganda Department and the central government in Peking is often enough not the case so that we can allow that they do sometimes appear to be expressing independence, or at least reflecting factionalism within the leadership. In 1979 when Deng Xiaoping, with cultural functionary Zhou Yang and journalist and novelist Bai Hua in supporting roles, launched his campaign against ideology and the harm it does to culture and thought (Garside 1981: 397–408), the media extrapolated the theme. However:

> one publication was absent in this discussion. It was none other than China's most important ideological journal, *Red Flag*. Why? . . . *Red Flag* was under the control of a faction differing in ideology and policy from Teng Hsiao-ping [Deng Xiaoping]. The discussion campaign on 'practice as the sole criterion for the verification of truth' was nothing but part of an overall plot to discredit and de-power this faction. Only after the leader of

this faction was purged and the journal editor-in-chief replaced, did *Red Flag* confess its mistakes and join the discussion.

(Chu 1983: 54)

The reverse was to happen a few years later.[4] During the months leading up to the Tiananmen massacre in 1989 the media reflected the confusion in the centre until May, when, as if they believed that the battle had been won by the reformers, most journalists appear to have come out in favour of the democracy move-ment. Immediately after the Tiananmen massacre, central control was imposed by force and the stock of the left rose as the reformers were discredited. So much was this the case that even Deng Xiaoping could not get his views publicized, for, although he could hardly be accused of having been soft on the demonstrators, as the minutes of leadership discussions have subsequently revealed (Nathan and Perry 2001), it was considered that his policies had inspired them. More-over, when Deng Xiaoping determined to strike out against the fear of reform which he felt to be damaging China's prospects, and went on his Southern Progress, he could get no publicity for it. For nearly two months the media did not report his activities, with the one exception of a report in *The Peking Daily* which was authorized by Jiang Zemin's political enemy (later indicted for cor-ruption), Peking Mayor Chen Xitong, possibly to undermine Jiang.

The media, in other words, do have some choice, or at least leeway, at certain times and within the circumscriptions of the faction system which determines, in the absence of other modes of expressing dissent, Chinese politics. Journalists can reflect and perhaps even influence these 'opposition' factions if the factions themselves can muster enough power, which power must also include power among journalists and institutions such as the Propaganda Department which have power over them.

Image and reality in journalists' identity

Of the ideas which have run through this book, another is that journalists tend to have an image of themselves which is at variance with observers' perceptions. True, those piloted in England for the case study contrasted with their Chinese counterparts in that they made no highfalutin claims, although the editor ex-pressed in (idealistic) terms the common belief that the kind of journalism he and his team were undertaking was a kind of 'service to the people' and indeed a more praiseworthy service than that claimed by the 'elitists', as he described them. Nevertheless over half of British journalists, like their colleagues world-wide, rate the role of adversary of public officials as very or extremely important and most thought that journalists should be investigating claims and statements made by the government (Henningham and Delano 1998). It is reasonable to assume that, if journalists believe these things important for their profession, they themselves believe they have a hand in realizing them, much as it is argued in Chapter 11 that Chinese journalists believe in a myth of their own profession even when they do not incarnate the myth in their daily work. At first sight this confusion over identity seems to be a ridiculous contradiction, but is it? Surely many teachers believe that teaching is about doing what the protagonist of *Dead Poets Society* did, yet recognize their own inability to be so inspirational. Why should it not be so with journalists? There is an ideal identity, which is not rendered null by the failure to achieve it. Many journalists in most countries may never *investigate* anything.

The higher calling

As we saw in Chapter 9, there is a cast of mind which is attracted to journalism on account of the variety of experiences it offers, the shallow nature of those experiences and of the amusement which can be derived from the processes of transforming them into popular communication. This gadfly approach contrasts both with the weight given to their activities, as constructors of reality, by academics and pundits, and with the ideals remembered when journalists are asked about 'journalism' in the abstract rather than about themselves and what they do.

In China, although journalists may become journalists for the fun of it, they soon come to believe themselves to have a higher calling, perhaps even analogous to the Good Official of yore; yet what they produce is usually just what the Party wants. So are they deluded? Or cowards? Or simply hedged around by the cultural boundaries which do not permit them to see the contradiction? Or is the contradiction in the eye of the (anglophone) beholder? After all, every journalist may need to perform the functions both of information finder ('gadfly') and, in other spaces, of sceptic and guardian of public virtue. Perhaps anglophone journalists appear similarly culture driven to non-anglophones, operating within their own a culture of assumptions and sourcing which they do not interrogate.

Following an international study of journalists' coverage of the same issues Lee (2000) has concluded that, no matter how varied may be their approaches and agendas in domestic affairs, journalists from a particular country tend to have homogeneous interpretations when it comes to international affairs. One explanation for this phenomenon is that, just as someone can have multiple 'territorial' identities (the Kurd who is Turkish and British, the Frenchman who is Jewish and North African) so the professional can have situational versions of his or her profession such that when dealing with domestic matters the reporter may be a Robin Hood whereas when in the wider world s/he may be a jingo. To borrow a term from psychology, they 'code-switch'. As to China, insulation within the 'Chinese world-view' is over. Chinese are also exposed to the forces which confuse identity and produce postmodern 'hybridity'. Why should we demand consistency of the Chinese journalists? Should they not be permitted to believe both that they represent the people and that they serve the state? Moreover, Chinese journalists may not consider it illogical to hold principles in their minds which they have little chance of practising in daily work. After all, they have the safety valve of current affairs when the frustrations of conventional news are too much.

Other explanations for the apparent contradiction in the Chinese journalists' espousal of values which they do not practise might include: the ability to implement has not developed as fast as the recognition that certain courses of action are desirable; news is not taken seriously by journalists, in comparison with other manifestations of journalism, because of the political controls exerted; public spirit is a more acceptable nostrum to trot out to a foreign interviewer than other possible motivations; job security and the emoluments of a rather privileged life are enough to stifle principles in a society in which, still, the alternative means of earning a living are few and where the power of politics to ruin careers and blight lives is well understood; factionalism; commercialism.

Nevertheless the mere fact that we can identify what appears to us as a contradiction may show that great changes have occurred in journalists' perceptions of their roles, changes which both reflect changes in attitude and identity in Chinese society and which will impact upon them. We noted earlier how journalists had, in the first decades of the People's Republic, tried to advance their right to be tribunes of the people but did so from the standpoint always that democratic centralism, or the right of the Party to have the last word, was *correct*. Today journalists have shifted, which accounts for the disparagement of Liu Binyan, seen not as a loyal Communist but as temporizer, no matter how good his exposés. Some of the, apparently contradictory, currents are illustrated in the way a reporter, Liu Chao, met in Chapter 10, described himself as a teacher with a sense of justice and an audience larger than that of a schoolteacher, both as the 'throat and tongue of the Party' and as 'serving the people first'.

On the one hand, Liu sees himself in that didactic role we associate with Deng Tuo; on the other hand he is helping the petitioners like the good officials of yore; he is interpreting the meaning of the petition in the manner of those social novelists of the 1920s and although he claims to serve the Party he (in public, before witnesses in this case!) believes he puts people before Party.

This may be indicative of the change in perceptions that are taking place, changes which are affecting all those loosely called 'the intelligentsia'. One young television reporter mentioned Fang Lizhi as someone whom she thought represented new attitudes (Kang Wei), likening him to Galileo, a reference Fang himself has employed. What social changes are influencing these perceptual ones?

Journalists and the reflection of social change and new expectations

There are many reasons for discontent in Chinese society and discontent is no longer muzzled by a system of comprehensive repression. One writer on 'Rights and Resistance' in China today quotes the well-known dictum of de Tocqueville that as repression relaxes, so demands grow (Pei 2000). In China they have and, although persecution of dissidents takes place it is admissible now to protest about local issues of corruption, maladministration, poverty or environmental blight (see also Lee, Ching Kwan 2000). From the president downwards, officials have wished to be seen as sincere in their condemnation of abuses and their example is taken by lower officials who tolerate complaints which only a few years ago would have been bludgeoned. Institutional changes, from village elections to the Administrative Litigation Law, have probably allowed people to be more courageous in commenting upon local affairs and in identifying perceived injustices or maladministration. And people are learning to use the media. For example, a group of students in Dianbei, Canton Province, tipped off a local newspaper about a plan by examination candidates to cheat using pagers. Reporters investigated the story, garnered and published the details, sparking a nationwide spate of investigations into similar practices (Beijing 2000). Environment pressure groups tip off journalists as a matter of routine and receive funds from western foundations for their campaigns against pollution and for local clean-ups and consciousness-raising activities (Shapiro 2001: 209). It is not so much the fact of the reports themselves which are a sign of the changes in Chinese journalism, but the fact that they were instigated by citizens and taken on board by the media. Officials too may be taking on a different role in relation to the media: responding to the high number of industrial accidents, the head of the State Administration for Production Safety called for 'more media participation in the investigation of major industrial accidents'. He considered that in almost every case corruption was involved and that the media could help expose this (Gittings 2002).

We saw in Chapter 6 that people are becoming more outspoken and that authority is, relative to the situation a few years ago, more tolerant. So when journalists claim to be taking up cudgels on behalf of some group which is not part of the political establishment, are they reflecting a development in popular consciousness, a real change in how people perceive themselves as well as a reaction to the oppression of the recent past? Certainly, there are problems to be dealt with: the struggle for resources or merely for consideration, between the east coast and the poor hinterland; unemployment; pollution and the destruction of the environment; appalling health problems, not least hepatitis, TB and HIV; a dramatically ageing population; the illusory prosperity born of selfish trade; contemptuous attitudes to the public weal and the flight abroad of money and talent; in culture, the obsession with national humiliation; the gulf between the wealthy and the disadvantaged; the lack of political participation; the risks of war with Taiwan. Will Chinese journalists confront these and the other problems of Chinese society? Will they illuminate the issues, analyse the options, provide evidence for the debates and oblige the politicians to attend? Journalists may be championing rights, but this does not necessarily mean that they are imbued with a democratic spirit.

Neo-conservatism

The emergence of a nascent discourse of rights does not necessarily mean that the Chinese are adopting anglophone notions of democracy. Immediately after the Cultural Revolution democracy was talked about as an essential instrument for the development of the nation, much as it had been back in the early years of the century, and adopted almost as a religious belief by some at least of the 1989 protesters. Today some observers consider that intellectuals have given up on democracy and are inspired by what Chen (1997) calls neo-conservatism. There are various varieties of neo-conservatives but they all share a scepticism about the appropriateness of democracy for China. This scepticism derives from a disdain for the unrealistic elitism of the 1989 demonstrators; a fear that Chinese development would be weakened or halted by the chaos democratic systems would bring; revulsion from what is seen as the failures of political reform in Russia; a desire to find an authentically Chinese way of managing society; a feeling that the objective conditions for making democracy a success do not exist in China today. This is not to say that neo-conservatives identify with the CCP; they have usually rejected Communism as a failed ideology, but consider that the CCP is the only force available which can push on China's development and prevent China from becoming, in Sun Yatsen's evocative phrase 'a sheet of sand'. An outsider might imagine that the Nationalist Party, which has come to terms with power-sharing and accepted democracy as an aspiration, might be the alternative, but this is probably a thought too far, even for the neo-conservative.

The neo-conservatives counter what appears to be, for whatever reason, a developing sense of rights, by championing authoritarianism. This they justify on grounds different according to personal preference. On the one hand the Chinese citizenry can be characterized as too backward (the 'development discourse') to be able to benefit from democratic rights, on account of thousands of years of debilitating 'feudalism'. Since the May 4 movement it has been conventional to denigrate traditional Chinese culture as enervating and to dismiss it as 'feudalism'. The Chinese people have been so hamstrung by this awful heritage, it is held, that democratic institutions and notions of rights would only impede the solution of the problems China faces and that the state's impetus to wealth and power must be allowed to override other considerations (the 'Lee Kwan-yew position'). Some journalists justify their patronizing attitudes, and their privileges, in these terms. Liu appears to be doing so when he talks about interpreting the citizens' needs for them and earning his high status with professional impartiality, a neat illustration of what Tuchman terms, in the US context, a 'strategic ritual' (Tuchman 1972).

> There's not really a contradiction between the social activist and the impartial journalist; your job is to work on behalf of the citizenry, to interpret their needs for them. In that way you are a social activist, your aims are activist. But in the way you deal with topics you must be impartial. That is what gives you your high status.
>
> (Liu Chao)

Those of this persuasion did not, unlike those lauded in the West, oppose the crackdown of June 1989.[5] Several prominent ones supported it. They approve of certain aspects of modernization such as private property and the emergence of a middle class but want strong government (Hao 1997: 187). They are not pluralists, their notions of civil society fall far short of Habermasian notions of a public sphere (Keane 2002: 786). When they critique their society they do so from a standpoint of traditional values, willingly described as authoritarian. Some go so far as to fall in with Jiang Zemin's own arguments against democracy which rest upon xenophobia in that they posit a 'Chinese way' against a 'western way' and oppose that which is claimed not to chime with *Chinese traditional values* which, conveniently, support the present order and tie in with the anti-foreignism evident from publications, fashionable in the late 1990s, such as *China Can Say No* and *Behind the Demonization of China*.[6] Chinese exceptionalism seems particularly attractive to disappointed intellectuals (Zhang, X. 1998: 4). The 'Wei Jingshen argument', that China needs its Fifth Modernization, democracy, if it is to develop the wealth and power which all Chinese are told to want for their society, is little represented except among some émigrés.

Countering this is the view that the Party intellectuals, those members of the intelligentsia with jobs in or commitments to the establishment, are becoming more fervently 'progressive' or reform orientated (Tang 1997, Liu and Link 1998). If this is the case it is perhaps because they are more exposed to the muddle of government and are grappling with how to implement policy without the transparency, accountability and rational decision-making processes that developed nations at least espouse. In a book which has aroused controversy in China, He (1998) argues that China has failed to get to grips with reforms which are fundamental if the country is to compete in the modern world.

Westernization?

Chinese journalists have been constructed by scholars in relation to anglophone assumptions (Curran and Park 2000), even Cold War assumptions, in that the focus has been on the events and situations which can be interpreted as manifestations of a struggle between a totalitarian state and journalists hankering for press freedom. At least that is one interpretation of many of the comments on journalists made after the Tiananmen massacre.

Chen (1998) has conceived of Chinese media after the Cultural Revolution as falling into three periods, first that of 1979–82 when, in reaction against the Cultural Revolution, journalists rediscovered respect for the audience and emphasized facts; second, 1983–6 when the concept of information, as distinct from propaganda, caught on; and third, 1987–9 when the movement for press freedom and media law got under way. Journalists are constructed as attempting to get closer to an ideal of what 'real' journalism is all about, namely, detached reporting of facts, the performance of a watchdog function and independence from powerful interests. Their slogans are interpreted, for instance by Polumbaum (1990), as showing Chinese journalists aiming for the roles associated with American reportage.

The reference made to Watergate by Wang Qianghua (quoted on p. 157) is not exceptional. Many, perhaps most, Chinese journalists display a familiarity with the formats and genres of anglophone journalism and often with the exploits too. It is tempting to ask whether, as some have assumed, apparent adoption of aspects of anglophone journalism's beliefs and practices amounts to 'westernization'.

The anglophone journalist has what is now a highly developed reading of his role as opponent of those in authority, virtually an opposition.[7] Are we seeing the beginnings of this in China? Research trying to establish whether American films affect the values of Chinese viewers suggest that certain themes such as the equation of freedom and wealth, responsibility and ambition predict a gradual internalization of 'American values' (Heisey and Gong 1998: xxvi).[8] Is this what is happening in the sphere of journalism?

If Chinese journalists really are investigating in the individualistic manner associated with their anglophone counterparts, we might agree. However, reporter Lee Chun dismissed the claims of various fellow journalists that they are investigative; the only courageous medium in the whole country is the Canton weekly, *Weekend South*, she said; she dismissed the claims of *Focal Point* as those of an operation which 'makes a big noise but is only swatting a fly'. She believes that a careful analysis of topics covered by the programme will bear her out. In evidence for her scepticism, she talked of a matter which had been constantly discussed in journalism circles since first it leaked out, the exposure of the Party Secretary in Ningpo for corruption.[9] She pointed out that the case was never investigated by the media, despite the fact that local journalists certainly knew about it (transfers of media buildings and other assets were involved) many months before the corruption came to light. Similar examples can be cited.

Current affairs programmes publish collections of their transcripts in book form. It is easy to take this merely as a symptom of a respect for the printed word, but interviewees claimed that such publication signified much more. 'They consider themselves much more than just journalists; this is the record of their works.' It was advised that 'If you analyse these publications over time you will find a pattern conforming to the government's interests of the moment' (Xie Yizhi) with the implication that journalists are functioning as do state press officers.

Lee Chun was also contemptuous of the suggestion that Chinese journalists were rediscovering the relative independence of the 1930s and were motivated by idealism:

> What you term idealism I call oppression. Some do regard themselves as resurrecting the suppressed professionalism of the 1930s, but they are quite wrong to do so, they do not deserve that 'mantle' as they are state servants.
>
> (Lee Chun)

A colleague went on to point out the limits within which would-be investigators work and which do make them appear like 'state servants':

> There are many subjects you cannot touch no matter where you work. But every journalist is also restricted to his/her level. We have our levels

[national, provincial, county, etc.] only at which, and below which, we can investigate.

(Fang Chih)

Journalists may take the risk of offending authority where popular demand and cultural pride coincide, for example, over historic buildings preservation. Where powerful interests are at stake and there is no groundswell of public concern, they may not, even if the public interest is clearly involved. To illustrate this there is the case of the contaminated milk of some areas of Zhejiang, the true situation of which was well known to journalists six months before it came out. For six months people were drinking contaminated milk, there was widespread suspicion but journalists who knew the reality did nothing because they had not been given the 'all-clear' by the authorities (Ye Xinghua).

In the case of the Shandong fertilizers (p. 144), CCTV spiked the programme at the urgent request of the provincial authorities; however, upon receiving representations from the journalists who had undertaken the investigation, the Head of the Station rescheduled it, although only after fierce battles which went right up to the Central Committee. It was finally shown after the abuses had been dealt with and the culprits punished and reference could be made to this fact at transmission.

Zhao (2000) argues that this kind of journalism may be investigative in terms of the approach to the topic and the methods deployed but that it lacks that individual initiative which would mark it out as prepared to pit itself against the most powerful.[10] She writes:

> To the extent that it exposes safe targets and investigates violations of exist-ing laws and policies, it fulfils the media's role of being the mouthpiece of both the Party and the people. While individual officials and businesses have everything to lose, both the Party and the people have something to gain from this practice.
>
> (Zhao 2000: 31–33)

This helps explain why high leaders today flatter journalists more than they castigate them.[11] Another reason may simply be that they need them, as is indicated by the popular expression 'Kings without crowns', used to suggest that politicians are to some extent dependent upon journalists for their media profiles and the success of their careers – 'journalists are the kingmakers' – just as ordinary people need them to raise issues (Kang Keming). This would explain the flattery heaped upon them by important politicians; quite a departure from Chairman Mao's master-and-servant approach.

Anglophones assume antagonism between power holders and journalists of the investigative variety. This is not the assumption in China. Yet, are we so different in the West? In considering the anglophone tradition of investigative journalism it is arguable that the inspiring myth of the investigative journalist as intrepid seeker after truth obscures the fact that most investigative journalism is well within the conventions of the society in which s/he operates[12] and that journalists always work closely with powerholders and can often be contained by them. This does not necessarily mean there is no agency. What the investigative journalist is doing is drawing our attention to infringements of the moral law that is generally accepted in the society. However, it can also attempt to extend the limits of the citizens' concern.

Similarly in China today reporters see themselves as finding aspects of society that had remained hidden; exposing them to earn the surprise and sympathy of the audience; using their findings to extend the moral horizons of that audience. In doing these things these reporters are as much the heirs of the 1930s socially concerned novelists (Hsia 1971) as anglophone investigators John Pilger, Paul Foot or Seymour Hersch are the heirs of Dickens, Zola and Sinclair Lewis. Although knowledgeable about western journalism, and complimentary, interviewees did not see what was happening in China as derivative. Typical was this statement:

> 'Public scrutiny' [*yulun jiandu*] is a concept which goes back as far as the Qin Dynasty [221 BC] in China. It is a way by which rulers boost political confidence without handing over control. When authority is pretty sure it's in charge it allows rein. The trouble is when you relax control society often responds unpredictably and government [forces a turn back to] social stability. Look at the example of the Hundred Flowers.
>
> (Li Zhengmao)

For Li, current developments fitted snugly within the Chinese order and, in criticizing, the modern journalist is performing a culturally sanctioned ritual, taking on a role defined by Chinese tradition rather than by western example.

Culture and journalism

In a comparison of Chinese mainland journalists in Hong Kong and their Hong Kong colleagues, Nip (1998) appears to suggest that differences in approach were not great but that news judgement was informed by reporters' perceptions of their relationship to authority. In discussions among observers in the late 1990s it was assumed at one point that confrontation between government and the new breed of investigative journalists was inevitable, although later Gordon (1997) and Zhao (1999) both came to the conclusion that an accommodation was being reached between the two 'sides' if that is what they were. From the government's point of view critical journalism is very useful, provided it does not get above itself. It can both alert the government to areas of controversy which other channels do not see and it can be used to give the appearance that 'authority' is concerned, that people are not ignored and that 'something is being done'.

Given the need to take into account the importance of informal power groupings and personal charisma which eclipse other loyalties and stymie attempts to develop a professional ethic detached from faction, that interpretation of the emergence of investigative journalism was realistic. It is when we cast around for a third party, another tradition of journalism against which to measure the Chinese variety, that the limitations of the anglophone touchstone become even more apparent. In other societies, particularly Mediterranean and Hispanic, journalists may characterize themselves using the discourses of anglophone journalism studies, yet, in practice, are very distant from them. In Italy and Spain where tyro journalists assiduously study the anglophone model, they nevertheless act in accordance with quite different sets of conventions.

Mancini (2000) argues that, in Italy, the 'professional model of journalism based on neutrality, autonomy and detachment from power' is widely accorded respect on account of the need, still forcefully felt by journalists, to prove that they are repudiating the fascist legacy. Another factor is media imperialism. The need to reject any whiff that the media of other countries are superior obliges non-anglophone media institutions to represent themselves as the same kind of institution, whereas the true fact may be that they are simply performing roles which are determined by and in their own cultures.

Mancini observes that the press in Italy has always been 'more literary, comment and advocacy orientated' as does Chalaby (1996) of the French press. Journalism is expected to be a tool in struggles for commercial or political gain. He also emphasizes that news organizations are closely tied to organized interests and political parties, and many suggest that this is the case in the Hispanic media too (Quesada 1997, La Fuente 2000, Perez-Ayerra 2000) although Waisbord has re-examined this question and come up with a more nuanced understanding (Waisbord 2001). Mancini argues that the objectives of the media channels are to 'transmit ideas, protect interests and organise people who already share the same point of view' and he accounts for this by saying that, whereas, in a two-party system such as those of the US and UK objectivity may be possible:

> Objectivity is almost impossible within an intricate and fragmented panorama in which a greater number of political forces act and in which even the slightest shades of meaning in a story risk stepping on the positions of one of the forces in the political field.
>
> (Mancini 2000: 273)

A common aspect of the journalisms described in these studies is that the journalist sees him or herself as a political actor in a way that has, over the last century, been inadmissible to all but the minority of committed partisans in the anglophone media. Most journalists are tied in some manner to a political party and owe greater allegiance to its political beliefs than to a conception of the impartial journalist. More studies need to be undertaken in this area before we can with confidence ascribe differences in journalistic practice to deep structure cultural traditions, but it is timely that scholars in media studies, as in other disciplines, are discovering that anglophone assumptions about behaviour may have but limited applicability even as close to home as the European mainland. This should not surprise us. We have seen how different are the origins of

Chinese and English journalism. Thus 'westernization' is not helpful if the concept obscures the differences between journalists' roles that persist even as certain practices converge.

Commercialization

> Journalism was not a popular choice in 1988, [and] at about that time the social status of teachers had begun to plummet after the 1985 reforms and I felt that journalism would regain its past high status because they are regarded as representatives of the government. I was wrong. They are not representatives of the government, more realistically they are representatives of big business.
>
> (Tang Musan)

In the introduction attention was drawn to the concerns which are expressed in the anglophone world about the detrimental effects upon the media of the free market, heretofore thought of as the guarantor of a free media. Later we saw that liberalizing the market in China has, by contrast, increased variety and done the opposite of what marketization is supposed to have done in the West, i.e., increased the quantity and quality of information and scrutiny. The same is claimed for several Latin American countries (Waisbord 2001).

If you talk to observers of the Chinese media scene it is to these lessons that they will point, not the anglophone jeremiads. That these matters are not issues in China is a function of the recent history of Chinese journalism from which the lesson has been drawn that the more financially independent the media can be from the government the better for everyone: plutocrats are better than Party people.

This is curious, since journalists also seem to be influenced by their belief in the 'hypodermic theory of effects' much as the authoritarian theory of teaching influences teachers.[13] It may not be true, it may be flawed even to its believers, but it dignifies and gives point to the profession and the myth thereof. Unfortunately, if it also prevents recognition of the dangers of, for example, highly commercialized media, so it may be dysfunctional. Journalists appear to believe that political propaganda is transmitted hypodermically, as in the Bolshevik model, but that commercial values are not propaganda, but freedom. The mental vestiges of the Bolshevik model ensure that, while journalists ascribe power and influence to the agents of political ideas (whether politicians or journalists) they discount the power of commercial pressures. These they equate with liberty and light to the extent that they fail to argue for a public service solution, and seem to have faith in privatization and a hoped-for media law as being the answers to the political troubles of the profession.

The throw away remark by Tang, above, that journalists are more the representatives of business was not necessarily intended to be negative. Yet as we have seen from revelations like that of Wen Weiping, above, and observations by others familiar with 'red envelopes'[14] and other modes by which Chinese journalists allow their copy to be dictated by rich people, Chinese journalism may be going much further than the anglophone media in abandoning the public service values we identified earlier and to which journalists claim to subscribe. There is a common saying: 'The first rate reporter is in the stock market; the second rate sells ads; the third rate moonlights to make money and only the fourth rate work exclusively for their employers' (Gu 2000) As far as is known, only the *Chengdu Business News* has taken measures to make corruption less likely, and it is interesting that it has done this through establishing a *system* which is supposed to make corruption unnecessary and unprofitable.

Monetary bribery is but one form of corruption. In anglophone countries today an increasing proportion of newspaper and screen space is given over to the concoctions of public relations offices and promotion agencies and less and less to the product of journalists' evidenced reflection (Franklin 2001). Proprietors use newspapers to propagandize (see Weymouth and Anderson 1999; CPBF 2000; Gaber and Barnett 2001) and investigative journalism survives where it is acceptable to those proprietors' agendas and where it is sufficiently sensational to offer a good return. The difference from China can seem more one of degree than of nature.

Cultural change: the loss of naivete

There is a contradiction of Chinese society which journalists, like their colleagues with other roles in the culture industries, have to live with and adapt to. A Marxist oligarchy, with supposedly lofty ideal of creating a society based on service to others and the end of the cash nexus, presides over the world's biggest Klondike: a greedy stampede for personal wealth which tramples underfoot all sense of social obligation, respect for others or consideration for the weak. Neither traditional ethics nor Communist internationalism have much sway to impede this.[15]

Thus it is not surprising that many observers of Chinese cultural life today have noted the abundance of irony and scepticism. Its manifestations are as various as the ironic use of political slogans in art, the proud adoption of the loafer attitude[16] illustrated in the film *Beijing Bastards*,[17] the pandering to western taste for art that is both sensational and 'dissident' and literature which celebrates meaninglessness and cynicism even while making its authors rich. These attitudes are not obviously shared by the interviewees for this study; journalists are neither fully of the cultural intelligentsia yet not quite functionaries either. Yet it is likely that they are affected by them and may help to explain the fact that some interviewees savaged their government's colonial and human rights policies in private conversation yet continued to take the government shilling for producing the kind of news described in the case study.

Barmé's interpretation of this kind of situation is convincing. Writing of cultural developments in the 1990s, he says:

Younger editors, writers, television production crews, and propagandists also played a more ambivalent role in the media. Many approached the task of making pro-Party TV specials or writing screeds in favour of some political line with a sophisticated cynicism: they greedily accepted official largesse (the pay for this sort of work increased in direct proportion to the decline in public interest) while sometimes sneaking subversive messages into their work. But when the bottom line was top dollar, subversion became little more than a piquant marketing ploy that also served to salve the conscience of the guilty toady. Others spared themselves such refinements and simply churned out the mind-numbing humbug, laughing all the way to the People's Bank. It was not outside the realm of possibility that a few of them sincerely believed in what they were doing.

(Barmé 1999: 116)

In sum such public service ethic as there is is too weak to counter either the state's propaganda or the imperatives of commercialism. The relevance to the anglophone media is illuminating. The lesson from China is that where there is neither public service obligation nor regulation then a dangerous collusion between the state – or the ruling Party – and business interests come to control the power to construct reality, unmediated by any concern for interests other than their own. There is some awareness of this. In conversation, older journalists referred to dumbing down and the relaxing of controls and there has been a very public controversy on just this topic.[18] But there is no concerted attempt to understand it, its dangers, causes and solutions. Naivete vis-à-vis the party has gone, but business can be idealized.

Improvisation

Pan Zhongdan proposes 'improvisation' to explain the situation in which Chinese journalists find themselves adapting to the new commercial imperatives, without any declared intention by the political authorities to change their beliefs or practices or any 'conceptual framework for reform'; he refers to 'the way in which journalists design, implement, and justify their nonroutine journalistic practices that function to *weaken, circumvent, and erode the hegemony of the commandist system associated with Communist ideology*' (Pan 2000: 73, original emphases). He believes that journalists' improvised activities are changing the 'map of reality in China's journalism institution [sic]'. They are also changing the 'map of meaning of journalism itself' (Pan 2000: 104).

From the preceding pages it would seem that the improvisation to which Pan draws our attention reflects less the step-by-step assimilation of a new world view, or, as the Chinese leaders sometimes say, 'crossing the river by feeling stone by stone', than the dissonance between beliefs about roles and actual daily practices, a dissonance they will live with as long as there are ideals about journalism to live up to. There has been a marked shift from the idea of journalist as servant of party and state towards a professional, tribune position. The distinction between the two approaches cannot be perfectly clear cut, nor can we point to a particular date on which the change came about. As we have seen,

Liu Shaoqi and others recognized the validity of aspects of the tribune position early in the life of the PRC; the evidence of the Hangzhou news programmes, taken alone, would have us believe that there was little or no real change, regardless of the interviewees' aspirations. Yet there has been development: Maoist ideology is ever weaker and instead, journalists increasingly measure themselves against moral norms which appear to have their ancestry in the 'good official' myth. Taking the analogy further, Chinese journalists can see themselves as repositories of social values, confronting or at least chiding an authority which claims moral right yet is shot through with inconsistency and corruption.

Evidence for change

Evidence for the change is two-fold. First, the kinds of journalism that have emerged. There are contrasting views, fuelling the emergence of a public opinion; there is revelation; there is investigation. The second piece of evidence is the language with which the journalists describe their functions: the preponderance of the 'public scrutiny' role over the 'throat and tongue of the Party' role is marked as is the preference for the non-political vocabulary demonstrated in the way 'audience' replaces 'masses' as the target of media efforts. They distinguish between interests of state and citizen. These changes demonstrate journalists' commitment to contribute to their society's development in a fundamentally different way from their predecessors; they correlate with Chen's research. The journalists see themselves as important and the Party and government to some extent acknowledge the moral claims for journalism; see how Gong Xueping encouraged the students at Fudan University and how Li Peng praised *Focal Point* (pages 25; 131).

A new self-image?

In the 1920s and 1930s journalists saw themselves as replacing traditional scholars and teachers in the reproduction of cultural values and their successors may be reappropriating and modernizing that role. They no longer see the task of the journalists as bringing together again rulers and ruled into harmony, an aim which may have been that of Liu Binyan and Deng Tuo's generation; although confrontation avoidance remains a value of Chinese society, yet people do confront and changes do take place, in proof of which we can cite both the development of public debate and, most significant of all, the achievements of Taiwan's democratic opposition. As to the, arguably enfeebling, influence of personal bonds of faction and friend, it can be countered that individuals may be increasingly willing to influence those bonds from below. After all, patrons can become reformers and reformers, patrons.

In our analysis of the news product of the Hangzhou reporters, we saw that those matters rated important by the reporters did not feature highly; those matters which did feature highly were not rated important by the reporters. The contrast between what they believed and what their masters wanted was striking.

The news, in other words, was what they had to do, and they do their best within the tight political constraints.

News may not be significantly different in approach from that of thirty years before, yet the content of *current affairs* is, and more obviously reflects the aspirations expressed by the journalists, aspirations which are being realized in ways that those of their predecessors were not. In this field they test the boundaries of self-censorship to the limit, fighting, as in the case of Zao Hungwen, for their stories. The Party has lost prestige, such that its demands are not perceived as exhortations but as bullying. The contradictions between how journalists believe, and how they behave, reflect the contradictions in the context within which they operate rather than their own confusion; their values seem increasingly seem clear-cut, even where their actions contradict them.

Of course Chinese journalists vary according to the channels in which they work, generation and many other aspects. By and large, however, the younger they are, the more detached they are from the '*throat and tongue*' idea of journalism, to the extent that two of the youngest were prepared to make subversive comments about the most sacred of all cows, Taiwan and the colonies. If we can generalize from this, journalists in the future are likely to be ever more iconoclastic.

Notwithstanding all that has been written above about the socio-cultural impediments to democratic ideas in Chinese society and the abstract nature of journalists' commitment to them, they have initiated their own dialogues with experts and ordinary people. Their ambitions can be on the side of the people, not authority. In these initiatives, their courage can be remarkable. Just as the *World Economic Herald*, although independent of state finance or hierarchies, still got shut down in 1989, so the state today closes down channels regardless of supposed independence and destroys the careers of journalists, or imprisons them.

How do these observations relate to the motivations we identified? Few, if any, tyro journalists enter the profession on account of their ideals; these are developed during training for it and initiation into it. They are part of the professionalization which is going on, in which a group ascribes to itself altruistic objectives and motives even while often failing to live up to them. In being so ambivalent they reflect the deep contradictions in Chinese society as a whole, where market individualism coexists with political authoritarianism. Chinese journalists believe they have social responsibilities but, to an outside observer, rarely fulfil them; they uphold moral standards with their words but accept red envelopes with their hands; have high ideals but perform conventional rituals; declare themselves for the people one minute and unreflectingly promote authority the next.

The model of professionalism which is developing today is different from the anglophone equivalent and can only partially be accounted for by Maoism. There may be scepticism, cynicism about the CCP; there certainly is irritation at official interference in professional work and an increasing tendency to distinguish between state and citizenry and to see themselves on the side of the latter.

Chinese journalists may be embarrassed at their failure to live up to their own ideals but this hardly shakes their overriding belief that they are serving the nation. Two of our interviewees may be cited to express this:

> To be a journalist today is to do a much respected job so that journalism is a profession to which many aspire. What people like about it is the independence that it gives, the fact that you can become very knowledgeable about society and have many contacts; from the point of view of an individual's career, it helps you to get on, it is glorious.
>
> (Deng Huo)

> Journalists in China have an extremely important position. Not only are they the mouthpiece of the Party but also its eyes and ears. We speak for the people and we speak for the government. We are the ears and eyes in the sense that we must understand what is going on; examine issues; translate issues; delve into matters; analyse, explain.
>
> (Liu Cihui)

On 15 October 2002, all newspapers in China carried the same story in exactly the same words – the eulogy of the leader who was supposedly 'retiring', but virtually nothing of the man who had succeeded him as General Secretary of the CCP. This is a useful lesson with which to conclude this review of Chinese journalists with the reminder that, notwithstanding many similarities in practice and apparent similarities in purpose, the roles of journalists in different countries are inextricably bound up with the often implicit expectations of their society's culture.

Appendix A: glossary of names and terms

Anti-Spiritual Pollution Campaign Campaign initiated by Deng Xiaoping in 1982 to counter western-inspired 'decadence' in the arts; echoed by similar campaigns through the 1980s instituted by Jiang Zemin.

Ba Jin (1904–) Sichuanese novelist and chronicler of family life. Obtained positions in CCP government 1950. Purged 1968. Rehabilitated 1977. Still active in cultural institutions of the PRC.

Canton An important trading city and capital of Canton province since the Tang Dynasty. Centre of Cantonese culture, with its distinct language and customs.

CCP Founded 1921 in Shanghai as a satellite of the Comintern. Until the death of Sun Yatsen, the CCP, on Stalin's orders, worked with the KMT.

Chengdu Capital of Sichuan Province. It was a capital of one of China's antecedent states, Shu, from AD 221–63, and has been an important city ever since.

Civil War Within months of the surrender of Japan in 1945, full civil war broke out and lasted until the KMT flight to Taiwan in 1949.

Communes, People's *Renmin Gongshe.* Tens of thousands of families were organized into these economic and political units during the GLF, re-emphasized during the GPCR, abolishing traditional units of administration and distribution.

Confucianism A school of thought based upon the teachings of Confucius (551–479 BC) and his successors, particularly Mencius and Hsun-tzu. The Confucian classics, which principally dealt with social relationships and hierarchy as the bases for successful family and social life, were the key tenets of the state ideology until 1911, notwithstanding many other religious and philosophical currents in the Chinese world. A discussion of the relationship of Confucianism to China's modern political development is to be found in Fung *In Search of Chinese Democracy* Cambridge: Cambridge University Press.

(Great Proletarian) Cultural Revolution Upheaval which supposedly lasted from 1966–76 but whose worst violence took place in 1966–9. Ostensibly a movement for a final clearing out of old ideas and habits, it was more an attempt by Mao once again to re-establish his waning authority as it was being marginalized by managers and experts more suited to guide a modern society than the ageing guerrilla and prophet. His prestige allowed him to call upon young people to first criticize and then attack those in authority, while commanding the forces of law and order to stand down. By the time those in authority realized what was happening they were beaten into submission, imprisoned or isolated. Most institutions ceased functioning as they were invaded and taken over by gangs of rebels and looters. The ruination of authority brought to local power cliques and thugs who vaunted their loyalty to Mao while enjoying the fruits of power. Over this mess the Gang of Four presided until 1976, although some of the old institutions and administrators gradually returned from around 1970.

Dai Qing   Adopted daughter of Ye Jianying. Missile engineer and (*Guangming Daily*) journalist. Now freelance. Much web information available.

Democracy Wall   1978–9 posters were displayed on a stretch of the wall of the Forbidden City calling for democracy. The best known was that of Wei Jingshen, who described democracy as the 'Fifth Modernization'. In the subsequent clamp down, Wei was imprisoned for fifteen years.

Deng Tuo (1911–67)   Editor-in-chief of *The People's Daily* until 1958. Purged in the Cultural Revolution. Committed suicide.

Deng Xiaoping (1904–)   Sichuanese. Active radical from 1919, in Sichuan, France, Jiangxi. Member of the CC in 1945. Senior member of the central government by the early 1960. Purged 1965. Recalled 1973, became third in the hierarchy. Purged 1976. Regained some positions 1977. Regained decision-making positions 1982–3. Implemented the Four Modernizations. Senior decision-maker at the time of the Tiananmen massacre.

East Turkestan   Large territory in Central Asia contiguous with Uzbekistan, Kazakhstan, Pakistan, Tibet and China. Under loose Qing Dynasty and Nationalist suzerainty until an independent state was declared in the 1930s. Culturally Turkic and Muslim although there has been substantial Chinese immigration since the 1960s. Occupied by the Chinese army in 1950 and soon after incorporated into the PRC as an 'autonomous region'. Although up to the Cultural Revolution it appears that the indigenous population was generally not anti-Chinese, there is now considerable unrest.

Falun Gong   Banned in 1999 following peaceful demonstrations in Peking, the Falungong or Falundafa has been persecuted and subject to vilification ever since. The movement claims to be a pacific organization devoted to meditation and exercises to develop personal qualities; no evidence as yet surfaced that convinces otherwise, although many, perhaps thousands, of unlikely dissidents have been imprisoned and maltreated, perhaps murdered. One possible explanation for the government's extreme reaction is that the movement too closely resembles that from which the Taiping and Boxer rebellions grew; another is that the government sees any nationwide organization, however informal, as a threat to its monopoly.

Fang Lizhi (1936–)   Academic and scientist. Best known for his book *We Are Making History* and for his criticisms of Chinese government.

Gang of Four   The group of people most associated, aside from Marshal Lin Biao, with the carrying out of Mao's Cultural Revolution, it consisted of Jiang Qing (Mao's wife), Yo Wenyuan, Wang Hongwen, Zhang Qunqiaio.

Great Leap Forward (1958–61)   The movement to raise productivity hugely and industrialize rapidly which Mao instituted in order to circumvent the specialists and experts who denied the primacy of will in economic development. Agriculture was collectivized and industry decentralized, with the result of chaos and widespread starvation.

Hangzhou   Developed as recently as AD 700 it was the imperial capital in the twelfth century and this spurred on its urban development and industrial progress. Under the Mongols Hangzhou developed as an international trading centre and was visited by French, Arab and Italian traders, some of whom left reports of the splendour and advanced state of the city with its large temples and palaces. Unfortunately many of these were destroyed during the Taiping Rebellion. The city has an extraordinarily beautiful setting of hills and water, and, conscious of this, the city authorities have in recent years done up or rebuilt large numbers of traditional teahouses, temples and famous cultural sites. They have been rewarded by more tourism than any Chinese city bar Peking, 21 million visitors a year.

Hu Feng   Marxist writer who believed that freedom of artistic expression was compatible with Communism. Disagreed with the conformist Zhou Yang and purged in 1955.

Hu Jiwei (1916–)   Sichuanese journalist. Deputy editor-in-chief, *The People's Daily*. Purged 1967. Chief editor 1977. Chairman, Journalists' Association 1980. Emerged in the 1980s as a champion of press freedoms. He was purged again in the summer of 1989 and held responsible for the involvement of many of his colleagues in the protests that led to the Tiananmen massacre. He has since been rehabilitated and perhaps serves as an icon to those still hopeful of the success of his ideas although he himself has, reportedly, despaired utterly.[1]

Hu Qiaomu (1912–)   Senior politician. CCP activist since 1935. Director of NCNA from 1948.

Hu Yaobang (1915–89)   CCP activist. Chairman of the YCYL in the 1950s and General Secretary of the CCP in 1981. Dismissed in 1986 for sympathy for student protests. His death in 1989 inspired demonstrations which only ended on 4 June 1989.

Hua Guofeng (1921–)   Political activist from the age of 15. Prime Minister 1976. Lost all senior posts in 1982.

Jiang Zemin (1926–)   Electrical engineer and CCP official. A Vice-Minister 1980. Mayor of Shanghai 1985. Politburo 1987. CCP Secretary General and Chairman of the Central Military Commission 1989.

Kang Youwei (1858–1927)   Scholar. Leader of the Hundred Days Reform Movement, aiming to modernize but retain Confucianism, repressed by the Empress Dowager in 1898.

KMT (*Guomindang*)   The Nationalist Party. Established 1912 from various smaller reform parties. Outlawed by Yuan Shikai 1914, it was recreated as the Keming Dang in exile in Japan. Re-established 1919.

Li Peng (1928–)   Adoptive son of Zhou Enlai. Engineer and party functionary. Prime Minister 1988.

Liang Qichao (1873–1929)   Disciple of Kang Youwei. Journalist and leading intellectual of the reform movement of the early part of the century.

Liu Binyan (1925–)   Investigative journalist and CCP activist from the age of 19. Famous for his stories exposing corruption. Purged 1957. Rehabilitated 1979. In Paris during the period 4 June 1989 joins student fugitives in denouncing the government's action and in setting up a 'Front of Democratic China' 1989. Lives in USA.

Liu Shaoqi (1900–74)   CCP activist from an early age. One of two Vice Presidents of the new PRC in 1949. Disagreed with Mao over Great Leap. Denounced in GPCR as a capitalist and vilified, probably badly maltreated. Lost all his positions 1968.

Mao Zedong (1893–1976)   Leader of the CCP 1935–76, in effect dictator for substantial periods 1949–76.

May 4 movement   Demonstrations which took place at Tiananmen 4 May 1919 against the Treaty of Versailles symbolize the greater movement for reform of institutions, culture and language which is labelled *May 4 Movement*.

Meiji Restoration   The 1868 palace coup in Japan which abolished the Shogunate and established in power a group of reformist nobles under the umbrella of the Meiji emperor.

Nanjing (also Nanking)   Capital of China under the Republic of China, 1922 to 1949.

PLA (People's Liberation Army)   Originally founded as the Red Army, the PLA remains the armed force of the CCP although it operates as if it were a state army.

Politburo   Powerful executive arm of the Central Committee, the central coordinating body of the CCP. From its members come the leading figures in Party and nation, the Standing Committee.

Qiao Shi (1924–)   CCP activist from the age of 16, senior politburo member by 1985.

Sichuan   South-westernmost province of China, bordering Tibet in the west. Its capital is Chengdu and it has a population of over 105 million.

Sun Yatsen (1866–1925)   A western-educated anti-Qing Dynasty activist, he founded several reform parties, some of which eventually merged to create the KMT. After the 1912 Revolution he became, briefly, first President of the Republic (ROC) in 1911, ceding his position to General Yuan Shikai for reasons of realpolitik. Thereafter he struggled for the remainder of his life to unite China; allied himself with the Soviet Union. His wife would become a Vice-President of the PRC, his sister-in law married his successor as President of the ROC, Chiang Kaishek. An inspiration to all modernizers and anti-imperialists, Sun is hero to both left and right and regarded as the father of modern China

Tiananmen incident   On 5 April 1976 demonstrations ostensibly expressing regret at the death of Zhou Enlai took place in Peking and were interpreted as critical of Mao and the Cultural Revolution.

Tibet   Country on China's south-west, bordering India and China's Qinghai Province. Nominally part of the Manchu Qing Empire, it remained ethnically homogenous and distinct both culturally and linguistically until quite recently. Invaded by China in 1950, its government overthrown, it has been subjected to some harsh colonial measures but may also have benefited from certain modernization. Its traditional government is in exile and there is an active liberation movement.

Tribune   In ancient Rome the common people elected a representative to champion their interests. By extension the expression means any similar office.

Wang Ruoshi (1926–2002)   Journalist and sometime deputy editor-in-chief of *The People's Daily*. Writer on humanism. Criticized Mao 1972 and sent for rectification. Reinstated 1976. Member of the official commission on interpretation of the Cultural Revolution. Dismissed 1983. Died in the USA.

Wei Jingsheng (1949–)   Editor of *Exploration*, activist in democracy movement of 1978–9, imprisoned 1979, exiled 1999.

Wu Han (1909–1969)   Scholar and administrator. Author of the oblique criticism, of Mao's purging of Peng Dehuai, *The Dismissal of Hai Rui from Office*, which stimulated responses from the left and so started the Cultural Revolution.

Yanan (also Yenan)   Shaanxi Province, small town in a mountainous area which was capital of the CCP 'state' from 1936 to 1947, when it was captured by government forces.

Yao Wenyuan (born 1931. Probably alive)   Shanghai journalist and associate of Jiang Qing who became one of the Gang of Four. He was author of the article which attacked Wu Han's *The Dismissal of Hai Rui from Office*, regarded as the start of the Cultural Revolution.

Zhang Chunqiao (1917–91)   Member of the Gang of Four. Journalist and leading Shanghai radical. Convicted in 1980.

Zhao Ziyang (1919–)   Official of Canton CCP when denounced and publicly humiliated in 1967. Rehabilitated 1971. Minister of the Commission for the restructuring of the Economic System 1982. Prime Minister who fell as a result of the student demonstrations of 1989.

Zhejiang   Province immediately south of Shanghai, with a population of over 40 million. Its capital is Hangzhou. It is one of the richest agricultural provinces and a major producer also of tea, fruit and silkworm cocoons and their derivatives. The textile, foods and chemical industries were well established before the Communist government came to power and have regained and surpassed their former importance since the economic liberalization of the early 1980s. The province has been successful in attracting foreign investment, most recently Italian clothing and leather goods producers and the authorities are conscious of the examples of high-tech enclaves in California and parts of Europe (Silicon Valley, Silicon Glen, etc.) and have set up equivalents.

Zhou Yang (1907–)   Communist activist and writer.

Appendix B: Chinese glossary

Ba Jin	巴金
Bao Qingtian	包青天
Bare Earth	赤地之爱,
Behind Official Openness	政务公开之后
Beijing Bastards	北京杂种
Bitter Love	苦爱
Canon of Filial Piety	孝经
Canton Daily	广州日报
Central People's Radio	中央广播电台
Central Propaganda and Ideological Work Group	央宣传和意识形态工作组
Central Propaganda Department	中宣部
Zhang Chunqiao	长春桥
Zhang Ailing	张爱玲
Chen Duxiu	陈独秀
Chen Xitong	陈希同
Chengchih University	政治大学
Chengdu	成都
Chengdu Business News	成都商报
Chiang Kaishek	蒋介石
China Can Say No	中国可以说不
China Democratic Party	中国民主党
China TV News	中国电视报
China Women's Daily	中国夫奴日报
Chinese traditional values	中国传统价值
Chong Ngoi Sam Bo	中外新报
Chu, Kingdom of	楚国 338–278 BC
chuanye	专业
Chungking	重庆
citizenry	老百姓
class society	阶级社会 a society with classes 有阶级的社会
Communist Youth Daily	共产青年报
county	(县)
creative adaptability	应变能力
Critique Department	评论部
Cultural Revolution	文化大革命

current affairs/investigative reports	深度报道
current affairs	时务部
Dadu	大渡河 River
Danwei	单位
Deng Tuo	邓拓
Deng Xiaoping	邓小平
disciplined	收纪录的
district level	(局)
ditan publications	地摊读物
East Radio	东方广播电台
Economics Half Hour	经济半小时
erudite essays	散文
falsehood, exaggeration and empty words	假大空
falungong	法轮功
Fang Lizhi	方励之
Fangfa	方法
Focal Point	焦点访谈
Foreign Affairs Department	对外部
Four Modernizations	四个现代化
Fudan University	复旦大学
Gang of Four	四人帮
Gengshen	更深
Golden Period	黄金时期
Gong Xueping	龚学平
Great Leap Forward	大跃进
Great Unity	大同
Guangming Daily	光明日报
Guo Moruo	郭沫若
Hai Rui	海瑞
Han Dynasty	汉朝 (206 BC–AD 220)
Helping the Poor	扶贫
High Leaders' Compound	中南海
Honorary Dean, Journalism School	新闻学院名誉院长
Hsin Pao	新报 in 1861
Hu Feng	胡蜂
Hu Jiwei	胡绩伟
Hu Qiaomu	胡乔木
Hu Shi	胡师
Hu Yaobang	胡耀邦
Hua Guofeng	花郭丰
Human Resources Reform	人力资源改革
Human Rights Observer	人权观察
Hundred Flowers	白花
inspiration	灵气儿 (Peking dialect)
(institutional) system	系统
Internal Reference	内部参考
Internal Situation	内部情况
iron rice bowl (permanent, secure posts)	铁饭碗
Jiang Qing	将青

Judge Di	狄公
Kang Youwei	康有为
Keda	科大
KMT	国民党
Kunming	昆明
latest news facts	最新发生的新闻事件
Law and Democracy Monthly	民主与法制
Leadership Small Group	领导小组
Li Dachao	李大潮
Li Po	李伯
Liang Qichao	梁启超
Liberation Army Daily	解放军报
Liberation Daily	解放日报
Liu Binyan	刘宾雁
Liu Shaoqi	刘少奇
loafer	流氓
Lu Xun	鲁迅
Lushan Conference	庐山代会
Mao Zedong	毛泽东
masses	群众 audience or receiving masses shou 收众
media commercialization	媒体商业化
mediators	中介人
Mencius	孟子
Middle Layer in Society	中等社会
Ming Dynasty	明朝 (1368–1644)
Ministry of Culture	文化部
Ministry of Finance	财政部
National Association of Journalists	中国记协
New China News Agency	新华新闻社
New Rome	新罗马
New Weekly	新周报
New Youth	新青年
News Criticism Department	新闻评论部
News from Inside the Paper	本报内部消息
non-political papers	街头报纸
non-profit making	事业
officials	干部
Opening	开放
Oriental Horizon	东方时空
Oriental Television	(OTV) 东方电视台
Ouyang Da	欧阳达
Party Principle	党性原则
Peking Broadcasting Institute	北京广播学院
Peking Daily	北京日报
Peking Youth News	北京青年报
Peng Dehuai	彭德怀
People's Daily, The	人民日报
PLA General Political Department	解放军总政部中宣部

political reports	政治报道
process the news	采制信息
Producer System Reform	制片人制度改革
profession	专业
profit-making	企业
province	省
public scrutiny	舆论监督
Pure Criticism Newspaper	清仪报
Qianjiang Wanbao	钱江晚报
Qiao Shi	乔石
Qin Benli	钦本立
Qin	秦
Qing	清朝 (1644–1911)
qinmei	亲美
Qiu Jin	丘金
Qu Yuan	屈原 (338–278 BC)
qualities	素质
Reading	读书
Rectification of Names	正名
Red Flag	红旗
Reference News	参考消息
regular graduates	本科生
Renmin University	人民大学
Research	第六次全国传播学研讨会
Rice Sprout Song	秧歌
River Elegy	河殇
Romance of the Three Kingdoms	三国演义
scum	无赖文人
Self-Sufficiency System	自营制度
sense of duty	责任感
Shao Piaoping	少票平
Shenzhen Pictorial Journal	深圳画报
social effect	社会的效果
Southern Progress	南巡
spirit of the nation	国魂
Spiritual Civilization	精神文明
Standing Committee of the Politburo	中共中央政治局党委会
State A'n for Radio Film and Television	国家广播电影电视总局
State A'n of Press and Publication	新闻出版署
State Council Information Office	国务院新闻办公室
State Office of Publishing	国家新闻出版社
Su Xiaokang	苏晓康
Sung Dynasty	宋朝
The Family	家
Three Family Village	三家村
throat and tongue of the Party	党的喉舌
Times	时报
township	镇
Vice General Secretary of the Shanghai CCP	中共上海市委副书记

Viewers	观众
Wahji Yatbo	花子日报
Wang Meng	王盟
Wang Shiwei	王市委
Warring States period	战国时代 (403–221 BC)
Water Margin	水浒巷
Weekend South	南方周末
Wei Jingshen	魏京生
Wenhui Daily	文汇报
Wenhui-Xinming Press Group	文汇新明
World Economic Herald	世界经济报
Wu Han	武汉
Xiang River Review	湘江评论
Xinao	洗脑
Xinghai	兴亥革命 (1911) Revolution
Xinjiang Daily	新疆日报
Xinmin Wanbao	新民晚报
Xu Liangyang	许良英
Yao Wenyuan	耀文元
Yenching	燕京大学
Yinglixing	营力性，
Yueh Fei	岳
Zhang Chunqiao	张春桥
Zhangjiagang	涨价港
Zhangjiagang	涨价港，
Zhou Yang	周扬，
Zhu Rongji	朱榕基
zhuanjieben	专节本
zhuankesheng	专科生

Sayings/expressions

seek truth from facts!	实事求是
our job is to serve the public weal	我们是为公众提供服务
jumping into the ocean	下海
above and below in harmony	上下一体
close to the citizenry	贴近老百姓
crossing the river by feeling stone by stone	摸着石头过河
does a child find its mother too ugly?	做孩子的不嫌娘丑
praise the vanguard	表扬先进
criticize that which is backward	批评落后
bring justice to society	生藏争议
Oh how odd, Oh how odd	真奇怪真奇怪
always printing lies, always printing lies	全是谎话全是谎话
It doesn't matter if it's a black cat or white cat as long as it gets the mouse!	不管白猫黑猫只要抓住老鼠就是好猫

Notes

Preface

1 The first story is 趙簡子問子貢 Chao Jiantzi wen Zigong, the second 刻舟求劍 Ke chuan qiu qian. I had the pleasure of translating them in my classical Chinese class with Mrs Y.C. Liu at SOAS many years ago. She published them (no translation, I am afraid) in Liu, Y.C. (1960) *Fifty Chinese Stories*, London: Lund Humphries.

1 Introduction

1 A typical article is Pratley (2002) which notes, among other things, that China has more mobile phone users than the USA and that the British DIY chain B and Q, soon to have fifty-eight stores in China, finds that average transaction values are double that in the UK. See, among others, Roberts, D. (2003) 'China's economy is no house of cards' in *Business Week* 16 January 2003; Winacott P. (2002) 'WTO entry spawns optimistic feeling at home' in *Wall Street Journal* 15 January 2002 or Sheridan, M. (2003) 'How China has become the world's new workshop'; London: *Sunday Times Business Section* 26 January 2003 and *The Economist* 'China forecast' 24 January 2003.

2 The two main areas, both of which had client status under the Qing and were incorporated into the PRC into the 1950s, are Tibet and East Turkestan (Xinjiang). There are of course many minorities, particularly in Sichuan, Guizhou and Yunnan; there are indigenous peoples of different cultures in Inner Mongolia, Manchuria (Dongbei) and Gansu and there are several different religions. But none of these groups will ever have the slightest influence on the majority, Chinese, community. CCP policy, aping the USSR, created the fiction that China is a multinational state in which the biggest race is the Han. Southern Chinese, however, call themselves Tang rather than Han and anyway every Chinese is by preference a *Zhongguoren* (Chinese).

3 For a reader interested in pursuing the challenge still posed to non-western societies by the western example and the experience of globalization, *The West and The Rest* by Roger Scruton (Wilmington: ISI Books 2002) will be stimulating.

4 Recent data are given in Thomas, Bella (2003) 'What the poor watch on TV' in *Prospect*, Issue 82, January 2003 pp. 46–51.

5 According to J. Abramsky, Director BBC Radio and Music, it is radio and not TV that is now the most used medium in the UK, catching up with Third World countries where this has long been so. She said this in the course of her address, the James Cameron Memorial Lecture, City University, London 25 November 2002.

6 Halloran, James, (ed.), (1990) *A Quarter of a Century of Prix Jeunesse Research*, Munchen: Stiftung Prix Jeunesse.

7 TV has been found to portray various groups and activities in ways at variance with with real life occurrences or demographic significance (Gunter 2000: 68). For example it underrepresents the elderly as compared with their number in real life (Gunter 1998, Kubey 1980, Harris and Feinberg 1977).

8 See for example Rajasundaram, C.V. (1981) *Manual of Development Communication* Singapore: Asian Mass Communication Research and Information Centre.

9 Although the ways in which they are influential can sometimes astonish the creators. See Thomas, Bella (2003) 'What the poor watch on TV' in *Prospect*, Issue 82, January 2003 pp. 46–51.

10 Or at least that they should do. See Philo, Greg and Miller, David (2000) *Market Killing* London: Pearson.

11 The writings of David Green and his colleagues at the UK think-tank Civitas are indicative. See http://www.civitas.org.uk

12 The *agora* was the forum in ancient Athens in which the debates took place that characterized Athenian democracy.

13 References: news reports often merely reproduce what reporters are told by established authority (Sigal 1999, Dickson 1992, Daley and O'Neill 1991); are ethnocentric (Gans 1979); create norms of deviance (Cohen 1990); give unwarranted prominence to violence and criminality (Roshier 1981); stereotype people (Glasgow University Media Group 1980, Tuchman 1978); sanitize content (Shephard 1993, cit. in Shoemaker, P. 1996; Phillips 1995, Bell 1998).

14 Michel Foucault, Richard Rorty and Jacques Derrida have charmed the academic world with their contention that all is relative, there is no truth, only opinion or story. This view is held in a religious manner, that is, is not subject to rational refutation, another manifestation of the longing that some have for abandoning their critical faculties in favour of belief.

15 In August 1974 US President Richard Nixon resigned when it was clear that he would be impeached by Congress both for trying to obstruct the official investigation of a burglary, using government resources for party political purposes and dishonestly denying his involvement in other illegal or unacceptable activities. The event which symbolized all the misdemeanours was the burglary at Democratic Party headquarters, based in a Washington office block called the Watergate.

16 The full story is told, and the professional techniques and attitudes well demonstrated, in the two reporters' own account, *All the President's Men* (Woodward and Bernstein 1979) and in a film of the same name.

17 Mark D'arcy, now a BBC parliamentary reporter, was for many years BBC Local Government Correspondent in the Midlands. He lectures on the extraordinary limitations placed upon reporters by their readers' laziness and their editors' lack of imagination, suggesting that 'the quango state' is largely unscrutinized, an area where rich friends of those in power slurp unwatched from the trough of public money. See also his (1994) *Abuse of Trust*, London: Bowendean and (2000) *Nightmare!*, London: Politicos.

18 See, for example, King, Anthony (2001) *Does Britain Still have a Constitution?* London: Sweet and Maxwell.

19 As leader of the opposition Tony Blair did a turn at News International's managers' freebee in Australia and, more important and almost as undignified, promised not to interfere in that company's position in the British media, in return for which favours News International's most influential titles supported the briber. As if that were not adequate Danegeld, in 2001 *The Sun* was even told the date of the General Election before anyone outside the leadership compound, and that newspaper repaid its debt with its support. Tony Blair also went to some lengths to please the pornographer Richard Desmond when he bought the *Express* newspaper.

20 When Robert Pinker, Chairman of the Press Complaints Commission, defended self-regulation in a speech at Goldsmiths College on 21 November 2002, the sceptics

who took him to task for failure to control the press came from the left; twenty years before, the positions would have been reversed.

21 See for example the publications of Britain's Campaign for Press and Broadcasting Freedom (http://www.cpbf.org.uk).

22 Conversations with Professor Peter Smith, Head of the Department of Psychology, Goldsmiths College, October to December 2000. Anthropology has long seen great differences in social behaviour and attitudes between, for example, north and south Europeans yet the challenge to the north European dominance of psychology has not come from the Mediterranean, where scholars have gone along with the homogenizing psychology, but from China.

2 The inheritance

1 Nanxun means 'southern tour' but has implications of the journey of inspection by an Emperor to his provinces, or even a royal progress. Hence my use of the term Progress which seem to me to give the right flavour while not being any less accurate than the other translations in use.

2 I am intentionally simplifying a drawn-out process. The CCP announced 'New Democracy', an alliance of classes, in 1949, which they replaced by 'Socialist Transformation' in 1953 and 'Socialist Construction' in 1956. The private sectors and the opportunities for initiative were progressively reduced. The process may be examined more deeply in Hsu 1995: Chapter 26.

3 Winstanley, M.J. *Ireland and the Land Question 1800–1922* London: Methuen.

4 See Hughes T.J. and Luard D.E.T. *The Economic Development of Communist China* London: 1962.

5 As Hsu has pointed out (1995: 657) Mao was probably inspired more by Kang Youwei's *Book of Great Unity* (*Datong Shu*) which advocated an end to private property and family life as well as a kind of cradle to grave welfare system, than by the European examples.

6 Because everybody wore a standard uniform, differing only slightly according to whether s/he was a peasant, soldier, industrial worker or official. The student in question was a painter and had achieved high status for his public art at that time; later he left China and made a career for himself in the USA, and worldwide, as a fine painter. He is Han Xin.

7 At least this is my interpretation, and it is of necessity brief and partial. For a more nuanced overview of the People's Republic of China before Deng Xiaoping, I suggest Jack Gray's (1990) *Rebellions and Revolutions* Oxford: OUP.

8 For an explanation of the Xitongs see Christiansen *et al.* (1998).

9 Subsequently renamed Information Department in the English version.

10 Li Peng retired in November 2002 but obtained the elevation of a least two of his protégés to the Standing Committee of the politburo as he did so.

11 However repression did not stop: in April 2000 an English-language weekly was closed down and the editor of another magazine sacked for what appear to be quite trivial reasons (Prisma 2001: 207).

12 For more on this, see Buruma (2001 Chapter 5).

13 All at http://www.igc.org/hric/crf/english

3 Media characteristics

1 Abridged from a very long reply full of instances.

2 The reader who is concerned with commercial data should refer to the following: China Media Intelligence http://www.eight-and-eight.com/internet.html or China Media Monitor Intelligence http://www.cmmintelligence.cm/. Also of interest may be Chinese Communications Research http://sjmc.cla.umn.edu/cca/history.htm

3 Zhongguo Shehui Kexueyuan Xinwen yu Chuanbo Yenjiusuo (ZSKXCY) (ed.) (2001) Zhongguo Xinwen Nianjian Peking: Zhonguo Xinwen Nianjian She, pp. 405–406. Some sources give higher figures.

4 Ibid., pp. 419–420.

5 The official Chinese sources make distinctions which are valuable but not relevant to the points made here. Figures may be obtained from Guojia Guangbo Dianyingshe Zongju, etc. (GGDZ) (2001) *Zhongguo Guangbo Dianshi Nianjian* Peking: Zhongguo Guangbo Dianshi Nianjian She, p. 45.

6 Prisma 2001: 202.

7 *Newsweek Magazine* 'Changing China. a special report' 2002.

8 The justification for Conglomeration appears to be that the Japanese zaibatsu are a model which China should attempt to emulate, not only for their function in national development but also for their believed efficiency.

9 Mr Pan refused to further comment on this matter, about which I had heard from several other sources.

10 Journalists' monthly paper *News Journalist* (*Xinwen Jizhe*) covered this with major articles in January 2002, February 2002, March 2002.

11 The story investigated by various UK journalists in the early 1990s, studied in depth by the *Scott Report* (1996) and which revealed that a UK Minister had sanctioned arms exports to Iraq against the expressed public policy of his own government.

12 Editors regularly receive directives from Party offices, originating from the Central Propaganda Department (CCP), the New China News Agency (NCNA) and the Propaganda Department of the PLA General Political Department. One of their principal jobs is to supply the appropriate formulations in regular circulars or in the newsletters for journalists, such as *Newspaper Trends*. There are weekly *post facto* evaluation sessions held at most media outlets, at which Party officials are present. The word 'propaganda' has recently been changed to 'information'; in English translations of the titles are referred to above.

13 For an explanation of Restricted Circulation Publications see Chapter 9.

14 The books are Wang Weici (2000) *Record and Explore* and Lu Xinyu *The Contemporary Television Documentary Movement in China*. Wang Ningtong is my informant.

15 C4TV was established in the UK in 1982 with a remit to be a publisher-broadcaster rather than a programme maker, one of the intentions of the government being to develop a programme production sector. While the policy was revolutionary, and initially much decried, since 1987 independent production has become much more general, with all broadcasters commissioning an ever rising proportion of programmes from the one thousand or so independents in the UK; however, there is a tendency to commission blocks of programmes from one supplier, or to deal only with a very few established suppliers. Probably only C4 has commissioned such a high proportion from such a variety of individual producers and only C4 has allowed independents to produce segments for its news programmes.

16 I am indebted to Jiang (2002) for the up-to-date information about the private production industry. Her essay cites various sources for her figures, Zhang Yi (2001) and Lu Di (1999).

17 This is not as different from western practice as it at first appears. In even the most entrepreneur-friendly regime, such as that operated in the early 1990s by C4TV, commissioning editors would agree, and sometimes propose, key personnel.

18 In Chengdu in June 2000 I was struck at finding a Burberry jacket for sale at a price which was the equivalent of a year's salary for a *senior* Chinese television reporter.

19 There is no exact equivalent to the UK term, but the nearest is probably Shendu Xinwen, literally 'news in depth'.

20 Curiously, simple people interviewed are often not captioned by name but as 'local peasant', 'villager', 'local woman', etc.

21 I had flown in with some of the Orbis team.

4 Burden of the past (Yanan–Cultural Revolution)

1 For example, Li's *Essentials of Journalism Theory* (1997).
2 It should not be imagined that these formulations are only for the masses; the leaders express themselves in this tortuous way, too. To make the point of just how far from reality and clear and rational thinking the Chinese leadership often is, Studwell (2002: 266) quotes from a report of the Central Committee. I suppose that two factors are at play in bringing about this kind of pseudo-speak; the fear of truth, identified so well by George Orwell's critique of left politicians' language in the 1930s (in 'Politics and the English Language') and the desire to pretend to being scientific.
3 Liu (1975: 30) identifies four principles of CCP mass persuasion. They are: insulation (from competing ideas), emotional arousal, simplification, politicization (i.e. soaking the targets' thoughts in political categorization).
4 Early observers of the mass media, typified by Matthew Arnold, were concerned at the supplanting of traditional cultures, seen as organically developed, by commercially and/or politically manufactured knowledge. Adorno (1991) and Arendt (1951) were concerned that the mass media were so influential as to be able to erase all traditional social decencies and cultural knowledge and to remake us as political slaves or the dupes of commercial interests. The mass media were 'narcotic' in effect, 'lobotomized' the recipients, who became possessed of false consciousness which made them 'one-dimensional'. This power of the mass media seemed obvious to generations which had seen the eyes of people from confined communities being opened to thousands of new stimuli (Seymour-Ure 1974) or the way in which totalitarian regimes had sought to use them for 'brain-washing' (McQuail 1994: 58). Their mistake was that they assumed that this power was exercised in a *hypodermic* manner. As suggested above, Mao and his colleagues inherited this idea through Lenin since when it became an article of faith in journalism education in China. Meanwhile in the West, by the 1950s empirical studies were showing that the mere fact of communication did not necessarily involve an effect, at least not the effect intended by the communicator; neither attitudes nor behaviour were easily susceptible to change; much depended upon the recipient, other influences upon that recipient as well as the message environment, mode of communication and so forth. Both media studies and psychology agreed upon that (de Burgh 1987: Chapter 2). Messages, in other words, were mediated. This was taken further in the 'uses and gratifications' approach, which suggested that it was the recipient who determined the significance of the message, accepting or rejecting it according to various conditions and criteria quite at odds with the parameters within which the message-maker worked (Blumler 1974). By 1973 a more balanced way forward had been proposed by Stuart Hall in his 'Encoding and decoding in the television discourse' (1973) in which he suggested that there was not necessarily a correspondence between the message encoded by the message-maker and that de-coded at the other end and that the communicative process had to be looked at as a whole. It was Hall's article that laid the ground for a new flowering of empirical work, concentrating upon the recipients' readings of the messages or texts, associated with the Birmingham School (Kitzinger 1999: 3). Morley's study of readings of the current affairs programme *Nationwide* confirmed that there were different possible readings of the text, that readings were related to class, gender, age and ethnicity (Morley 1980). Comparable studies were subsequently undertaken on readings of soap operas (Katz and Liebes 1985).

On a slightly different tack, various studies were undertaken in the early 1990s which suggested that the media did influence, but by no means always in the way which might have been predicted by the message-makers, and pointing to a need to understand the construction of the messages themselves as much as the recipients (Jhally and Lewis 1992; Gamson 1992; Corner *et al.* 1990). Soon after Morley's 1980 study Cohen and Young (1981) were arguing that effects were not amenable to analysis, for one result of this new understanding was that the very idea of effects was doubted. That the media professionals and the public both appeared to believe still in the hypodermic model is evident from the reaction to the Bulger case (in which it was suggested that the murderers had been stimulated by their media viewing; discussed in Kitzinger 1999). Academics reacted by publishing several titles, including *Ill Effects* (Barker 1997), which broadly argued that the idea of effects was a myth and that the media were being made scapegoats for social behaviour in reality influenced by other factors.

However, the Glasgow University Media Group was, in the 1990s as in the 1980s, carrying out a series of studies into the television audience reception process which were suggesting that the dismissive attitude to effects was misguided. There was impact upon recipients, they concluded, since certain types of information were conveyed very effectively and could be used in daily life by the recipients just as associations were made between situations mediated and real-life situations, causing fear of danger, for example. Moreover recipients could recall dialogue and used their recall of the situations 'as common reference points to explain or justify certain points of view' (Kitzinger 1999).

Impact was mediated by the environment, the personality of the recipients and many other factors and was linked to the message construction. Until recently these debates largely passed by Chinese journalists and even media academics. Jiang Weihua is worth quoting as he remains an exponent of what anglophones might call the hypodermic approach. 'Once the masses understand what the Party wants then society is in order and the journalists have done their job' (Jiang Weihua).

5 The process was not quite so clean-cut and some independent newspapers survived but so hamstrung by political dictates or lack of advertising funding that they did not last long.

6 The most terrifying aspect of this, often overlooked by foreign observers, was that it was in effect hereditary. That the political actions or words (and 'political' had very broad meanings) of one member of a family could determine the life chances and perhaps survival of all relatives to several degrees of consanguinity and for generations to come was a feature of CCP terror particularly awful in a society in which the family has typically been the only support of individuals; its existence is one particularly dramatic example of how draconian was the CCP's terror.

7 In Taiwan a resurrection along these lines was being attempted and is expressed in a document which would not have been out of place on the mainland in relatively relaxed times. The 1950s Code of Ethics adopted by the (Taiwan) *Press Association*, *Newspaper Society* and *Reporters' Society*, appears intended to provide a framework acceptable to the political leadership which might yet allow some scope for journalistic responsibility to develop. It declares, among other things 'We deeply believe that national independence and world peace transcend all other interests. We pledge not to indulge in any expression of opinion or reporting which may be prejudicial to national reconstruction . . . We pledge to work for the promotion of the people's knowledge, the promotion of the people's morals . . . We pledge to go deeply among the people to seek improvement in their livelihood, to propagate production and reconstruction and to organise social service' (Zhang 1968: 21).

One of the problems that journalists on the mainland had from which their counterparts in Taiwan suffered less, is that the splits in the CCP leadership were severe, often involved the media and had repercussions on the media.

8 I use two of them in final paragraph of Chapter 1. To supplement 'feudal' notions carried by the traditional *chengyu* or sayings, the CCP created thousands more as each campaign or new theory sprouted its mnemonics and slogans. More information on this technique can be found in Liu (1971) and Liang and Shapiro (1984).

9 According to my informant, his father was a 'mere' fisherman around Shaoxing but was able to progress to being the manager of a fish farm. His mother's family benefited similarly from the CCP. His older brother and sister became doctors and

he studied philosophy. The only brother who did not go to university, the youngest, became an entrepreneur whose fortune now subsidizes other members of the family. The latter is quite likely to want faster change, the members of the family in state jobs are doubtless chary of it. He himself is ambivalent, as befits an 'intellectual' in the culture industries!

10 As to the motivations of Mao's loathing for intellectuals, Liu (1971: 26), as with others, points to Mao's own account of the manner in which he was treated when a lowly functionary at Peking University.

11 Almost every journalist I have met in China I have asked to tell me the attractions of journalism to him/her. All of them cited the freedom to travel within China, something which until the mid-1980s was very difficult for all but quite senior officials and journalists and is still expensive for most people. Thus travel is a great perk and privilege and journalists have probably always been very sensible of this.

12 Marx believed that consciousness was the product of material conditions which man had little power to change; Lenin saw the Party as the agent by which those conditions would be changed because the Party would alter consciousness. Maoists, like European fascists, inherited this idea from Lenin and took it a stage further, suggesting that transformation of the consciousness of the masses could itself be all that was needed. 'To a Bolshevik the Maoist conviction that backward peasants, by believing the right thoughts (those of Mao) could change a nation, irrespective of the development of its productive forces and social structure, is the heresy of voluntarism' (Liu 1971: xii).

5 Burden of the past (Cultural Revolution–Tiananmen)

1 Hsu (1995: 691) gives agricultural and industrial output statistics for the Great Leap.

2 According to Zhao Yuezhi, *min-ban* newspapers were advocated in this period; they were not again to be advocated until the 1990s (Zhao 1998 Chapter 2).

3 'At court' is a rather apposite expression as the high leadership mostly lived at Zhongnanhai, the 'leadership compound' which is a section of the Forbidden City in Peking.

4 There is a political biography of Yao, by Lars Ragvald (1980).

5 I am indebted to Professor Roger Bromley for this analogy.

6 Falsehood and exaggeration should not, however, be thought to have been merely a product of the GPCR. They were endemic to the Leninist conception of reportage. See Zhang Ailing's novel *Yang ge* (*The Rice Sprout Song*), cited in Chapter 4 (Zhang 1960: 98–99).

7 I am grateful to Professor David Morley for providing me with the Howard articles.

8 The first statement is from a man in his forties, the second from a woman aged 24. The man had already played a role in policy development and was a co-author of *Heart to Heart*, the book which most clearly exposed Jiang Zemin's thoughts; the woman is an iconoclast from a provincial TV station.

9 In 1983–4 there was a campaign against 'spiritual pollution' or influences from abroad and in 1987 a campaign against 'bourgeois liberalization'. Although Wang Ruoshi, for example, lost his post in 1984 the mass persecutions of the past were not replicated.

10 See for example *Beijing Review* 10 April 1989: 5–8.

11 This has been widely discussed. See, e.g., Zhao (1998: 35). She also reminds us that Hu Jiwei had suggested that the press ensured that people had the right to be kept informed, to be consulted, to involvement and to supervise government. Wang Ruoshi and others moreover argued that a free press is essential to a stable and prosperous country (Zhao 1998: 37).

12 The majority Turkic people of Eastern Turkestan are referred to by the Chinese government as the 'national minority' of the 'Uighurs'. They are ethnically and culturally virtually Uzbek and speak Uzbek Turkish with a local accent.

13 And still is. In theory the subject is very much alive, with experts gathering information and, in the case of the NPC Media Law Advisory Committee at least, visiting the UK for extensive briefings (at Nottingham Trent University 1–28 February 1999).

14 This documentary provoked lengthy and virulent controversy as it lambasted Chinese traditional society and appeared to advocate sweeping westernization and rejection of the rest of Chinese culture.

15 The term is used here in its technical, CCP, sense as meaning the thought reform (through study and/or punishment) of the deviationist.

16 Conversations at Zhejiang University, September 1999.

17 Reported throughout the media, week beginning 20 September 1999.

6 Political context for journalism today

1 Economic data cited in this chapter derives from Fewsmith (2001), Studwell (2002), Kurlantzick (2002) and Sheridan (2003).

2 The philosopher Confucius lived 551–479 BC. His reflections evolved into a body of precepts which guided the Chinese state and society down to the twentieth century when the CCP sought systematically to destroy its remnants. Confucius emphasized a moral order to which, if we wish for happiness, we should submit or fit ourselves; he harked back to the humanity and good conduct of past rulers and called upon contemporary man to model himself upon the example of the ancients. He believed that there are natural relationships of superiority and inferiority to which we must adhere. We must make our activities conform to what is natural; thus his philosophy is the antithesis of the modern view of man as conqueror and master of the universe.

3 Studwell (2001: 252–253) goes into this, illustrating the vast greed of the crooks and their intimacy with the highest leaders.

4 His clearest exposition of this belief was published in *The People's Daily* of 12 May 1995.

5 It's widely held that most Chinese economic data is suspect, and accounts particularly irrelevant. See Chang (2001) and BBC (2002).

6 A great many interesting observations can be made about these issues and in particular of the pernicious influence of politics. The government has allowed favoured bankrupts to repudiate debt and thus set an example which is being followed at all levels. Another kind of political interference is when the government simply annuls the sale of companies to please local politicians (Chang 2001: 162).

7 The most articulate proponent of this point of view is the Harvard scholar Yu Yingshi who wrote: 'Since 1949, a group of marginal people in China, relying on an especially radical theory and using a new type of totalitarian organisation, completely destroyed the traditional social structure of China'.

8 Subsequently this whole question has been thought through and argued over by US academics. See Harrison *et al.* (2000).

9 According to *Southeast China* (Shanghai) 4 March 1999 the top-ten bestselling books in February 1999 included this academic work.

10 This took place at the launch of the London Chinese Association and the remarks were made by the Leader of the Conservative Party on 4 March 2002. It is only fair to remark that the Chinese are quite eccentric in their desire to hark back to past slights (what successful countries have so deep seated and easily exposed a sense of resentment?) and forget the many positive aspects of their relations with western countries, to say nothing of the failures of Chinese in this area.

11 He Qinglian sees the new companies being set up simply as ways of stealing state assets. Fewsmith (2001:171) notes that she describes the process of selling of land as 'the equivalent of England's Enclosure Movement'.

12 He Baogang (1997: 81) makes the interesting point that the disaster of the Tiananmen incident in Peking, when compared to the compromise solution achieved in Shanghai,

has taught Chinese intellectuals the necessity for bargaining and compromise. He writes: 'The transition to democracy is a transition in modes of conflict resolution. The first stage is characterized by a switch from command and imposition to intense bargaining and compromise . . . thus the civility of political opposition may come to mature' (He 1997: 81).

13 In opposition to this it might be argued that the Chinese rethinking of their relationship with the state will fall short of the demands made in anglophone countries because of the absence of a similarly developed sense of rights. Wang Gongwu has argued (1991: 172) that the Confucian catalogue of duties also implies rights which flow therefrom and Pei (2000) asks why the pervasive Chinese sense of reciprocity should not be understood as one of mutual rights. This topic has attracted increasing interest recently, with the work of Yu Yingshan and Yan Yunxiang (2003; 1996) being the best known. Pye contributes a chapter on the Chinese case to Harrison (2000), which takes a global and cross-disciplinary approach to the relationships between culture and political and economic development.

14 These parties, astonishingly, have survived the last fifty years or so, but are dormant. They have been allowed an office each, seats at various congresses and an increasingly geriatric membership in order to give the appearance of pluralism when such an appearance has been diplomatically convenient. They have not been allowed to recruit new members since 1949 (!).

15 One important unresolved issue in modern China is the institutional position of the military, which is an arm of the CCP, rather than of the state. After the Tiananmen massacre, Deng Xiaoping dropped the ideas with which he had been playing, of the need to subject the armed forces, both the People's Liberation Army (PLA) and People's Armed Police (PAP), to institutional 'public scrutiny', reduce its involvement in civilian affairs and generally push it to the margins of public affairs where armies habitually reside in advanced countries. Such changes would presumably have included incorporating the armed forces into the state, and subjecting them to that state. However, his successors in power found themselves obliged to the army for their survival and Jiang in his early years of power was in a weak position in relation to the military, to the extent that observers talked of the subjection of the state to the generals (Lam 1999). The power of the PLA augmented as a result of various uncoordinated developments which, taken together, illustrate not only the problems of China's policy-making systems but also the inability of the media to draw attention to a very significant and very far-reaching development in the Chinese polity. After the shock of Tiananmen and the anti-western backlash, the army was promoted as a bastion of correct values, the defender of spiritual civilization and a model of good behaviour for the populace at large. Indoctrination campaigns were also held within the military in conditions of total separation from the outside world and the PLA's own media registered strong disapproval of 'western' decadence and parliamentary democracy. The armed forces were characterized as not merely the defenders of China against foreign aggression ('the Washington anti-China alliance') but also as responsible for upholding real Chinese values at home and resisting western corruption. In return for protestations of purity and loyalty and for taking the leading responsibility, at least in rhetoric, for the defence of the motherland from cultural contamination, army generals took upon themselves an increasingly active role in economic policy-making. Although there were sporadic attempts to limit the PLA's involvement in economic development, especially when the scale of corruption being practised by army units became evident, nothing serious was done, arguably because Jiang had allowed himself increasingly to become hostage to the military in the faction-fighting at the top. In fact, by 1997 the PLA was able to get its privileged position enshrined in the National Defence Law which gave priority to PLA requirements in economic policy and gave carte blanche for open-ended expansion of military budgets. It also declared that the army had the domestic duty of keeping order

and imposing stability. Taking these responsibilities seriously, and infuriated by Jiang's relatively accommodating approach to the Taiwan question, the PLA usurped his foreign policy-making functions on occasions and threatened Taiwan with war, denying the then sitting NPC and the media access to information about its activities (Lam 1999). The military appeared to be out of the control of the politicians. Journalists dared not report the doings of even quite minor examples of corruption or intimidation or dereliction of duty by military units (T'ao 2000), let alone keep the people informed of the generals' challenges to Jiang and the Foreign Ministry's supposed policy prerogatives. Moreover the PLA used its own media to publicize its own line. However, it is possible that the PLA had gone too far and that the civilian leadership took measures to rein it in, since the new Central Committee selected at the NC contained fewer military personnel than before and there were none on the Politburo Standing Committee (Fewsmith 2001). Jiang has also been able to call for a reduction in military personnel; it may be that he was able to exploit disagreement within the military, whose leaders may be as divided about the reform and opening programmes as their civilian counterparts. It is widely thought that Jiang's successor will make the institutional reorganization of the PLA an early objective.

7 The patriot journalists

1 There were a few who did not wish to engage with these questions, sceptics who saw their futures abroad, preferably in the USA, before which journalism could be used as a way of having an interesting time and making some money. The interviewees quoted here were among the media professionals, mainly journalists, whom I have interviewed on various aspects of their work. The full report is contained in a unpublished Ph.D. thesis by me, Nottingham Trent University, 2001.

2 By 'grand narratives' I mean the orthodoxies of historical writing since 1949, for example the belief that China was 'semi feudal, semi colonial' before socialism; that it was saved from ruin by the peasant–worker–soldier movement and other such religious mumbo-jumbo.

3 'Literatus' is the expression commonly used in Chinese studies to designate those conventionally regarded as 'educated' in traditional China, namely those who had, or had had, aspirations to take national examinations for the magistracy or persons from families typically so aiming. It is used here in preference to 'intellectual', which has implications of 'free-thinking' or event 'iconoclastic'.

4 The Mandarin transcription of these Cantonese names is: Zhongwai Xinbao, Huazi Ribao and Xinbao.

5 See Hsia (1971), still an excellent account of the interaction between politics and literature in the period.

6 See, in particular, Schwartz, B. (1964) *In Search of Wealth and Power: Yen Fu and the West* Cambridge, MA: Harvard University Press.

7 For my general background I am drawing upon past reading, particularly of the wonderful books on the period by Benjamin Schwarz, and also upon lectures at the LSE by Professors Stuart Schram and Jean Chesnaux 1970–72.

8 See also Cheng, Jason (1963) p. 50.

9 Owing to some missionary connections, the University of Missouri established a programme for young Chinese journalists in about 1908. I believe this university was the first in the world to offer education in journalism. Many Chinese took advantage of it, although the definitive history has yet to be written.

10 And translated into English several times.

11 There is an amusing series of scenes in Chapter 29 depicting the rather half-hearted attempts of the local warlord to close down the paper. With hindsight, it contrasts vividly with the savagery of CCP oppression that would follow.

12 For a critical account of the period, see Daruvala (2000).

13 Nanjing (Nanking) was capital of China under the KMT.

14 Conversations at Zhejiang University School of Journalism, 17 September 1999.

15 'Marxist terminology was eschewed; but the ideas of a vanguard party above the state and society, of imperialism, of class struggle, and of the power to deprive political opponents of their rights were all asserted. The ideology and organization of the Nationalist Party were transformed by these decisions, many of which proved as useful in justifying Chiang Kaishek's later dictatorship as in justifying totalitarian socialism' (Gray 1990: 212).

16 These rather sweeping statements will be found backed up by very interesting studies in social psychology of recent years, of which representative work is collected in Bond (1999).

17 The ideal of great unity and harmony is traced back by Chinese traditionalists to the Shang Dynasty of the Golden Age (which historically may have ruled parts of Heibei and Henan). As Fitzgerald writes 'The sense of unity, of belonging to a civilization rather than to a state or nation, was thus very ancient . . . It formed, in later times, the foundation for the acceptance by the Chinese peoples as a whole of the firm, strong and enduring central government which first united the country in the third century BC. It was an ideal which could be transmitted . . .' (Fitzgerald 1969: pp. 6–7). Always a powerful concept in Chinese thinking, it was further developed by the nineteenth-century reformer Kang Youwei who wrote a book devoted to how the great unity would once again be realized, the *Datong Shu*. Gernet summarizes his idea thus: 'humanity must experience in the course of its evolution three stages, the last of which will see the disappearance of frontiers and social classes, the formation of a universal civilization, and the inauguration of a definitive peace' (Gernet 1996: 596). Unity is thus the state to come and Confucians await it as they seek social harmony.

18 Joseph Levenson has argued that Communism suited Chinese intellectuals because it enabled them to feel superior to the hated West and more advanced. They could 'reject Confucianism from a superior position, while rejecting capitalism too' (Levenson 1958: 134). I would add that another appeal of Communism was surely that it offered that great unity which the messy compromises of anglophone democracy did not. While not assuming that Levenson would agree with that, I will quote from him to back up my point:

> To suggest, therefore, that Chinese communism has a role to play as a device for an intelligentsia in its efforts to escape an intellectual dilemma is not to deny but to confirm the fact that Chinese communism has come to the fore because of awesome social pressures. Alienation from Chinese tradition is inseparable from restlessness in Chinese society; and a revolutionary effort to cure the malaise which alienation engenders is the inescapable counterpart, in intellectual history, of the effort, by revolution, to pass through social restlessness to a social equilibrium.

> (Levenson 1958: 145)

19 This limitation, it can be argued, helps to account for China's tortured, even disastrous, relationship to the modern world. Where its origins lie is outside the scope of this study, but anthropology and developmental psychology will doubtless eventually throw light upon them. That journalists shared this blindness is not surprising, after all, they are of their culture. However, they have made attempts to overcome it, to establish themselves as professionals with a clearly demarcated role in Chinese society.

8 The journalist as tribune

1 Several academics in journalism departments mentioned this essay as influential. Weber tried to develop an idea of a responsible political leader, above interests of family or

class to replace the partial leaders who lacked awareness of common underlying interests. See Beetham (1974: 240–245).

2 The date 4 May 1919 was the occasion of demonstrations throughout China asserting the country's rights in the teeth of humiliation by foreign powers. The term 'May 4 movement' is, however, shorthand for a modernizing movement with more domestic than foreign policy ramifications, of which perhaps the core idea is the need utterly to transfigure traditional Chinese culture. Today this orthodoxy, common to both CCP and KMT, is being challenged as never before. For a thoughtful critique, see Daruvala (2000).

3 Journalists such as Deng Tuo and Liu Binyan both exemplify the desire to enrich their socialist faith with their high sense of personal responsibility.

4 The expression RCP is my own, there is a variety of ways in which the various Chinese terms are rendered into English.

5 During the Cultural Revolution Red Guards published files 'liberated' from government and CCP offices.

6 The importance attached to readers' letters was inherited from the USSR. In the 1980s a newspaper such as *Pravda* (the institutional equivalent of *The People's Daily*) received thousands of letters a week and maintained a special department to process them. Many would be referred to the 'appropriate authorities'. McNair reports a Soviet commentator as saying that 'the Soviet media receive 60–70 million letters each year, and [that] about 12 million people (6 per cent of the population) have contributed to the press in one form or another' (McNair 1991: 25).

7 Lecturers in journalism at Fudan, said that they could get their hands on any such RCPs if they wanted to.

8 Although in a sense it is that too. Note how people change their vocabulary in accordance with fashion in anglophone society ('chair' for 'chairman', 'Beijing' for 'Peking', 'operative' for 'worker' and you get a flavour of what happens with dramatic rapidity and thoroughness in China.

9 In the case of the use of the traditional English name for the Chinese capital, Peking, some media outlets bowed to Chinese government request that the substitute 'Beijing' be used; imagine what they would have said if the Italian government had requested we say Napoli or Roma!

10 The theory behind the attention to formulations is that there is a 'scientific' explanation of everything. When the CCP says that something is 'scientific' it does not mean that it is empirically verifiable but that it accords with the policies of the moment and will contribute to their realization – 'efficacious' might be a more suitable word. The theory underlying this is that 'scientific' explanation has a 'class character' but the selection of who or what is of any particular class is arbitrary. Today this seems to all westerners and many Chinese just so much religious mumbo-jumbo, yet this mumbo-jumbo has ruined the lives of many and distorted the thinking of millions of Chinese, not only through the media but because all academic research and pedagogy has been subject to rules which supposedly reflect this 'scientific approach'. Thus Chinese historians have been forced to describe past societies in terms which are, to modern historians elsewhere (and to many Chinese, privately), laughably simplistic. Chinese cultural life generally has been deadened by the requirement to see everything in politically correct formulae. However, the Central Committee itself has moved away from this position, declaring that it is not possible to see the Cultural Revolution in such class terms although it still remains mandatory to formulate the Cultural Revolution in a certain way that is restrictive of analysis and interpretation (Schoenhals 1992: 107–108).

11 Kang did in fact return to Shanghai in December 2000.

12 Zhang Ximin is director of the Centre for Media and Mass Communications Law Studies at the Chinese Academy of Social Sciences and author of many articles, of which two are cited in the bibliography.

13 A recent and nuanced examination of these questions is found in Yan (2003).

14 Adopted daughter of Ye Jianying. Missile engineer. *Guangming Daily* reporter. Sacked from *GD*; now freelance journalist.

15 The difference is of course that UK journalists do from time to time draw our attention to such manipulation and falsification. See the C4 Dispatches *Cooking the Books* 1989 and more recently, BBC Panorama *Politics of Spin* 2000.

16 The synopsis of this programme, though not Zao's description of its gestation, appears in the *collected* treatments of *Focal Point* which are cited in the bibliography.

17 Kang is here *NOT* referring to the Mayor of Shanghai conurbation but of a much smaller unit.

18 The expression 'cadre' translates *ganbu*, a singular or plural term for 'official' or 'functionary'.

19 Stephan Feuchtwang argues that these are returning. See Perry (2000).

20 In Eastman's words, 'some of the dominant traits of Chinese social behaviour proved to be particularly inimical to the development of effective government administration' (Eastman 1975: 309).

21 Blaming others for China's problems has been a distinguishing feature of Chinese political life and relations with other countries for at least a century. While it is understandable, in the light of the humiliations visited upon China in the nineteenth century, that Chinese should be critical of imperialism and the West, the refusal to acknowledge the immense help given to China by often disinterested and dedicated educationalists, officials and philanthropists is quite extraordinarily mean-minded. Truly, Communism provided a good excuse for despising the West as Levenson noted in his great early study of Chinese intellectuals (Levenson 1958). Considering the troublesome relationships that other societies have had with imperialism, or with competitors, China has little to complain about compared to much of colonized Africa or European countries exploited by their neighbours. However, the inability to empathize with others or to relativize things Chinese is familiar to students of modern Chinese history.

9 Becoming a journalist

1 He said 'between the rich and powerful and the poor and weak there's often only journalists, and the only weapon we have is shame'. However, these declarations were qualified by admissions that he came into journalism for social advancement and by the fact that his reputation as a journalist rests not upon radical exposures but upon pleasant light features. The one journalist who had worked on a radical left periodical made no claims of idealism, although he thought he had originally been pleased to work on a political paper because 'journalists are all leftish really' and 'it was the way students thought at the time'.

2 The sources of the above four quotations are CVs sent directly to me by the authors.

3 There are still many Chinese journalists who are not graduates, but this is not because of lingering reliance on the 'apprenticeship' approach as in Britain, but owing to the disruption of university courses during the Cultural Revolution 1965–75.

4 This aspect of Chinese society is the reverse of the anglophone case where it is I believe generally assumed that applicants 'from the sticks' are disadvantaged. Chinese explain the phenomenon of the peasant children outperforming city children as being not because of economic desperation but (1) domestic security (2) relatively good nutrition (3) an educational system with few variations from place to place (4) respect for learning among people of all classes.

5 Jenner (1994) has several interesting observations on this phenomenon.

6 The roles of these bodies are changing as I write and so are their names. Before the 1980s the craft unions were paramount.

7 As in the UK, the early years of television saw many people entering the profession without degrees (particularly in the technical side, from which they could progress

to direction and production as easily as journalists). However, Shanghai TV has declared that its professionals will in future all be graduates. There is therefore a demand for night-school classes in Shanghai's schools of journalism.

8 Those who took their first degree in Chinese language and literature or economics (the two main rivals to journalism) appear mostly to have made up for it by taking the MA in journalism which all the top universities offer. The fact that the MA takes three years does not appear to be a disincentive since it would seem that virtually nobody can be employed as a reporter until the late twenties so that getting an MA is a good way to bide time.

9 Interview with Professor Ivor Gaber, University of London, 28 March 2000.

10 The data on journalism education has been provided for me, most generously, by the Association. In his covering letter, my informant warned me that the information could not be comprehensive.

11 The main classifications of undergraduate degrees in China are: *Benkesheng* or regular, four-year degree candidates; *shuangkesheng* or 'double-degree' candidates doing two years of journalism with two years of, say, law or economics; *zhuankesheng* take a three-year degree only and usually do so by distance learning; *zhuanjieben* or technical college graduates.

12 I use the term 'distance learning' to translate the expression '*zixue kaoshi dianshi daxue*'.

13 There are 61 members listed on the tables, but only 55 have supplied data.

14 Two lectures given by Hugo de Burgh for the Department of Media, Renmin University, Peking on 14 April 1998.

15 At Renmin in 1998 the minimum level was 400 points (He 1998) and at Fudan 380 points (Huang *et al.* 1997).

16 On a visit to one of China's biggest and most important TV stations, the lecturer accompanying me bumped into twenty-four people who had been her students or whom she knew as having graduated from her school of journalism, one of whom was the chief executive (who asked her to lecture the following month on what she had learned from a recent overseas trip) and others in the senior management team.

17 Three pro-CCP American journalists who reported from China during the Civil War and the early years of the PRC, Edgar Snow, Agnes Smedley and Anna-Louise Strong.

18 Lee Chin-ch'uan, personal communication, 5 May 2000.

19 Useful explanations of the hypodermic and other approaches to media effects can be found at www.cultsock.ndirect.co.uk/MUHome/cshtml/index/html

20 A glance through the reports of the Campaign for Quality Television or Media Watch will confirm this.

21 This is by no means a Chinese speciality. Many British journalists and even some people teaching the subject in universities believe that all the tyros need are a few handy knacks. See my article 'Skills are not enough: the case for journalism as an academic discipline' *Journalism* autumn 2002.

10 Who do they think they are?

1 The idea that there is such a thing as 'western' media has been challenged by, among others, Chalaby (1998) and Mancini (2000). What is often called 'western' in fact means 'anglophone', if not American (de Burgh 2000). Thus I prefer to use the term 'anglophone'.

2 The Chinese expressions normally thus translated are *Shendu Baodao* or, less commonly, *Diaocha Xinwen*. The English expression is often used.

3 The newspaper *Nanfang Zhoumo*, the TV shows *Shihua Shishuo* and *Jiaodian Fangtan*.

4 The synopsis of this programme, though not the quoted description of its gestation, appears in the collected treatments of *Focal Point* (CCTV 1998).

5 These issues are discussed in, e.g., Ettema and Glasser (1985), Protess (1991) and de Burgh 2000 (Chapter 1).

6 In conversation with David Ross, editor of *File on Four* in January 2002, the familiar description of these kinds of topics as 'difficult' came up again.

7 Wu Jiaming, Shanghai IBS, letter to Paul Fox, Goldsmiths College, undated but received February 2002.

8 Friedman (1995) coins this expression. It is explained in Chapter 11.

9 One journalist put it to me that what his colleagues were doing was to call upon Chinese to awake and to change, a new *nahan* or call to arms, as in Lu Xun's celebrated book title, by those seeking to re-establish Chinese values after decades of subjection to western ones (i.e. Marxism-Leninism).

10 This refers to a topic well known in media studies and discussed in Scannell (1996).

11 Another indication of the trend was the fate of Marshal Peng Dehuai. When the Marshal blamed the GLF for the sufferings of the peasantry at the Lushan Conference of 1959 he was dismissed and his supporters purged at every level; many observers have pointed out that after Lushan there was no more real discussion or acceptable dissent in the CCP. Peng Dehuai was rehabilitated in 1979, presumably to symbolize the return of open discussion.

12 However, they were maltreated, his house was taken and his possessions stolen by the chief of police (Cheek 1997: 281).

13 See, for example, *The Journalist (Xinwen Jizhe)*, August 1984–February 1985.

14 Shaoxing is the hometown of Zhou Zuoren and his brother Lu Xun, as well as the ancestral home of Zhou Enlai and the source of China's best wine.

15 When I lived in Hong Kong for short periods in the 1970s and 1980s, I enjoyed reading newspapers and magazines using Cantonese vocabulary. This was a delight not available to 100 million-odd Cantonese in the PRC. Although programmes in the other Chinese languages are available on radio and to a lesser extent on cable TV, I understand that no mainstream media reflect spoken languages other than Mandarin.

16 See Chapter 11, p. 170.

17 Liu can be disparaged because he lives as a refugee in the USA as much as for the reasons I propose in the chapter. However, from the context of the conversation, I believe my reading to be correct.

18 Hu Yaobang was a protégé of Deng Xiaoping, expected to succeed him until 1987 when he was dismissed from his post of CCP General Secretary on account of his failure to suppress the student democracy movement. It was his death in April 1989 that precipitated massive demonstrations culminating in the Tiananmen massacre. He was respected for his frugality, openness and passion.

19 For a wise and informed view of Liu's associates and generation, see Mirsky, J. (2002) 'The life and death of Wang Ruowang' in *China Brief* 2(2): 17.

20 To refer to More's myth is not to subscribe to it. More was a pig-headed politician who supported overseas interests in purely administrative matters over against those of his own country, according to a critical interpretation. That he was vain and silly is hardly in doubt and it seems that he did everything he could to make himself a martyr.

21 The *Canon of Filial Piety (Xiaojing)* is one of the Confucian classics studied by all literate persons until 1911 at least, and treated with as much respect as the Holy Bible in Protestant societies. It is a dialogue upon the ethics of human relationships carried on by Confucius with his disciples. A translation is available in the series *Translations of the Confucian Classics* by Fu Genqing (1993) Jinan: Shandong Friendship Press.

22 See Hobsbawm, E.J. (1969) *Bandits* London: Weidenfeld.

23 I am mainly indebted to Schneider, and his excellent book of 1980, for my understanding of Qu Yuan.

24 The emphasis upon passion and individual expression, the sentimentalism and the emotionalism associated with the romantic movement in European literature, art and music seems to have appealed to the Chinese of that generation in particular.

25 Inspired by the radical writers of the 1930s, I was distressed, in 1973, to meet Guo Mojuo the Minister. He was at Peking airport to meet Prince Sihanouk, surrounded by the flunkeys and trappings of his high rank, dignified as any court chamberlain of another century and quintessentially of the established power.

26 Translated by Gordon (2000) as *Candid Talk*.

27 In saying this, I do not wish to ignore the 'Treaty Port' or commercial press, nor even the ancestors sometimes claimed for Chinese journalism, the *tongbao* of yore. However, just as a qualitatively different kind of journalism appeared in England in the eighteenth century from that which preceded it, so what emerged after the failure of Kang Youwei's 100 days bears little relation to its predecessors. See Britton, R. (1933) *The Chinese Periodical Press 1800–1912* Shanghai: Kelly & Walsh; and Gray, Jack (1990) *Rebellions and Revolutions* Oxford: Oxford University Press.

28 For example, the two distinguished journalists from BBC Radio's *File on Four*, Heggie and Ross, interviewed elsewhere (de Burgh 2000 pp. 200–202).

29 This newspaper is roughly the equivalent of (UK's) *Guardian*, in that its appeal is to teachers, lecturers and intellectuals generally. It is one of the most important three or four national newspapers.

11 Making news: a case study

1 Seventeen television journalists were interviewed of whom eight worked on the four weeks of product examined. The technique used was that of the semi-structured interview, since quantitative methods tend to apply in well-mapped territory where agreed categories of questions and fine definitions are possible.

2 In looking at news content, sociologists have established that news programmes are dependent upon established authority (Sigal 1973, Dickson 1992, Daley and O'Neill 1991), are ethnocentric (Gans 1979), create norms of deviance (Cohen 1990, Hertog and McLeod 1988), give undue prominence to violence and criminality (Roshier 1981) and stereotype people (GMG 1980, Tuchman 1978). Furthermore Phillips (1995), Bell (1998) and other working journalists have accused the media of sanitizing content as has at least one academic study (Shepard 1993, cit. in Shoemaker 1996). McQuail (1994) and Shoemaker (1996) are among the scholars who have taxonomized the influences upon content.

3 Mead (1926), Hughes (1968), Tuchman (1973), Carey (1976), Barthes (1977), Fiske and Hartley (1978), Brundson and Morley (1978), Silverstone (1981), Mazzolini (1987), Poecke (1988), Bennett (1988), Bird (1988), Zelizer (1993) and Langer (1998).

4 Any more than are those of the newsrooms with which I am most familiar, Scottish Television (reflecting a dissenting and cultural minority within the UK) or C4 News (an elite, small-audience, opinion-former programme with slant and format very distinct from mainstream news).

5 Figures from the Municipal Foreign Economic Relations and Trade Commission, November 1999.

6 In the UK, I spent one week (after initial exploratory visits) in the Birmingham newsroom of Central Television attending all news conferences and noting the discussion of stories and running orders; taped each evening's news programme for analysis; interviewed sixteen journalists, covering all roles, in eighteen interviews. Following the fieldwork I had further discussions with the Editor of Central News; analysed the interviews and texts recorded; and also invited two groups of students to examine the texts.

7 Signification: 'the relationship of a sign or sign system to its referential reality' (Saussure) although Barthes (1972) makes more of the concept, relating it to cultural values or myths. See O'Sullivan, Tim (1994) *Key Concepts in Communications and Cultural Studies* London: Routledge, p. 286.

8 The Chinese word '*xinwen*' has a broader sense than the English word 'news', although it encompasses it. It is better translated as 'journalism'.

9 These have been described in greater depth in a paper delivered to the Media Research Seminar of the School of Oriental and African Studies on 1 November 2001, entitled 'Investigative journalism as a social and cultural practice'.

10 The reason for the discrepancy is that, having worked in UK newsrooms and lived for many years in the UK, I felt confident that the English week was representative, I could not feel so confident about one week in China.

11 I have not classified as corruption the several packages dealing with traders flouting laws on health or environmental protection.

12 A question mark denotes that this theme or topic may be considered to have been covered also by a package which has been classified under another, more clearly appropriate, classification.

13 As note 4.

14 There are distortions of the period to be taken into account, distortions which qualify any comments which may be made: there was heavy reporting of the Wenzhou floods, accounting for over one-third of the items in the category 'problem-solving'; although the CCP and its history was reported on only 11 times, these totalled 54 minutes, or about 15 minutes per week, comprising features on the CCP's achievement in occupying Zhejiang in 1949, presented as a prelude to the 1 October national day celebrations; English packages vary much less in length than Chinese; there were 36 packages making government announcements, but over 75 per cent of these dealt with one topic, the Falungong.

15 Editors regularly receive directives from Party offices, originating from the CCP Central Propaganda Department, the New China News Agency (NCNA) and the Propaganda Department of the PLA General Political Department. One of their principal jobs is to supply the appropriate formulations in regular circulars or in the newsletters for journalists, such as *Newspaper Trends*. There are weekly *post facto* evaluation sessions held at most media outlets, at which Party officials are present. The word 'propaganda' has recently been changed to 'information' in English translations of the titles referred to above.

16 Do people in China rely upon the media? Do they trust them? anecdotal evidence suggests that most Chinese are very sceptical about the public media and in particular the news, even though they may be avid consumers. It is informal channels of information that they trust most, their families and friends. This is born out by such studies as there are. Bishop (1989: 27) concludes: 'All available evidence indicates that family influence is very high . . . and that the mass media have little influence when these two channels of information disagree. The media and official channels are important in publicizing official demands, and they have been quite influential for relatively short periods . . . but this influence seems to be declining'.

17 There is a clear idea in UK professional lore as to what is and is not 'televisual'.

18 Lee Chinchuan was examining a study by Chen (1998) in Weaver (1998) in the light of a contemporary one carried out from within China (Yu 1997).

19 The opposing trend in anglophone journalism is towards describing professionalism as the ability to catch and please the audience. Rather than holding on to some abstract notion of duty to the public sphere, 'socially responsible' journalism may be being subtly redefined as that which the audience wants. The editor of Central News, John Boileau, was quite unashamed of this approach, believing that the pre-eminent function of the programme is to entertain. This vision is a kind of radicalism – it is absolutely against the old public service ethos and contrasts with the idea of the journalist as serving the people's 'interests rather than their desires'.

20 See de Burgh (2000) pp. 69–70.

12 Conclusion

1 The main study dealt exclusively with news, yet the reporters invariably preferred to talk about other programmes they (might have) worked on.

2 That is not a put-down; anglophone individualism may have as many dysfunctional aspects as positive. However, it is difficult for anglophones to see them.

3 Alone, of course, the scribblers could not do this, but Mao had manoeuvred his supporters into leading positions in the army around the capital so that he was able to back his media attack with the threat of a *coup d'état*.

4 Liu Binyan writes 'The degree of boldness at *The People's Daily* is (determined by) the presence or absence of support by a politically important individual. . . . During the 1981 Bai Hua incident, for example, although newspapers of the People's Liberation Army published one critical article after another, *The People's Daily* remained on the sidelines, without publishing a single criticism of Bai Hua' (Liu 1990: 88).

5 This is not a reference to Liu, whose views on the crackdown I do not know.

6 Anti-foreignness is manifested in other ways too; Kurlantzick brings to our attention the fears of some foreign business people in China in Kurlantzick, Joshua (2002) 'Asia Minor' in *The New Republic* 16 December 2002 pp. 20–25.

7 See de Burgh (2000: 69–70) for some examples.

8 There are other interesting observations in this area for example from Sun Wusan and Huang Yu (1997) from which comes this: 'Another study carried out in 76 countries notes that the direct influence education and urbanization have upon a person's political outlook is minimal. Only when access to the media is enhanced can education help in the progress of democracy and political participation' from Sun Wusan and Huang Yu (1997) 'Effects of media behaviour on modernization of ideas – the case of China' in *China Report* 33(1): 93.

9 See *China Daily* week beginning 19 September 1999.

10 Asked to recommend the best examples of investigative journalism in 2002, a senior editor at BTV suggested *Counterfeit Transfusion Apparatus*; *Corruption in The Hope Project*; *Monopoly Power in Petrol Distribution* and *Stock Fraud*. All four of these investigations are lengthy exposés of dishonest dealings and the latter three touch on quite powerful interests with political connections. However, the only really 'political' story is that dealing with the *Hope Project*, set up with high-level backing (as well as sponsorship from US company Motorola) to provide schooling for poor families losing out from market reforms and headed for a time by Hu Jintao, subsequently elected General Secretary in November 2002.

11 Magazines have continued to be proscribed, either indefinitely or for short periods, because they offended the government and unwary journalists risk prison (IFEX 1999, Prisma 2001).

12 A much-promoted 2001 BBC investigative series on TV, *Sleepers*, covered such topics as the 'false weddings' of immigrants; racial abuse of Asians by whites and counterfeit passports.

13 For a synopsis of the hypodermic and other effects models see http://www.cultsock.ndirect.co.uk/MUHome/cshtml/media/fdevdet.html. As to the authoritarian assumption, some very interesting research is being done on Chinese children's upbringing and the significance of authoritarian behaviour towards them. For example Chen, X, Dong, Q. and Zhou, H. (1997) 'Authoritative and authoritarian parenting practices and social and school performance in Chinese children' *International Journal of Behavioural Development* 21, 855–873.

14 'Red Envelope' is a gift from a patron, sometimes, more precisely, a bribe.

15 And yet China is a big country, rich in so many traditions that the CCP may have failed to smash. The emergence and persistence of the Falungong illustrates a counter-trend. Professor Stephan Feuchtwang tells me that, even in Pudong, materialist China's Holy of Holies, temples may be found wherein young men are being trained,

as Daoist monks, to reject all worldly temptations (one of the LSE doctoral candidates whom he supervises is studying this phenomenon, 9 November 2002).

16 This term and its associations are discussed in Barmé (1999: 62).

17 *Beijing Bastards* (*Beijing Zahong*) is a 1993 film directed by Zhang Yuan and starring rock musicians Cui Jian and Dou Wei. It is compiled of clips from concerts, interspersed with 'bits' of stories as the band is expelled from its rehearsal rooms or has family problems and random shots of everyday Peking. It is interpreted as an expression of alienation.

18 The problems being brought about by commercialism gradually dawned on some of the intellectuals in the 1990s, when Culture Minister Wang Meng's championship of the novelist Wang Shuo was held by some to be a sell-out to commercial values.

Appendix A: Glossary of names and terms

1 Lee Chin-chuan, 1 November 2000, London, personal communication following his interview with Hu Jiwei. Lee considered that Hu's call to young journalists to 'make money' and 'work for yourself' was the symptom of a broken heart.

Bibliography

Abbott, Andrew (1988) *The System of Professions* Chicago: University of Chicago Press.
AC Nielsen (2002) Asia Pacific (http://asiapacific.acnielsen.com.au/news.asp?newsID=17).
Adorno, Theodore (1991) *The Culture Industry. Selected Essays on Mass Culture*. Edited with an introduction by J.M. Bernstein, London: Routledge.
Ahern, E. (1981) *Chinese Ritual and Politics* Cambridge: Cambridge University Press.
Allan, S. (1997) 'News and the public sphere: towards a history of news objectivity' in Bromley, M. *et al. A Journalism Reader* London: Routledge.
Allinson, R. (1986) *Understanding the Chinese Mind* Oxford: Oxford University Press.
Altschull, J.H. (1998) *Agents of Power* London: Longman.
Anderson, Benedict (1983) *Imagined Communities* London: Verso.
Anon (1996) 'How CCTV covered June 1989' in *Journalism Monographs* of the Association for Education in Journalism and Mass Communications University of S. Carolina, April.
August, Oliver (2002) 'Catchprase is the name of the game' in *The Times* 18 November, p. 12.
Ba Jin 巴金 (1956) 家 The Family 香港南國出版社
Bai Hua 白樺 (1986) 白樺的中篇小說 Bai Hua's Novellas 北京中國文聯出版公司
Bao Ruowang and Chelminski, Rudolph (1973) *Prisoner of Mao* Coward.
Bardoel, J. (1996) 'Beyond journalism: a profession between information society and civil society' *European Journal of Communication* 11(3):283–302.
Barker, Martin and Petley, Julian (eds) (1997) *Ill Effects: The Media–Violence Debate* London: Routledge.
Barmé, Geremie (1993) 'History for the masses' in Unger, J. (ed.) *Using the Past to Serve the Present: Historiography and Politics in Contemporary China* London: ME Sharpe.
Barmé, Geremie (1999) *In the Red: On Contemporary Chinese Culture* New York: Columbia University Press.
Barnett, Steven and Seymour, Emily (1999) *A Shrinking Iceberg Travelling South: Changing Trends in British Television* London: Campaign for Quality Television.
Barnett, Steven and Seymour, Emily (2000) *From Callaghan to Kosovo: Changing Trends in British Television 1975–99* London: University of Westminster.
Barthes, Roland (1972) *Mythologies* London: Cape.
Barthes, Roland (1990) *New Critical Essays* Berkeley: University of California Press.
Bartke, Wolfgang (1991) *Who's Who in the PRC* 23rd edn, Munich: KG Saur.
Bary, W.T. du and Tu Wei-Ming (1998) *Confucianism and Human Rights* New York: Cambridge University Press.
Baum, Richard and Shevchenko, Alexei (1999) 'The "state of the state"' in Goldman and MacFarquhar (1999).

BBC (2002) 'China and the WTO' *In Business* 16 June, London: BBC Radio 4.

BBC (2002a) 'From our own correspondent' 16 November, London: BBC Radio 4.

BBC (2002b) (http://zem.squidley.org.weblog/article/2228 and 1920).

Bechelloni, G. (1996) *Il Mestiere di Giornalista* Liguori Editori.

Becker, Jasper (1996) *Hungry Ghosts: China's Secret Famine* London: John Murray.

Becker, Jasper (2000) *The Chinese* London: John Murray.

Beetham, David (1974) *Max Weber and the Theory of Modern Politics* London: Allen and Unwin.

Beijing (2000) 'Page me the exam answers, teacher' in *The Straits Times* 17 July, p. 19.

Bell, M. (1998) 'The journalism of attachment' in Kieran, M. (ed.) *Media Ethics* London: Routledge.

Berkowitz, D. (1997) *Social Meanings of News: A Text Reader* Thousand Oaks, CA: Sage.

Bernstein, Richard and Munro, Ross H. (1998) *The Coming Conflict with China* New York: Alfred A. Knopf.

Bertuccioli, Giuliano (1981) 'Una melodramma di Liang Qichao sul Risorgimento italiano, Xin Luoma' *Catai* 1(2).

Bird, S.E. (1988) 'Myth, chronicle and story: exploring the narrative qualities of news' in Berkowitz (1997).

Bishop, Robert L. (1989) *Qi Lai! Mobilizing One Billion Chinese: The Chinese Communication System* Ames: Iowa State University Press.

Black, George and Munro, Robin (1993) *Black Hands of Beijing: Lives of Defiance in China's Democracy Movement* New York: John Wiley.

Blumler, Jay G. and Katz, Elihu (1974) *The Uses of Mass Communications: Current Perspectives On Gratifications Research* London: Sage.

Bodman R.W. (1991) *Death Song of the River: A Reader's Guide to the Chinese TV Series 'Heshang'* Ithaca, NY: Cornell University Press.

Bond, M.H. (1991) *Beyond the Chinese Face* Hong Kong: Oxford University Press.

Bond, M.H. (1996) (ed.) *A Handbook of Chinese Psychology* Hong Kong: Oxford University Press.

Bond, M.H. (1999) *The Psychology of the Chinese People* Oxford: Oxford University Press.

Boorman, Howard L. (ed.) (1970) *Biographical Dictionary of Republican China* VIII New York: Columbia University Press.

Bourdieu, P. (1998) *On Television and Journalism* London: Pluto.

Boyd Barrett, Oliver (1997) (ed.) *International Communication and Globalization: A Critical Introduction* London: Sage.

Brahm, Laurence J. (2001) *China's Century: The Awakening of the Next Economic Powerhouse* New York: Wiley and Sons.

Briller, Bert (1993) 'The Tao of tabloid Television' *Television Quarterly* 26:51–61.

Britton, Roswell (1933) *The Chinese Periodical Press. 1800–1912* Shanghai: Kelly and Walsh.

Brook, T. and Frolic, B.M. (eds) (1997) *The Ambiguous Challenge of Civil Society* New York: ME Sharpe.

Broyelle, Claudie, Broyelle, Jacques and Tschirhart, Evelyne (1980) *China: A Second Look* Brighton: Harvester.

Brugger, Bill (1994) *Politics, Economy and Society in Contemporary China* London: Macmillan.

Brundson, C. and Morley, D. (1978) *Everyday Television: 'Nationwide'* London: British Film Institute.

Cai Xiansheng 蔡賢盛 (1996) '制片人制式電視節目生產管理的一次改革' A Radical Reform of Television Programme Management 電視研究 1996/2.

Cao Qing (2000) 'Journalism as politics: reporting Hong Kong's handover in the Chinese press' *Journalism Studies* 1(4), November.

Carey, J. (1975) 'A cultural approach to communication' *Communication* 2:1–22.

Carey, J. (1998) 'Political ritual on television: episodes in the history of shame, degradation and excommunication' in Curran, James and Liebes, Tamar (eds) *Media, Ritual and Identity* London: Routledge.

CCTV Current Affairs Department (1998) 中央電視台新聞評論部編：新聞背后的新聞— — —新聞調查'97實錄 The stories behind the news – a collection of the 1997 stories written by the journalists of CCTV's News Probe 北京：中央編譯出版社

CCTV Current Affairs Department (1998a) 中央電視台新聞評論部編：焦點訪談系列叢書：焦點訪談—改革卷 Focus Reports: the book of the series, 'The Reform Collection' 北京：中國政法大學出版社

Chalaby, J.K. (1996) 'Journalism as an Anglo-American invention: a comparison of the development of French and Anglo-American journalism 1830s–1920s' *European Journal of Communication* 11(3):303–326.

Chalaby, J.K. (1998) *The Invention of Journalism* London: Macmillan.

Chan, J. (1994) 'National responses and accessibility to STAR TV in Asia' *Journal of Communication* 44(3).

Chan, Joseph Man (1994) 'Commercialization without independence: media development in China' in Cheng, Joseph and Brosseau, Maurice (eds) *China Review 1993* Hong Kong: Chinese University Press.

Chang, Gordon (2001) *The Coming Collapse of China* New York: Random House.

Chang, Jung (1991) *Wild Swans* London: HarperCollins.

Chang, Man (1969) The People's Daily *and the* Red Flag *Magazine during the Cultural Revolution* Hong Kong: Union Research Institute.

Chang Won Ho (1989) *Mass Media in China* Ames: Iowa State University Press.

Cheek, Timothy (1986) 'Deng Tuo: a Chinese Leninist approach to journalism' in Hamrin, C.L. and Cheek, Timothy *China's Establishment Intellectuals* New York: Buena Vista.

Cheek, Timothy (1989) 'Redefining propaganda' *Issues and Studies* 2.

Cheek, Timothy (1997) *Propaganda and Culture in Mao's China: Deng Tuo and the Intelligentsia* Oxford: Clarendon.

Chen Chongshan *et al.* (1998) 'The Chinese journalist' in Weaver, David H. (ed.) *The Global Journalist* New Jersey: Hampton Press.

Chen, F. (1997) 'Order and stability in social transition' *China Quarterly* 51, September.

Chen Huailin and Chan, Joseph Man (1998) 'Bird-caged press freedom in China' in Cheng, Joseph (ed.) (2000) *China After Deng* Hong Kong: City University Press, pp. 23.1–23.19.

Chen Huailin and Lee Chin-chuan (1998) 'Press, finance and economic reform in China' in *China Review* Hong Kong: Cambridge University Press.

Chen Huailin and Huang Yu (2000) 'Reversal of fortune: uneven development in China's press commercialization' in Lee Chin-chuan (ed.) *Money, Power, and Media: Communication Patterns in Cultural China* Evanston, IL: Northwestern University Press.

Chen, J. (1975) *Inside the Cultural Revolution* London: Sheldon.

Chen, L. (1991) 'The door opens to a thousand blossoms: a preliminary study of communication and rural development in China (1979–88)' *AJ Communication* 1(2):103–121.

Cheng, Jason (1962) 'Walter Williams and China', unpublished MA thesis, University of Missouri.

Cheng, Joseph Y.S. (2000) *China in the Post-Deng Era* Hong Kong: Cambridge University Press.

Cheng, W.K. (1998) 'Contending publicity: state and press in late Qing China' *Asian Thought and Society* XXIII(69).

Cheung, Peter Tsan-yin (1994) 'The case of Guangdong in central–provincial relations' in Jia Hao and Lin Zhimin (eds) *Changing Central–Local Relations in China* Boulder, CO: Westview, pp. 207–238.

Chinoy, Mike (2000) *China Live: People Power and the Television Revolution* Oxford: Rowman and Littlefield.

Christian, H. (ed.) (1980) *The Sociology of Journalism and the Press* (Sociological Review Monograph 29) pp. 341–369, Keele: University of Keele.

Christian, Harry (1976) 'The development of trade unionism and professionalism among British journalists: a sociological enquiry' London: University of London (LSE), Ph.D. thesis.

Christiansen, Flemming and Rai, Shirin (1998) *Chinese Politics and Society: An Introduction* New Jersey: Prentice Hall.

Chu, G.C. (1992) *The Great Wall in Ruins* Albany: State University of New York Press.

Chu, James (1975) *The PRC Journalist as a Cadre* CS XIII(11) S.1–14.

Chu, Leonard C. (1994) 'Continuity and change in China's media reform' *Journal of Communication* 44(3), summer.

Chu, Leonard, L. (1983) 'Communications, press criticism and self-criticism in Communist China: an analysis of its ideology, structure and operation' *Gazette* 31:47–61.

CIA *World Factbook* 2001.

Clarke, D. (1983) *Corruption: Causes, Consequences and Control* London: Frances Pinter.

Clifford, Mark (2002) 'China's experiment: read all about it!' *China Journal* 13 September (http://www.businessweek.com/bwdaily/dnflash/sep2002/nf20020913_0198.htm).

Cohen, S. (1981) *The Manufacture of News: Deviance, Social Problems and the Mass Media* Beverly Hills: Sage.

Cohen, S. (1990) *Folk Devils and Moral Panics* Guildford: Billing.

Cohen, Stanley and Young, Jock (eds) (1981) *The Manufacture of News: Social Problems, Deviance and the Mass Media* London: Constable.

Colley, Linda (1996) *Britons: Forging the Nation 1707–1837* London: Vintage.

Corner, John, Richardson, Kay and Fenton, Natalie (1990) *Nuclear Reactions: Form and Response in 'Public Issue' Television* London: John Libbey.

Cottle, S. (1993) *TV News, Urban Conflict and the Inner City* Leicester: Leicester University Press.

CPJ (Committee to Protect Journalists) (1999) *Attacks on the Press in 1999, China Section* (http://www.cpj.org/attacks99/frameset_att99/frameset_att99.html).

Cranfield, J. (1978) *The Press and Society* London: Longman.

Crook, Tim (1997) 'Radio in China today' talk to the GB–China Centre, London, 17 November.

CSM (2002) *Television in China* CVSC Sofres Media (CSM).

Cullen, Richard and Hua Lingfu (1998) 'Seeking theory from experience: media regulation in China' *Democratization* 5(2), summer.

Curran, J. ([1985] 1997) *Power without Responsibility* London: Routledge.

Curran, J. and Park, Myung-jin (2000) *De-Westernizing Media Studies* London: Routledge.

Dahlgren, P. and Sparks, C. (1991) *Communication and Citizenship: Journalism and the Public Sphere* London: Routledge.

Dai Qing (1989) *Yangtze! Yangtze!* London: Earthscan.

Dai Qing (1994) *Wang Shiwei and 'Wild Lilies': Rectification and Purges in the Chinese Communist Party 1942–44* New York: ME Sharpe.

Dai Qing (1999) 'Guiding public opinion' *Media Studies Journal* 78, winter.

Daley, P. and O'Neill, D. (1991) 'Sad is too mild a word: press coverage of the Exxon Valdez oil spill' *Journal of Communication* 4194:42–57.

Daruvala, Susan (2000) *Zhou Zuoren and an Alternative Chinese Response to Modernity* Cambridge, MA: Harvard University Press.

de Burgh, Hugo (1975) 'Glimpsing the new China' *Blackwood's Magazine* 318(1922):541–556, December.

de Burgh, Hugo (1980) 'China: then and now' *Blackwood's Magazine* 328(1981):378–387, November.

de Burgh, Hugo (1998) 'China: new public sphere, new journalists?' *Media Development* XLV:64–66, April.

de Burgh, Hugo (1998a) 'Audience, journalist and text in television news', paper delivered at the Annual Conference of the International Association for Media and Communications Research, 29 July.

de Burgh, Hugo (ed.) (2000) *Investigative Journalism: Context and Practice* London: Routledge.

de Burgh, Hugo (ed.) (2000a) 'Of the Party and in the market: Chinese journalism today' *Journalism Studies*, special issue, 1(4), November.

de Burgh, H. (2000b) 'Scrutinising social policy at C4 *Dispatches*' in de Burgh (2000), pp. 231–244.

de Burgh, Hugo (2001) 'The beliefs and practices of Chinese regional television journalists', unpublished Ph.D. thesis, Nottingham Trent University CRICC, July.

de Burgh, Hugo (2002) 'What Chinese journalists believe about journalism' in Rawnsley, Gary (ed.) *Political Communication in Greater China* London: Macmillan.

de Burgh, Hugo and Steward, Tim G. (1987) *The Persuasive Screen: Video Applications in Business* London: Century Hutchinson.

Deng Liqun (ed.) 鄧力群 (主編) (1997) 當代中國叢書：當代中國的新聞事業 The Current Profession of Journalism 北京：當代中國出版社

Deng Tuo (1999) 猱相容 (主編) 鄧拓散文選集 Selected Works of Deng Tuo 天津：白花文化出版社

Dickson, S.H. (1992) 'Press and US policy towards Nicaragua 1983–7' *Journalism Quarterly* 69:562–571.

Dikotter, Frank (1992) *The Discourse of Race in Modern China* London: Hurst.

Ding Fazhang (ed.) (1997) 丁法章主編 新聞評論學 Journalism Critique 上海：复旦大學出版社

Ding Ling ([1947] 1984) *The Sun Shines over the Sangan River* Peking: Foreign Languages Press.

Dittmer, Lowell (1994) 'The politics of publicity in reform China' in Lee (1994), pp. 89–112.

Dong Qingwen, Tan Alexis and Cao Xiaobing in Heisey and Gong (1998).

Drège, Jean-Pierre (1978) *La presse commerciale de Shanghai 1897–1949* Paris: Collège de France.

Duke, Michael S. (1985) *Blooming and Contending: Chinese Literature in the Post-Mao Era* Bloomington: Indiana University Press.

Eastman, Lloyd E. (1975) *The Abortive Revolution, China under Nationalist Rule 1927–37* Cambridge, MA: Harvard University Press.

Ekirch, Arthur (1974) *Progressivism in America: A Study of the Era from Theodore Roosevelt to Woodrow Wilson* New York: New Viewpoints.

Ettema, J.S. and Glasser, T.L. (1985) 'On the epistemology of investigative journalism' *Communications* 8:183–206.

Ettema, J.S. and Glasser, T.L. (1988) 'Narrative form and moral force' *Journal of Communication* 8–26, summer.

Fang Lizhi (1987) 方勵之 我們在做曆史 We are making history 台北：經濟與生活

Fang Lizhi (1990) *Bringing down the Great Wall* New York: Alfred A. Knopf.

Fang Yew-Jin (1994) '"Riots" and demonstrations in the Chinese press: a case study of language and ideology' *Discourse and Society* 5(4):463–481.

Fei Xiaoting (1992) *From the Soil: The Foundations of Chinese Society*, trans. Hamilton, G. and Wang Zheng, Berkeley: University of California Press.

Fen Fengjian (ed.) (1996) 分馮健總主編中國新聞實用大辭典 A dictionary of Chinese journalism 北京：新華出版社

Feng Chen (1997) 'Order and stability in social transition: neo-conservative political thought in post-1989 China' *China Quarterly* 151, September.

Fewsmith, Joseph (2001) *China Since Tiananmen* Cambridge: Cambridge University Press.

Fiske, John and Hartley, John (1978) *Reading Television* London: Methuen.

Fitzgerald, C.P. (1969) *The Chinese View of their Place in the World* Oxford: Oxford University Press.

Fitzwalter, R. *et al.* (1981) *Web of Corruption: The Story of John Poulson and T. Dan Smith* St Albans: Granada.

Franklin, Bob (1997) *Newszak and News Media* London: Arnold.

Franklin, Bob (2001) 'The government and the media', address at the Conference of the Campaign for Press and Broadcasting Freedom, London, 24 February.

Friedman, E. (1993) 'A failed Chinese modernity' in Tu Wei-Ming (1993).

Friedman, E. (1995) *National Identity and Democratic Prospects in Socialist China* New York: ME Sharpe.

Friedson, Eliot (1994) *Professionalism Reborn* Cambridge: Polity.

Fudan University (1998) 復旦大學 新聞學類專業教學計划 Course Plan for Professional Practice modules offered by The Journalism Department 上海：復旦大學

Fudan University [n.d.] 復旦大學 復旦大學新聞學遠間接 Prospectus of the Fudan Faculty of Journalism 上海：復旦大學

Fukuyama, Francis (1993) *The End of History and the Last Man* London: Penguin.

Fung, E.S.K. (2000) *In Search of Chinese Democracy* Cambridge: Cambridge University Press.

Gaber, Ivor and Barnett, Steve (2001) *Westminster Tales: The Twenty-first Century Crisis in Political Communication* Poole: Continuum.

Galtung, J. and Ruge, M. (1965) 'The structure of foreign news' in Tunstall (1970).

Gamson, William A. (1992) *Talking Politics* Cambridge: Cambridge University Press.

Gan Xifen (1994) 'Debates contribute to the development of journalistic science' *Journal of Communication* 44(3), summer.

Gans, H. (1979) *Deciding What's News: A Study of CBS Evening News, NBC Nightly News, Newsweek and Time* New York: Pantheon Books.

Garnham, Nicholas (2000) *Emancipation, the Media and Modernity* Oxford: Oxford University Press.

Garside, Roger (1981) *Coming Alive! China after Mao* London: André Deutsch.

Gernet, J. (1996) *A History of Chinese Civilization* Cambridge: Cambridge University Press.

GGDZ 国家广播电影社总局 (2001) 中国广播电视年间 China Broadcast Yearbook 北京：中国广播电视年间社

Gilley, Bruce (1998) *Tiger on the Brink: Jiang Zemin and China's New Elite* Berkeley: University of California Press.

Gitlin, T. (1985) *Inside Prime Time* New York: Pantheon.

Gittings, John (1996) *Real China, from Cannibalism to Karaoke* London: Simon and Schuster.

Gittings, John (2002) 'Workers gagged by Chinese censorship' in *Guardian* 2 April.

Gold, Thomas, B. (1990) 'The resurgence of civil society in China' *Journal of Democracy* 1(1):18–31.

Goldberger, Nancy and Veroff, Judy (1995) *The Culture and Psychology Reader* New York: New York University Press.

Goldfein, Jacques de (1989) *Personnalités Chinoises* Paris: L'Harmattan.

Golding, P. (1977) 'Media professionalism in the third world: the transfer of an ideology' in Curran, J. *et al. Mass Communication and Society* London: Edward Arnold.

Golding, P. (1999) 'The political and the popular: getting the message of tabloidization', paper delivered at the annual conference of the Association of Media, Cultural and Communications Studies, Sheffield, December.

Goldman, M. (1981) *China's Intellectuals: Advise and Dissent* Cambridge, MA: Harvard University Press.

Goldman, M. (1994) *Sowing the Seeds of Democracy in China: Political Reform in the Deng Xiaoping Era* Cambridge, MA: Harvard University Press.

Goldman, M. and Cohen, P. (1990) *Ideas Across Cultures: Essays on Chinese Thought in Honour of Benjamin I. Schwartz* Cambridge, MA: Harvard University Press.

Goldman, M. and MacFarquhar, Roderick (1999) *The Paradox of China's Post-Mao Reforms* Cambridge, MA: Harvard University Press.

Goldman, M., Link, P. and Wei, Su (1987) 'China's intellectuals in the Deng era: loss of identity with the state' in Goldman, M., Cheek, T. and Hamrin, C.L. (eds) *China's Intellectuals and the State: In Search of a New Relationship* Cambridge, MA: Harvard University Press.

Goodman, David S.G. (1994) *Deng Xiaoping and the Chinese Revolution: A Political Biography* New York: Routledge.

Gordon, Kim (1996) 'China's TV reform and the $9.95 salad shooter', unpublished MA thesis, London, City University.

Gordon, Kim (1997) 'Government allows new public sphere to evolve in China' *Media Development* XLIV:20–34, April.

Gordon, Kim (1999) 'The Chinese media – between Party and market', address at the First European Symposium on the Chinese Media, held at Nottingham Trent University, February.

Gordon, Kim (2000) 'China speaks out' *China Review* 17, autumn.

Grant, Jennifer (1988) 'Internal reporting by investigative journalists in china and its influence on government policy' *Gazette* 41:53–65.

Gray, Jack (1990) *Rebellions and Revolutions* Oxford: Oxford University Press.

Gray, John (1995) *Enlightenment's Wake* London: Routledge.

Griffith, William (1973) 'Communist esoteric communications', in Pool and Frey (1973).

Gu Xuebin (2000) 'The blight of the king without a crown in China', draft essay for submission as part of the MAIJ degree, Nottingham Trent University.

Gu Xuebin (2000a) e-mailed communication, 29 March.

Gu Xuebin (2000b) 'Make the fourth power of society powerful', essay in partial fulfilment of the requirements of the MAIJ degree, Nottingham Trent University, 10 April.

GUMG (Glasgow University Media Group) (1980) *More Bad News* London: Routledge and Kegan Paul.

Gunter, B. (1998) *Understanding the Older Consumer: The Grey Market* London: Routledge.

Gunter, B. (2000) *Media Research Methods* London: Sage.

Gunter, B. and Svennevig, M. (1987) *Behind and in Front of the Screen: Television's Involvement with Family Life* London: Libbey.

Guo Zhenzhi 郭鎮之 (1999) 關于(焦點訪談)的'焦點訪談' 'About (Focal Point's) "Focal Point"' (paper) (論文)第六次全國傳播學研討會 上海，复旦大學 1999/11.

Hall, S. (1973) 'Coding and encoding in the television discourse' in Hall, S. *et al.* (1980) *Culture, Media, Language* London: Hutchinson.

Hallett, S. (1999) 'A new nationalism?' *China Review*, autumn–winter.

Hallin, Daniel C. (1993) *We Keep America on Top of the World: Television Journalism and the Public Sphere* London: Routledge.

Hamrin, Carol Lee and Cheek, Timothy (1986) *China's Establishment Intellectuals* New York: Buena Vista.

Hamrin, Carol Lee and Zhao Suisheng (1995) (eds) *Decision Making in Deng's China* New York: ME Sharpe.

Hao Zhidong (1997) 'The changing politics of intellectuals in China' *Asian Thought and Society* XXII(66), September–December.

Harris, A. and Feinberg, J. (1977) 'Television and ageing: is what you see what you get?' *Gerontologist* 17:464–468.

Harris, B. (1996) *Politics and the Rise of the Press* London: Routledge.

Harrison, Lawrence E. and Huntingdon, Samuel P. (2000) *Culture Matters: How Values Shape Human Progress* New York: Basic Books.

Hay, C. (1996) 'Narrating crisis: the discursive construction of the "Winter of Discontent"' *Sociology* 30(2):253–277.

Hazelbarth, T. (1997) *The Chinese Media: More Autonomous and Diverse – Within Limits* Washington, DC: CIA.

He Baogang (1997) *The Democratic Implication of Civil Society in China* London: Macmillan.

He, Bochuan (1991) *China on the Edge: The Crisis of Ecology and Development* San Francisco: China Books.

He, P. (1995) 'Perception of identity in modern China' *Social Identities* 1(1).

He Qinglian 何清廉 (1998) 中国的陷阱 China's Pitfall 香港：民譽出版社

He Zhou (2000) 'Chinese Communist Party press in a tug of war: a political–economic analysis of the *Shenzhen Special Zone Daily*' in Lee C.C. (2000).

He Zhou (2000) 'Working with a dying ideology: dissonance and its reduction in Chinese journalism' *Journalism Studies* 1(4):599–616, November.

He Zihua (2002) Two private letters, one to Ms Qiu Ling of BJDST and one to me, both dated 18/9/02.

Heisey, D.R. and Gong Wenxiang (1998) *Communication and Culture: China and the World entering the 21st Century* Amsterdam: Editions Rodopi.

Henningham, John and Delano, Anthony (1998) 'British journalists' in Weaver, D.H (ed.) *The Global Journalist* New Jersey: Hampton Press.

Herman, E. and Chomsky, N. (1995) *Manufacturing Consent* London: Vintage.

Hertz, Noreena (2001) *The Silent Takeover: Global Capitalism and the Death of Democracy* London: William Heinemann.

Ho, D.Y.F. (1989) 'Socialisation in contemporary mainland China' *Asian Thought and Society* 14(41–2):136–149.

Hobsbawm, E. (1969) *Bandits* London: Weidenfeld and Nicolson.

Hobsbawm, E. and Ranger, T. (1992) *The Invention of Tradition* Cambridge: Cambridge University Press.

Howard, Roger (1971) 'Chinese message' *New Society* 18 November.

Howkins, John (1982) *Mass Communications in China* New York: Longman.

Hsia, C.T. (1971) *A History of Modern Chinese Fiction* New Haven: Yale University Press.

Hsiao Ching-chang and Cheek, Timothy (1995) 'Open and closed media: external and internal newspapers in the propaganda system' in Hamrin and Zhao (1995).

Hsiao Ching-chang *et al.* (1990) 'Don't force us to lie: the case of the *World Economic Herald*' in Lee C.C. (1990).

Hsu, Francis L.K. (1963) *Class, Caste and Club* New York: van Nostrand Reinhold.

Hsü, Immanuel C.Y. (1995) *The Rise of Modern China* New York: Oxford University Press.

Hu Yaobang 胡耀邦 (1985) 我們的記者工作 Our Work in Journalism 北京：人民 大學出版社

Hua Xu (1999) personal communication from SMTP:huaxu@email.msn.com on 23 September.

Hua Xu (2000) 'Morality discourse in the marketplace: narratives in the Chinese television news magazine *Oriental Horizon*' *Journalism Studies* 1(4):649–664, November.

Huang Chengjiu (2000) 'The development of the semi-independent press in post-Mao China: the future for Chinese journalism as exemplified in *Chengdu Business News*' *Journalism Studies* 1(4):649–664, November.

Huang Hu 黃瑚 (1998) Media Law and Professional Ethics 新聞法規与新聞職業道德 成都 四川出版社.

Huang, Y., Hao, X. and Zhang, K. (1997) 'Challenges to government control of information in China' *Media Development* XLIV:17–22, February.

Huntingdon, Samuel P. (1996) *The Clash of Civilizations and the Remaking of World Order* New York: Simon and Schuster.

IFEX (1999) China Alert: IFEX welcomes release of Gao Yu (etc.) (http://www.ifex.org/alerts/view.html?id=4257).

Index on Censorship (1996–7) entitled 'China Can Say No', London: Index on Censorship.

Ishihara, Shintaro (1991) *The Japan That Can Say No: Why Japan Will Be First among Equals* New York: Simon and Schuster.

Jenner, W.J.F. (1994) *The Tyranny of History: The Roots of China's Crisis* London: Penguin.

Jernow, A.L. (1993) *Don't Force us to Lie* China Times Center for Media and Social Studies.

Jhally, Sut and Lewis, Justin (1992) *Enlightened Racism: The 'Cosby Show', Audiences, and the Myth of the American Dream* Boulder, CO: Westview.

Jiang Hong (1995) 'Chinese television and its transformation of Chinese lifestyle', unpublished M.Phil. thesis, London: City University.

Jiang Qiudi (2002) 'The future of private TV in China', unpublished essay in partial fulfilment of the requirements of the MA in television journalism, Goldsmiths College, University of London.

Jin, Jun (1989) 'Dam project ignites China's intellectuals' *Asian Wall Street Journal* 20 March.

Johnson, Terence, J. (1972) *Professions and Power* London: Macmillan.

Judge, Joan (1996) *Print and Politics, 'Shibao' and the Culture of Reform in late Qing China* Stanford, CA: Stanford University Press.

Keane, Michael (2001) 'Broadcasting policy, creative compliance and the myth of civil society in China' *Media Culture and Society* 23:783–798.

Keating, P. (1991) *The Haunted Study* London: Fontana.

Kedourie, E. and Mango, A. (1988) 'Talking about the BBC' *Encounter* 71:60–64, September–October.

Keller, Perry (2001) 'Rules without law' *China Review* 18, spring.

Kelly, David and He Baogang (1992) 'Emergent civil society and the intellectuals in China' in Miller, Robert (ed.) *The Development of Civil Society in Communist Systems* NSW: Allen and Unwin.

King, Anthony (2001) *Does the United Kingdom Still Have a Constitution?* London: Sweet and Maxwell.

Kitzinger, Jenny (1999) 'Effects of the media', talk to members of the Chinese National Media Legislation Working Group held at Nottingham Trent University on 10 February.

Klein, Naomi (2001) *No Logo* London: Flamingo.

Knightley, P. (1975) *The First Casualty* London: Hodder.

Knightley, P. (1997) *A Hack's Progress* London: Jonathan Cape.

Kolas, Ashild (1998) 'Chinese media discourses on Tibet: the language of inequality' *Tibet Journal* XXII(3):69–77.

Kubey, R. (1980) 'Television and ageing: past, present and future' *Gerontologist* 20:16–25.

Kuhn, Raymond (1985) *The Politics of Broadcasting* London: Croom Helm.

La Fuente, Sandra (2000) 'Theory and practice of investigative journalism in Venezuela', dissertation submitted in partial fulfilment of the requirements for the degree of MA at Nottingham Trent University, 11 May.

Lam, Willy (1999) *The Era of Jiang Zemin* New Jersey: Prentice Hall.

Lam, Willy Wo-Lap (2002) 'Hu Jintao', lecture delivered at the Royal Institute of International Affairs, Chatham House, 25 April.

Lam, Willy Wo-Lap (2002a) 'The new Chinese leadership and the prospects for political reform', lecture delivered at the Institute of Asia-Pacific Studies, University of Nottingham, 25 April.

Langer, John (1998) *Tabloid Television: Popular Journalism and the 'Other News'* London: Routledge.

Lardy, Nicholas R. (2002) *Integrating China into the Global Economy* Washington: Brookings.

Larson, Magali (1977) *The Rise of Professionalism: A Sociological Analysis* Berkeley: University of California Press.

Lau Wei-San (1949) 'The University of Missouri and journalism of China', unpublished MA thesis, University of Missouri.

Lee Chin-chuan (ed.) (1990) *Voices of China: The Interplay of Politics and Journalism* New York: Guilford Press.

Lee Chin-chuan (1990a) 'Mass media: of China, about China,' in Lee C.C. (1990), pp. 3–29.

Lee Chin-chuan (1994) *China's Media, Media's China* Boulder, CO: Westview Press.

Lee Chin-chuan (1994a) 'Ambiguities and contradictions: issues in china's changing political communication,' in Lee (1994), pp. 3–22.

Lee Chin-chuan (1999) 'Chinese communications: prisms and trajectories' opening lecture given to the First European Symposium on the Chinese Media, held at Nottingham Trent University, February.

Lee Chin-chuan (ed.) (2000) *Power, Money and Media: Communication Patterns and Bureaucratic Control in Cultural China* Evanston: Northwestern University Press.

Lee Chin-chuan (2000a) 'Servants of the state or the market? Media and journalists in China' in Tunstall, J. (ed.) *Media Occupations* London: Oxford University Press, 2001.

Lee Chin-chuan (2000c) 'In search of the "Audience": press models in modern China', paper presented to the International Conference on Chinese Audiences across Time and Space, City University of Hong Kong, 1–2 April.

Lee Chin-chuan, Chan, Joseph Man, Pan Zhongdan and So, Clement Y.K. (2000b) 'National prisms of a global "media event"' in Curran, James and Gurevitch, Michael (eds) (2000) *Mass Media and Society* 3rd edn, London: Edward Arnold.

Lee Ching Kwan (2000) 'The "revenge of history": collective memories and labour protests in Northeast China' *Ethnography* 1(2), December.

Lee, L.O. (1985) 'The beginnings of mass culture: journalism and fiction in the late Qing and beyond' in Johnson, D. (ed.) *Popular Culture in Late Imperial China* Berkeley: University of California Press.

Lee, P.S. (1994) 'China' in Wang, G. (ed.) *Treading Different Paths: Informatization in Asian nations* Norwood, NJ: Ablex Publishing.

Lee-Hsia Hsu Ting (1974) *Government Control of the Press in Modern China 1900–1949* Cambridge, MA: Harvard University Press.

Lent, John A. (ed.) (1987) 'The daily press of china: a symposium' *Asian Thought and Society* XII(36), November.

Levenson, Joseph R. (1958) *Confucian China and its Modern Fate* vol. 2, London: Routledge.

Leys, Simon (1971) *Les Habits Neufs du Président Mao* Paris: Editions Champ Libre.

Leys, Simon (1974) *Chinese Shadows* London: Penguin.

Leys, Simon (1979) *Broken Images* London: Allison and Busby.

Leys, Simon (1983) *The Burning Forest* New York: Holt.

Li, Cheng (2001) *China's Leaders* Lanham, MD: Rowman.

Li Dongsheng (ed.) 李東生 (1999[?]) 焦點的變遷 (焦點訪談改革開放20周年特別報道) Focal Point's Vicissitudes (A 20 Year Commemorative Record of Focal Point's Special Reports) 北京：中國政法大學出版社

Li Liangfong (1997) 李良榮西方新聞事業概論 A brief introduction to journalism in the west 上海：复旦大學出版社

Li Lubo (1984) 'Shao's words' feature article in *China Daily*, 13 November.

Li, P. (1991) *Culture and Politics in China* New Brunswick: Transaction.

Li Tsze Sun (1993) *The World Outside When the War Broke Out* Hong Kong: CUHK.

Li, X. (1991) 'Chinese television system and television news' *China Quarterly* 126:340–355.

Li Xiaoping (1989) 'Sino-British comparisons of TV news', unpublished MA thesis, University of Leeds.

Li Xisuo (ed.) (1993) 李喜所（編)梁啟超卷 On Liang Qichao 北京：人民出版社

Li Zhuojun (1997) 李卓鈞編著新聞理論綱要 Essentials of Journalism Theory 漢大學出版社

Li Zhurun (1998) 'Popular journalism with Chinese characteristics' *International Journal of Cultural Studies* 1(3), December.

Liang Heng and Shapiro, Judith (1984) *Son of the Revolution* London: Fontana.

Lin Jing (1994) *The Opening of the Chinese Mind: Democratic Changes in China since 1978* Westport: Praeger.

Lin Yutang (1936) *A History of the Press and Public Opinion in China* Shanghai: Kelly and Walsh.

Link, Perry (1992) *Evening Chats in Beijing* New York: Norton.

Liu, Alan, P. (1975) *Communications and National Integration in Communist China* Berkeley: UCLA Press.

Liu Binyan (1989) 劉賓雁 劉賓雁自傳 My Autobiography 台北：時報文化出版企業有限公司

Liu Binyan (1989) 劉賓雁 作品精選 Selected Works 香港：文學研究社

Liu Binyan (1989) *Tell the World; What Happened in China and Why* New York: Pantheon.

Liu Binyan (1990) 'Press freedom: particles in the air' in Lee C.C. (1990).

Liu Binyan (1990a) *A Higher Kind of Loyalty* London: Methuen.

Liu Binyan (1990b) *China's Crisis, China's Hope* Cambridge, MA: Harvard University Press.

Liu Binyan and Link, Perry (1998) 'A great leap backward?' review of He Qinglian *Zhongguo de xianjing* in *New York Review of Books* 8 October.

Liu, James (1967) *The Chinese Knight Errant* London: Routledge and Kegan Paul.

Liu Mei Ching (1983) 'Liang Chi-chao and the Media' *Gazette* 31:35–45.

Liu Shaoqi (1984) *Selected Works of Liu Shao-ch'i* Peking: FLP.

Lu Di (1999) 中国电视产业发展张略研究 A Study of China's Television Production 北京：新华出版社

Lu Xinyu (2002) 纪录中国—当代中国的新纪录运动 Recording China: The New Documentary Movement in China Today 上海：文艺出版社

Lu Ye 陸曄 (1998) '造度競爭辨調：上海廣播電視改革模式探討 An Examination of Aspects of TV Reform in Shanghai: the Creation of Competitive Coordination' in *Studies in Journalism and Communications* Peking 1998/2.

Lull, James (1991) *China Turned On* London: Routledge.

Luo Ming *et al.* (eds) (1998) 羅明胡運芳主(編)中國電視觀眾現狀報告 Chinese Current Affairs TV Reports 北京：社會科學文獻出版社

Ma, Eric Kit-wai (2000) 'Rethinking media studies' in Curran (2000).

Ma Guangren (ed.) (1996) 馬光仁主編上海新聞史 (1850–1949) A History of Shanghai Journalism 复旦大學出版社

Macdonald, Keith, M. (1995) *The Sociology of the Professions* London: Sage.

MacFarquhar, R. (1997) *The Origins of the Cultural Revolution* London: Oxford University Press.

MacFarquhar, R. (1997a) *The Politics of China 1949–89* Cambridge: Cambridge University Press.

McNair, Brian (1991) *Glasnost, Perestroika and the Soviet Media* London: Routledge.

McQuail, D. (1972) *Sociology of Mass Communications* London: Penguin.

McQuail, D. (1994) *Mass Communication Theory* London: Sage.

Mamo, David and Upson, Laurie (1977) *Dizionario Storico Bibliografico della Cina Moderna* Florence: Vallechi.

Mancini, Paulo (2000) 'Political complexity and alternative models of journalism' in Curran (2000).

Mao Zedong (1961) *Selected Works of Mao Tse-t'ung* vol. IV Peking: FLP.

Mao Zedong 毛泽东 (1967) 轮文艺 An Essay on Literature and Art 北京：中國人民大學出版社

Mark, S. (1991) 'Observing the observers at Tiananmen Square' in Li (1991) *Culture and Politics in China* New Brunswick: Transaction.

Merritt, D. (1995) *Public Journalism and Public Life: Why Telling the News is not Enough* Hillsdale, NJ: Lawrence Erlbaum Assocs.

Metzger, Thomas (1977) *Escape from Predicament: Neo Confucianism and China's Evolving Political Culture* New York: Cambridge University Press.

Millerson, G. (1984) *The Qualifying Associations: A Study in Professionalization* London: Routledge and Kegan Paul.

Monbiot, George (2000) *Captive State: The Corporate Take-over of Britain* London: Macmillan.

Moore, Gillian (2000) 'The English legal framework for investigative journalism' in de Burgh (2000), pp. 126–155.

Morley, David (1986) *Family Television: Cultural Power and Domestic Leisure* London: Comedia.

Morley, David (2000) Inaugural Professorial Lecture delivered at Goldsmiths College, 5 December.

Mu Chengzhou (2001) 'Foreign media penetrate China in Hong Kong Trade Development Council' (www.tdctrade.com/report/indprof/011101.htm).

Nathan, Andrew, J. (1985) *Chinese Democracy* Berkeley: University of California Press.

Nathan, Andrew, J. (1990) *China's Crisis: Dilemmas of Reform and Prospects for Democracy* New York: Columbia University Press.

Nathan, Andrew J. and Link, Perry (2001) *The Tiananmen Papers* New York: Little, Brown and Company.

Nathan, Andrew J. and Ross, Robert S. (1997) *The Great Wall and The Empty Fortress – China's Search for Security* New York: Norton.

Negrine, R. (1985) 'Great Britain: end of the public service tradition' in Kuhn, R. (ed.) *The Politics of Broadcasting* London: Croom Helm.

News Probe (1998) 新聞調查我們在做曆史 We're Making History [a collection of treatments/script synopses] 正在發生的曆史北京：光明日報出版社

Newsweek (2002) 'Changing China: a special report' *Newsweek Magazine* (http://school.newsweek.com/online_activities/changing_china.htm).

New York Times (2002) 'Critic of corruption in rural China is arrested' 14 June (http://zem.squidly.org.weblog/article/1661).

Nip, Joyce Y.M. (1998) 'Clash and compatibility of journalistic cultures: mainland China and Hong Kong' in Heisey and Gong (1998).

Nye, Joseph S. (2002) *The Paradox of American Power: Why the World's Only Superpower Can't Go It Alone* Oxford: Oxford University Press.

Nye, Joseph S. (2003) 'Propaganda isn't the way: soft power' *International Herald Tribune* 10 January.

O'Brien, Kevin (1995) 'The politics of lodging complaints in rural China' *China Quarterly* 143, September.

O'Sullivan, Tim *et al.* (1994) *Key Concepts in Communications and Cultural Studies* London: Routledge.

Oborne, Peter (1999) *Alastair Campbell, New Labour and the Rise of the Media Class* London: Aurum.

Ogden, S. (1992) *China's Unresolved Issues* New Jersey: Prentice Hall.

Oi, Jean C. and Walder, A.G. (1999) *Property Rights and Economic Reform in China* Stanford, CA: Stanford University Press.

Overholt, William H. (1993) *China: The Next Economic Superpower* London: Weidenfeld and Nicolson.

Page, B. (1998) 'A defence of "low" journalism' *British Journalism Review* 9(1).

Pan Zhongdan (1986) 潘忠党（民86年）'大陸新聞改革過程中象徵資源之替換形態' The Revolution in Mainland China's Journalism as Symbolic of the Formation of Interchanging Resources 新聞學研究第五十四集頁 111–139.

Pan Zhongdan 潘忠党 (1997) '新聞改革与新聞體制的改造─我們新聞改革實踐的傳播社會學的探討' The Journalism Revolution and the Reformation of Journalism – studies in communication sociology from our practice in the journalism revolution 新聞与傳播研究第四卷第三期頁 62–80.

Pan Zhongdan (1998) 'Venturing into unknowns with bounded innovations: institutional reconfigurations in China's journalism reforms', paper presented at the International Conference on 20 Years of China's Reforms, 12–13 December.

Pan Zhongdan (2000) 'Improvising reform activities: the changing reality of journalistic practice in China' in Lee C.C. (2000).

Parris, Matthew (1999) *Parris on TV*, a series for Radio 5 Live London: BBC.

Pei Minxin (2000) 'Rights and resistance: the changing contexts of the dissident movement' in Perry and Selden (2000).

Perez-Ayerra, Raquel (2000) 'The performance of investigative journalism in Spain: the case of national TV', dissertation submitted in partial fulfilment of the requirements for the degree of MA at Nottingham Trent University.

Perkin, Harold (1996) *The Third Revolution: Professional Elites in the Modern World* London: Routledge.

Perry, Elizabeth J. and Selden, Mark (eds) (2000) *Chinese Society: Change, Conflict and Resistance* London: Routledge.

Peterson, G. (1997) *The Power of Words: Literacy and Revolution in South China* Vancouver: UBC Press.

Phillips, Melanie (1995) 'The BBC and its values' *Observer* 17 April, p. 25.

Philo, Greg (ed.) (1997) *Message Received* Harlow: Longman.

Philo, Greg and Miller, David (2000) *Market Killing* London: Longman.

Pollard, David (1973) *A Chinese Look at Literature. The Literary Values of Chou Tso-jen in Relation to the Tradition* London: C. Hurst.

Polumbaum, Judy (1990) 'The tribulations of China's journalists after a decade of reform' in Lee C.C. (1990).

Polumbaum, Judy (1994) 'Striving for predictability: the bureaucratization of media management in China,' in Lee C.C. (1994), pp. 113–128.

Pool, Ithiel de Sola (1973) 'Communication in totalitarian societies' in Pool and Frey (1973).

Pool, Ithiel de Sola and Frey, Frederick, W. (eds) (1973) *Handbook of Communication* Chicago: Rand McNally.

Porter, Robin (1992) 'Shaping China's news: Xinhua's Duiwaibu on the threshold of change' in Porter (1992).

Porter, Robin (1992) 'A day in the life of the Duiwaibu' in Porter (1992).

Porter, Robin (ed.) (1992) *Reporting the News from China* London: RIIA.

Pratley, Nils (2002) 'Welcome to the last frontier' *Sunday Times Business* 3 November, p. 3.

Prisma (2001) *Report 2001: Freedom of the Press Throughout the World* Paris: Reporters sans Frontières.

Protess, D. *et al.* (1991) *The Journalism of Outrage: Investigative Reporting and Agenda Building in America* New York: Guilford.

Pusey, James, R. (1969) *Wu Han: Attacking the Present through the Past* Cambridge, MA: Harvard University Press.

Pye, Lucian (1968) *The Spirit of Chinese Politics* Cambridge, MA: MIT Press.

Pye, Lucian (1988) *The Mandarin and the Cadre* Ann Arbor: University of Michigan Press.

Qian Shaochang (1987) '*People's Daily* and *China Daily*: a comparative study' *Asian Thought and Society* XII(35):145–151.

Qian Weifan (1987) 'Rapport of "Jiefang Ribao" with the public through letters to the editor column' in Lent, John A. (1987) 'The daily press of China: a symposium' *Asian Thought and Society* XII(36):252–266.

Qiu Ling (2002) 'Comparing investigative news programmes as between China and the UK', unpublished essay in partial fulfilment of the requirements of the MA in Television Journalism, Goldsmiths College, University of London.

Quesada, M. (1997) *Periodismo de investigacion o el derecho a denunciar* Barcelona: CIMS.

Ramanathan, S. and Servaes, J. *Asia Reporting Europe and Europe Reporting Asia: A Study of News Coverage* Singapore: AMIC.

Randall, David (1996) *The Universal Journalist* London: Pluto Press.

Redding, S.G. (1990) *The Spirit of Chinese Capitalism* New York: Walter De Gruyter.

Renmin Daxue (1998) 中國人民大學新聞學院簡況 An Overview of the Journalism Faculty 北京：人民大學

Reuters (2001) http://zem.squidley.org.weblog/article/344, 20 August.

Reuters (2002) 'China lifts block on Net wall' 16 May.

Rojek, C. (1998) 'Stuart Hall and 40 years of cult studies' *International Journal of Communication* 1(1).

Roshier, B. (1981) 'The selection of crime news by the press' in Cohen (1981), pp. 148, 155.

Rowe, William T. (1990) 'The public sphere in modern China' *Modern China* 16(3):309–329.

Rudolph, Jorg-Meinhard (1984) 'Cankao Xiaoxi' *Occasional Papers/Reprint Series Contemporary Asian Studies*, Baltimore.

Rutherford, Smith R. (1979) 'Mythic elements of TV news' in Berkowitz (1997).

Sang Yilin (1996) 桑義嶙 著新聞報道學 The Study of News Reports 杭州：杭州大學出版社

Scannell, Paddy (1996) *Radio, Television and Modern Life: A Phenomenological Approach* Oxford: Blackwell.

Scannell, Paddy and Sparks, Colin (1992) *Culture and Power* London: Sage.

Schell, O. (1991) Introduction to Fang Lizhi *Bringing Down the Great Wall: Writings on Science, Culture, and Democracy in China* New York: Alfred A. Knopf.

Schell, O. (1995) *Mandate of Heaven* London: Warner.

Schell, O. (1998) 'Maoism vs media in the marketplace' *Media Studies Journal* 9(3):33–42.

Schlesinger, Philip (1987) *Putting Reality Together: BBC News* London: Routledge.

Schneider, Laurence A. (1980) *A Madman of Ch'u: The Chinese Myth of Loyalty and Dissent* Berkeley: University of California Press.

Schoenhals, Michael (1992) *Doing Things with Words in Chinese Politics: Five Studies* Berkeley: University of California Press Institute of East Asian Studies.

Schram, S. (1989) *The Thought of Mao Tse-t'ung* Cambridge: Cambridge University Press.

Schudson, M. (1992) 'Watergate: a study in mythology' *Columbia Journalism Review*, May–June.

Schwartz, B. (1964) *In Search of Wealth and Power: Yen Fu and the West* Cambridge, MA: Harvard University Press.

Schwartz, B. (1985) *The World of Thought in Ancient China* Cambridge, MA: Harvard University Press.

Schwartz, B. (1993) 'Culture, modernity and nationalism' in Tu (1993).

Schwartz, V. (1986) *The Chinese Enlightenment* Berkeley: University of California Press.

Seymour-Ure, Colin (1974) *The Political Impact of Mass Media* London: Constable.

Shapiro, Judith (2001) *Mao's War against Nature: Politics and the Environment in Revolutionary China* Cambridge: Cambridge University Press.

Shoemaker, P. (1996) *Mediating the Message* London: Longman.

Shue, Vivienne (1988) *The Reach of the State: Sketches of the Chinese Body Politic* Stanford, CA: Stanford University Press.

Sigal, Leon, V. (1999) 'Reporters and officials: the organization and politics of newsmaking' in Tumber, H. (ed.) (1999) *News: A Reader* Oxford: Oxford University Press.

Silverstone, Roger and Hirsch, E. (eds) (1992) *Consuming Technologies* London: Routledge and Kegan Paul.

Smith, Roger (1992) 'Television and Tiananmen' in Porter (ed.) (1992).

Sparks, C. (1991) 'Goodbye, Hildy Johnson: the vanishing "serious press"' in Dahlgren, P. and Sparks, C. (1991) *Communication and Citizenship: Journalism and the Public Sphere* London: Routledge.

Spence, J.D. (1982) *The Gate of Heavenly Peace: The Chinese and their Revolution* London: Faber and Faber.

Spence, J.D. (1990) *The Search for Modern China* London: Hutchinson.

Splichal, R. and Sparks, C. (1994) *Journalists for the 21st Century* Norwood, NJ: Ablex.

Stephenson, Hugh and Mory, Pierre (1990) *La Formation au Journalisme en Europe* Brussels: AEFJ.

Stranahan, Patrica (1990) *Molding the Medium: The Chinese Communist Party and the Liberation Daily* Armonk, NY: ME Sharpe.

Strand, David (1990) 'Protest in Beijing: civil society and the public sphere in China' *Problems of Communism* 34:1–19.

Studwell, Joe (2002) *China Dream* London: Profile.

Sun Xupei (1994) 孫許配新聞學新論 A New Study of Journalism Studies 北京現代中國出版社

Swanson, David L. and Mancini, Paulo (1996) *Politics, Media and Modern Democracy: An International Study of Innovations in Electoral Campaigning and their Consequences* Westport, CT: Praeger.

Tang Wenfang (1997) *Party Intellectuals' Demand for Reform in Contemporary China* Washington: Hoover (www-hoover.stanford.edu/publications/epp/97/97a.html).

Tang Zongli *et al.* (1996) *Maoism and Chinese Culture* Nova Science Publishers.

Thomas, Bella (2003) 'What the poor watch on TV' *Prospect* 82:46–51, January.

Thussu, Daya (1998) *Electronic Empires* New York: Arnold.

Tomlinson, John (1991) *Cultural Imperialism* London: Frances Pinter.

Tomlinson, John (1997) ' "And besides, the wench is dead": media scandals and the globalization of communication' in Lull, James and Hinermann, Steve (ed.) *Media Scandals* Cambridge: Polity.

Tomlinson, John (2000) *Globalization and Culture* London: Polity.

Tracey, M. (1985) 'The poisoned chalice? International television and the idea of dominance' *Daedalus* 114(4): 7–56.

Tu Wei-Ming (1993) *China in Transformation* Cambridge, MA: Harvard University Press.

Tu Wei-Ming (1995) *The Living Tree: The Changing Meaning of Being Chinese Today* Stanford, CA: Stanford University Press.

Tuchman, G. (1972) 'Objectivity as a strategic ritual' *American Journal of Sociology* 77(4):660–679.

Tuchman, G. (1978) *Making News: A Study in the Construction of Reality* New York: The Free Press.

Tunstall, Jeremy (ed.) (1970) *Media Sociology: A Reader* London: Constable.

Tunstall, Jeremy (1993) *Television Producers* London: Routledge.

Unger, J. (1993) 'Introduction' in Unger, J. (ed.) *Using the Past to Serve the Present. Historiography and Politics in Contemporary China* London: ME Sharpe.

Vogel, Ezra, F. (ed.) (1997) *Living with China: US–China Relations in the Twenty-first Century* New York: W.W. Norton.

Waisbord, Silvio (2001) *Watchdog Journalism in South America: News, Accountability and Democracy* New York: Columbia University Press.

Wakeman, F. (1993) 'The civil society and the public sphere debate: western reflections on Chinese political culture' *Modern China* 10:108–138, April.

Wang Gongwu (1991) *The Chineseness of China, Selected Essays* Hong Kong: Oxford University Press.

Wang Hongyang (ed.) (1997) 王洪樣中國現代新聞史 A History of Modern Chinese Journalism 北京：新華出版社

Wang Ningtong (2003) 'A comparative study of audience discussion programmes in China and the UK', unpublished dissertation in partial fulfilment of the MA in film and television production at the University of Bristol.

Wank, David L. (1995) 'Civil society in Communist China?' in Hall, J.A. (ed.) *Civil Society: Theory, History, Comparison* London: Polity.

Wank, David L. (1999) *Commodifying Chinese Communism: Markets, Power, and Culture in a South China City* Cambridge: Cambridge University Press.

Wasserstrom, J. (1989) 'Afterword: history, myth and the tales of Tiananmen' in Wasserstrom, J. (ed.) *Popular Protest and Political Culture in Modern China* Boulder, CO: Westview.

Watson, Tony and Harris, Pauline (1999) *The Emergent Manager* London: Sage.

Weaver, David H. (1998) 'Journalists around the world: commonalties and differences' in Weaver, David H. (ed.) *The Global Journalist* New Jersey: Hampton Press.

Weici Wang (2000) *Jilu yu Tansuo – Yu Dalu Julupian Gongzuozhe de Shiji Duihua*, Taibei: Yuanliu Chubanshe.

Wen Diya (1999) 'The Chinese TV revolution – an inside view' address at the First European Symposium on the Chinese Media, held at Nottingham Trent University, February.

Weymouth, Tony and Anderson, Peter, J, (1999) *Insulting the Public? The British Press and the European Union* New York: Addison Wesley.

White, Lynn, III (1990) 'All the news: structure and politics in Shanghai's reform media' in Lee C.C. (1990), pp. 88–110.

Wilkinson-Latham, R. (1979) *From Our Special Correspondent* London: Hodder.

Williams, Francis (1957) *Dangerous Estate* Cambridge: Stephens.

Williams, Granville (2000) *Britain's Media: How They are Related, Ownership and Democracy* London: Campaign for Press and Broadcasting Freedom.

Wilson, Richard W. (1974) *The Moral State: A Study of the Political Socialization of Chinese and American Children* New York: Free Press.

Winstanley, Michael J. (1984) *Ireland and the Land Question 1800–1922* London: Methuen.

Wolfe, Tom (1998) *Ambush at Fort Bragg* London: BBC Radio 4.

Womack, Brantly (ed.) (1996) *Media and the Chinese Public: A Survey of the Beijing Media Audience* New York: ME Sharpe.

Woodward, Bob and Bernstein, Carl (1979) *All the President's Men* London: Quartet Books.

Wu Guoguang and Liao Xiaoying, 'One head, many mouths: diversifying press structures in the reform China,' in Lee C.C. (2000).

Wu Haimin (1996) 吳海民著新聞出版風云 Rapid Change in Journalism Publishing 濟南：濟南出版社

Wu Mei (1999) 'Uncovering Three Gorges Dam' *Media Studies Journal* 122, winter.

Xu Xiaoou (1996) 徐小鸽著新聞傳播學原理与研究 Theories and studies on journalism and communication 桂林：廣西師大學出版社

Yan Jiaqi (1995) 'The nature of Chinese authoritarianism' in Hamrin and Zhao (1995).

Yan Yunxiang (1996) *The Flow of Gifts: Reciprocity and Social Networks in a Chinese Village*, Stanford, CA: Stanford University Press.

Yan Yunxiang (2003) *Private Life under Socialism*, Stanford, CA: Stanford University Press.

Yang, Mayfair Meihui (1994) *Gifts, Favors and Banquets: The Art of Social Relationships in China* New York: Cornell University Press.

Ying Chan (1999) 'Hong Kong' *Media Studies Journal* 84, winter.

Yu Huang and Xu Yu (1997) 'Broadcasting and politics: Chinese television in the Mao era 1958–76' *Historical Journal of Film, Radio and Television* 17(4).

Yu Jinglu (1990) 'The structure and function of Chinese television, 1979–1989,' in Lee C.C. (1990), pp. 69–87.

Yuan Jun (1997) 袁軍著新聞事業導論 An Approach to the Profession of Journalism 北京：北京廣播學院出版社

Zelizer, B. (1993) 'Has communication explained journalism?' in Berkowitz (1997) .

Zeng, Xubai 曾虛白 (ed.) (1989) 中國新聞史 A History of Chinese Journalism 台北：三民書居

Zha, J. (1995) *China Pop: How Soap Operas, Tabloids and Bestsellers are Transforming a Culture* New York: New Press.

Zhang Ailing (1954) 張愛玲著赤地之愛 Bare Earth 台北：皇奎出版社

Zhang Ailing (1960) 張愛玲著秧歌 The Rice Sprout Song. 台北：皇奎出版社

Zhang Guangtu (ed.) (1999) 張光逢主編20年記憶—中國改革開放20年人物志 A twenty-year record: Personalities of 20 years of Reform in China [in the CCTV programme East] 北京：華夏出版社

Zhang Guoxing (1968) 長郭興著中國報紙改觀 An Outline of Chinese Newspapers 香港：國際新聞

Zhang Longxi (1988) 'The myth of the other' *Critical Inquiry*, autumn.

Zhang Longxi (1992) 'Western theory and Chinese reality' *Critical Inquiry* 19, autumn.

Zhang Weiiguo (1999) 'Journalists, spies and martyrs' an essay by former Peking bureau chief of *World Economic Herald*, received from SMTP: Zhangwg@aol.com on 7 July.

Zhang Ximin (1998) 'Media law' *China Review* 9, spring.

Zhang Ximin (1999) 'Media law in China', talk to the First European Symposium on the Chinese Media, held at Nottingham Trent University, February.

Zhang Ximing, Weng Jieming, Zhang Qiang, Qu Kemin (eds) (1996) 与總書記談心 Peking: Zhongguo Kexue Shehui CBS.

Zhang Xudong (1998) 'Intellectual politics in post-Tiananmen China: an introduction' *Social Text* 16(2):55, summer.

Zhang Yi (2001) 'Zhongguo Minying Dianshi' in *Xinmin Zhoukan* 3 September, p. 48.

Zhang Yong (2000) 'From masses to audience: changing media ideologies and practices in reform China' *Journalism Studies* 1(4):649–664, November.

Zhang Zhihua (ed.) (1999) 張之華主編中國新聞事業史文選 (公元724年–1995年) An Anthology of the History of the Journalism Profession 北京：中國人民大學出版社

Zhao Yuezhi (1998) *Media, Market and Democracy in China: Between the Party Line and the Bottom Line* Urbana: University of Illinois Press.

Zhao Yuezhi (1999) personal communication.

Zhao Yuezhi (2000) 'Watchdogs on Party leashes? Contexts and implications of investigative journalism in post-Deng China' *Journalism Studies* 1(4): 577–598, November.

Zheng Baowei (1990) 鄭保衛著新聞學導論 An introduction to journalism 北京：新華出版社

Zhou Jinhua (1997) 周金化全國盛市級電視台制片人狀況分析 An Analysis of the Situation of Television Producers, Nationally and by Level 電視研究 1997/11.

Zhou Lifang (1998) 'Education in development journalism and communication' *Journal of Development Communication* 3(2):74–81.

Zhu Jian-hua (1988) 'Public opinion polling in China: a descriptive view' *Gazette* 41:27–138.

Zhu Jian-hua (1990) 'Information availability, source credibility and audience sophistication: factors conditioning the effects of communist propaganda in China', doctoral dissertation, School of Journalism, Indiana University.

Zweig, David (2000) 'The "externalities of development" Can new political institutions manage rural conflict?' in Perry, Elizabeth J. and Selden, Mark (eds) *Chinese Society: Change, Conflict and Resistance* London: Routledge.

ZXJX 中国新闻教育学会 (2001) Bulletin of the Chinese Association for Journalism Education 中国新闻教育学会通讯 北京：学会秘书编印 16 October 2001.

Index